Decorative
Knitting

Decorative Knitting

100 practical techniques, 200 inspirational ideas and 18 creative projects

Kate Haxell and Luise Roberts

Trafalgar Square Publishing
North Pomfret, Vermont

With love and thanks to our fantastic husbands,
Philip and David.

First published in the United States of America in 2005
by Trafalgar Square Publishing
North Pomfret, Vermont 05053

Printed in the U.S.A.

EDITOR: Kate Haxell
DESIGNER: Luise Roberts
PHOTOGRAPHER: Matthew Dickens
ILLUSTRATOR: Kate Simunek
PATTERN CHECKER: Marilyn Wilson

ISBN: 1-57076-306-2

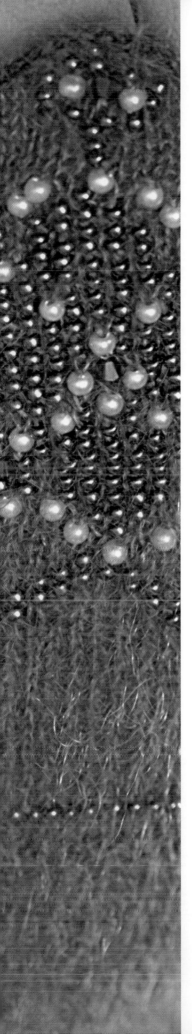

contents

introduction

The first, and one of the most important things to say about this book is that decorative knitting is not necessarily complicated knitting. A straightforward pattern can be richly embellished using easy-to-work techniques to produce a wonderfully decorative result.

The recent resurgence of the traditional craft of knitting has generated an enormous number of "easy knits" books aimed at teaching beginners the few simple techniques needed to start knitting. Essential and admirable though these books are, they are – as they are supposed to be – just a starting point.

With the basics mastered, the vast majority of knitters want more – more techniques, more ideas, more inspiration. *Decorative Knitting* supplies all of these in abundance. With 100 practical techniques, 200 inspirational knitted swatches and 18 creative projects, this book will expand the horizons of all knitters.

Within the five chapters that make up this book you will find techniques, ideas and projects suitable for those of you who have taken just the first few steps into the world of knitting, as well as more complex patterns for those who are already masters of the craft. For example, novices will be able to tackle the Caterpillar Baby Snuggler on page 62 with ease, while lovers of multi-texture, multi-stitch patterns will revel in the Helix Fur Scarf on page 31.

This book requires a basic level of skill: you need to be able to cast on using the cable and thumb methods; to be able to knit and purl; and to be able to bind (cast) off. In addition, you should understand intarsia and Fair Isle color knitting, as there is not a section devoted to these techniques. This is because, once the methods are mastered, the way forward is to knit different charted designs, and there are already many excellent books that offer hundreds of such designs.

There are five chapters in this book, each of which looks at a different aspect of decorative knitting. Firstly, Three-dimensional Yarn Effects offers different ways of creating surface texture and adding three-dimensional elements to a knitted fabric. Chapter Two, Yarn Plus, looks at the many possibilities for combining yarns, and what else you can knit with. Next is Knitting In, a chapter looking at the myriad of different embellishments that can be added to a knitted fabric. This is followed by Embroidery, where you can experiment with different stitches. Finally, Edgings and Trimmings looks at all important, but too often overlooked, ways of giving a project designer detail.

Each of these chapters is divided into three sections. The first section deals with techniques, and contains clear illustrations and detailed text to guide you through each and every one.

The second section is the Swatch Library, where you will find the techniques expanded upon to produce glorious knitted fabrics. Each swatch has full instructions, either a pattern or text, so that you can copy it.

The last section in each chapter contains the projects. Here you will find techniques and swatch ideas combined and taken further to produce a range of knitted items.

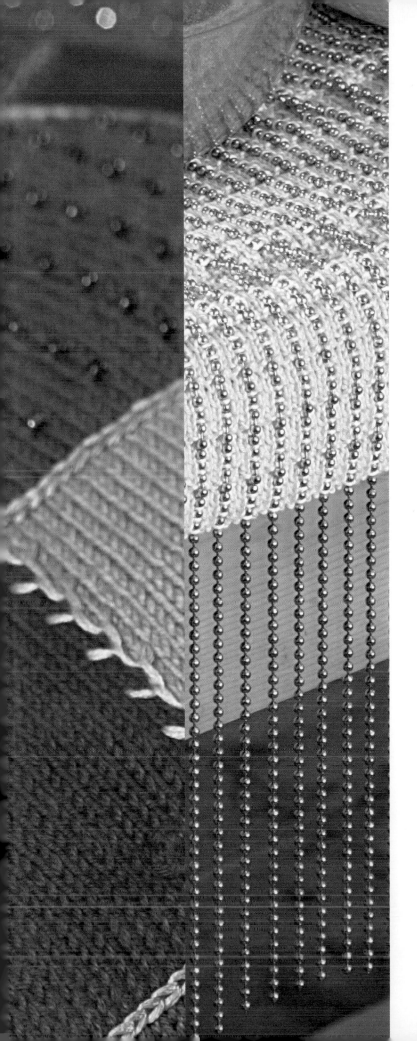

How to use this book

Decorative Knitting is designed to help you expand your knowledge and range of techniques and, above all, to experiment and create your own unique pieces of knitwear. Therefore, there are several ways of working with this book.

You can choose a project you would like to make and go from there. Each project gives a materials list and at the bottom of the pages you will find cross references to the techniques used in its construction. Turn to these and read them through to understand them or refresh your memory as appropriate.

It may be that a project appeals to you, but you don't want to use some of the techniques involved. Look through the swatch libraries, choose something you like instead and work a swatch to see how it will fit into the project you have chosen.

Alternatively, if you want to work from a favorite pattern you already have, read through techniques that appeal to you and incorporate them into your pattern. Some of the techniques can affect gauge (tension) or the dimensions of an item, and you will find notes on these problems and advice on how to get around them as appropriate.

The swatch libraries, too, can be plundered for ideas to augment your own patterns. Again, there are notes on potential problems, and it is always wise to look at the technique illustrations for the swatch as well. Within the swatch library text you will come across this symbol[1]. Look at the bottom of the page and you will find the cross reference to the appropriate technique.

Many of the swatch ideas can be used to embellish existing knitting. Embroidery is an obvious choice, but you could work fur cuffs and a collar, or add an edging, attach-later bobbles, or appliquéd shapes to a much-loved garment that is in need of a make over.

However you choose to use this book, experiment, create, embellish, and have a lot of fun doing it.

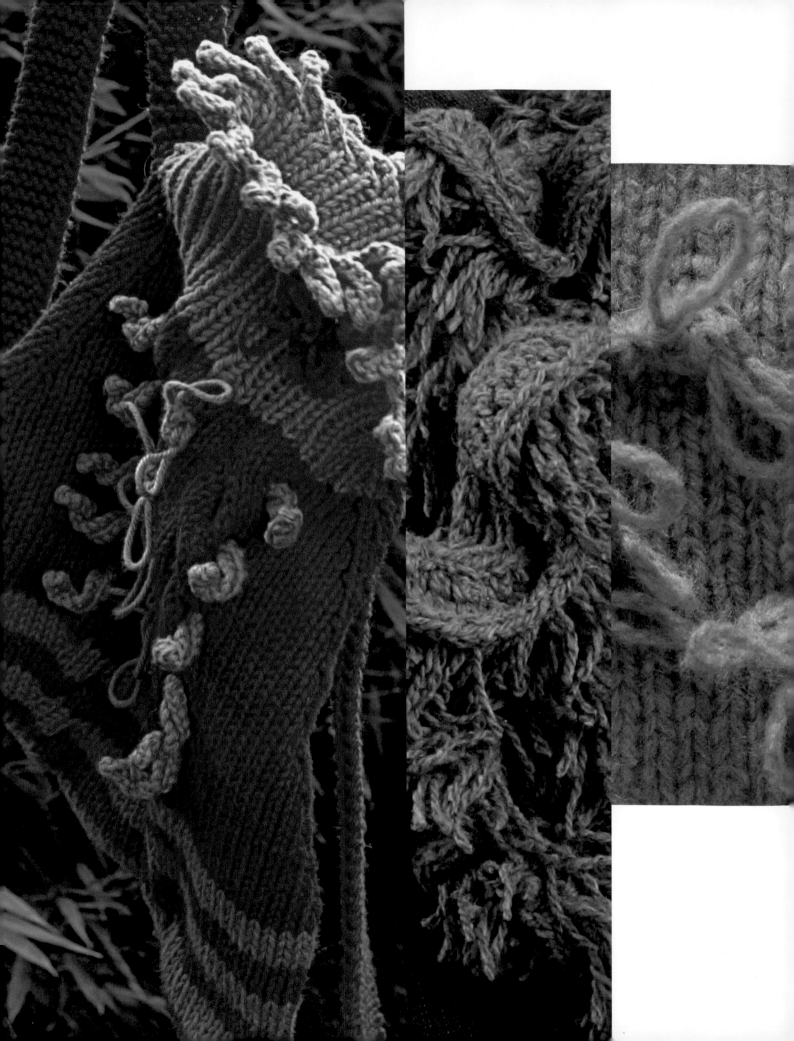

three-dimensional yarn effects

THE TERM "THREE-DIMENSIONAL" COVERS KNITTING techniques that range from basic shaping – which in one form or another finds its way into all but the simplest projects – through decorative stitches, such as loop stitch, bobbles, and cables, to quite complex techniques, such as short row shaping. This chapter will teach you how to work and apply all of these techniques to good effect.

Many knitters will be familiar with some of these techniques, but turn to the swatch library for ideas on how to expand them further. If you already know loop stitch, try working it on a bobble. If cables leave you cold, will beading them reawaken your interest?

If all of these techniques are new to you, then you will find plenty to learn and to try out. Following the instructions in the Techniques section, work swatches to master the various stitches, then move on to the Swatch Library and the projects to find new and exciting ways of putting them into practice.

Three-dimensional yarn effects
TECHNIQUES

Texture and shape

The most basic knitted items are pieces of flat fabric shaped by sewing them together. However, there are many techniques for adding texture and three-dimensional shapes to the surface of knitted fabric, and indeed for shaping it on the needles.

Surface texture is almost always knitted into the fabric as it is created, so some planning is required. The attach-later bobble is an exception as it can, as its name says, be attached to a finished project.

Some techniques, such as cables, will alter the gauge (tension) of the fabric, while others, such as pintucks, will affect the drape. It is important to swatch such techniques before starting a project.

Perfect shaping depends in part on choosing the right increases and decreases. Here, they are shown in matching pairs, making it easier for any knitter to achieve a professional finish.

Traditional Aran techniques

Traditional Aran knitting patterns originated in the Aran islands off the west coast of Ireland. They are characterized by their raised, rich-textured patterns, full of twists and turns.

The basic stitch combinations that create these textures are bobbles, cables and twists. Aran sweaters tend to have a dense knitted fabric because the patterning draws the stitches closely together. The traditional cream wool emphasizes the texture, but these designs can look equally good in more than one color or type of yarn.

BOBBLE

Bobbles are a group of stitches increased from one stitch and worked more times than other stitches in the row to create a pocket of stitches. The number of stitches created can vary, as can the stitch combinations and number of rows. Bobbles can be beaded, worked in a contrasting color to the background or in a different yarn, stranded across the back of the row. It is important to work bobbles tightly otherwise they may droop.

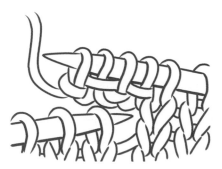

1 Work to the position of the bobble. Increase into the next stitch as many times as the pattern requires by working into the front and back of it.

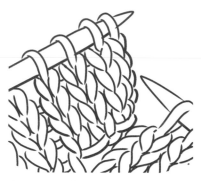

2 Turn the knitting and work the increase stitches only. Turn the knitting and work them again. Continue working the stitches in this way until the knitted pocket is the required depth, ending with a right-side row.

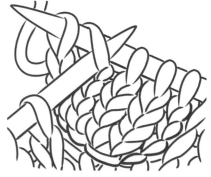

3 One at a time, slip the increase stitches over the first one. Continue working along the row to the next bobble. On the next row, work the bobble stitch firmly.

Alternatively, work the increase stitches until the pocket is the required depth and end with a wrong-side row. Slip one, knit one and pass the slipped stitch over, work one stitch and pass the first stitch over the second.

Continue to bind (cast) off the bobble stitches until two remain on the left-hand needle, knit two together, pass the first stitch over the second on the right-hand needle. Continue working along the row to the next bobble.

I-CORD BOBBLE

The I-cord bobble is worked in a similar way to the bobble above, but instead of turning the work to work several rows to make the pocket, the work remains right-side facing and the increase stitches are transferred onto the left-hand needle and worked again. These stitches are then transferred to the left-hand needle again and worked again, pulling the yarn tight after the first stitch is worked. Continue in this way until a pocket of the required depth is formed. The stitches are then decreased as described above. This bobble does have the advantage of not requiring frequent turning of the work – especially useful when the project is quite heavy – but also the bobble has a very neat form with the edges pulled together by the I-cord technique.

ATTACH-LATER BOBBLE

This bobble is made from a small knitted square that is gathered up to create a bobble that can then be attached to a knitted fabric. An excellent way to add a last-minute focal point to a project, and an easier way to add a bobble in a contrast color, these bobbles are also more controllable than those made by the traditional method, so the results are more consistent.

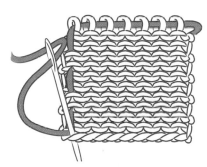

1 Cast on the required number of stitches and work a few rows to create a square of knitted fabric. Cut the yarn 4in (10 cm) from the square and thread a knitter's sewing needle with it. Pass the needle through the stitches and then work a small running stitch around the other three sides of the square. Pull the yarn tight to draw the edges together. Attach the bobble to the project with a few small stitches and secure the end on the back of the work.

TWISTS AND CROSSES

These techniques involve moving the position of one or more stitches to change their direction on a knitted fabric. They are sometimes called traveling stitches, as they do indeed travel across the background.

Crosses involve stitches are of the same type – for instance, two knit stitches – while twists involve stitches of different types – knit and purl stitches.

For twists of one or two knit stitches a cable needle can be used to hold the knit stitches front or back while the next stitch, usually one purl stitch, is worked. The traveling stitches can appear randomly to create a texture, vertically to create a mock cable, or as part of motif.

Twists and crosses will affect the gauge (tension) across the width of the fabric, so it is important to work a swatch and calculate the number of increases or extra stitches to be cast on. The technique for swapping two stitches is the same whether you are working a twist or a cross; it is illustrated here for a cross.

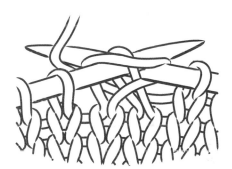

1 **To cross one stitch right**, work to the stitch before the one to be moved. Insert the right-hand needle into the second stitch on the left-hand needle and knit it. Then knit the first stitch on the left-hand needle.

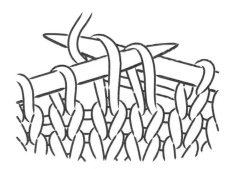

2 **To cross one stitch left**, work to the position of the stitch that is to be moved. Insert the right-hand needle into the second stitch on the left-hand needle through the back of the loop and knit it. Then knit the first stitch on the left-hand needle.

CABLE BACK OR BACKWARD

Cabling is moving groups of stitches across a knitted fabric. The same stitches can be moved repeatedly to create a rope-like pattern, or different stitches can be moved within a panel to create a more complex texture. Any yarn weight can be used, and cables can match the background fabric, be a contrasting color, or multicolored.

Cables are usually worked on a background of reverse st st to create the maximum contrast with the st st cable, but there are no rules.

Moving a group of stitches means that they will lose their elasticity and will draw the fabric up slightly. With a cable that swaps two groups of two stitches, an extra three stitches across the width of a project are often required. To be sure, work a plain swatch and a cabled swatch and measure the difference in width between them.

There are variations on the basic cable technique: the cable needle and stitches can be rotated by 180 degrees before the stitches are worked. Another variation is to have two sets of stitches on cable needles. One needle holds the center one or two stitches, and the other holds two groups of side stitches that will pass front or back of each other either side of the center stitches. A rope made with cable back appears to turn anti-clockwise on a knitted fabric.

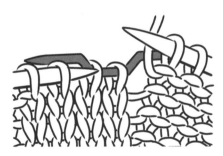

1 Work to the position of the cable and slip the required number of stitches onto a cable needle. Hold this needle at the back of the work.

2 Firmly work the required number of stitches from the left-hand needle.

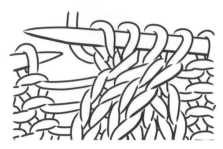

3 Then work the stitches on the cable needle to produce a crossover to the right.

CABLE FRONT OR FORWARD

The decorative possibilities and the variations that are described under Cable Back can all be applied equally well to cable front.

A rope made with cable front appears to turn clockwise on a knitted fabric.

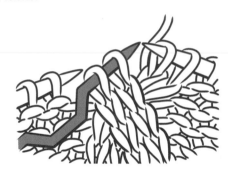

1 Work to the position of the cable and slip the required number of stitches onto a cable needle. Hold this needle at the front of the work. Work the required number of stitches from the left-hand needle, and then those on the cable needle to produce a crossover to the left.

Loops and strands

Fake fur on cuffs and collars or as an update for a classic shape has been part of our wardrobes for some time, and it is no surprise that knitting has the techniques and the materials to successfully create its own version of fur.

The loops that make up knitted fur are very yarn hungry: for example, looped fur worked on every second stitch around a thumb will use approximately three times as much yarn as plain st st. The density of the fur can be varied by altering the number of stitches between each loop. It is surprising how few loops are required to create a thick, luscious texture.

LOOPED FUR

Looped fur is a series of single loops emerging from a knitted fabric. It is called looped fur because the loops can be cut to create a fur texture, or they can be left intact. Loops can be beaded, but then they cannot be cut or the beads will fall off.

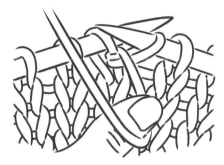

1 Right-side facing, work to the position of the loop. Insert the right-hand needle into the next stitch on the left-hand needle as if to knit, wrap the yarn round the right-hand needle and draw the loop through, without dropping the stitch off the left-hand needle. Bring the yarn to the front between the two needles and wind it clockwise round your free thumb.

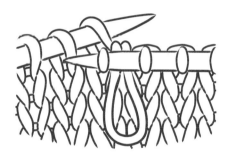

2 Take the yarn to the back of the work between the needles, knit the stitch again, and then slip it off the left-hand needle.

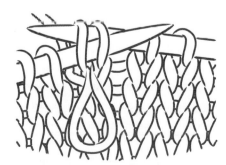

3 Slip both stitches onto the left hand needle, give the loop a sharp tug, and then knit the stitches firmly together through the backs of the loops.

LOOP CLUSTERS

Loop clusters are a series of loops created out of one stitch. Unlike single loop stitch, the loops cannot be cut to create a fur fabric, but their dense grouping looks very much like tight curls, and makes an excellent edging or all-over texture. This stitch works well if the cluster rows are worked in different yarns and different colors.

The number of loops can be varied but, depending on the yarn weight, too many loops may be difficult to draw through the stitch. The only way to find out is to try.

1 Wrong-side facing, take the yarn to the back and insert the right-hand needle knitwise into the next stitch on the left-hand needle. Wind the yarn round the fingers of your free hand and the tip of the right-hand needle in a clockwise direction, ending with the yarn on the needle. Hook the yarn between the needle and your fingers.

2 Use the tip of the right-hand needle to draw the ends of the loops through the stitch, leaving the original stitch on the left-hand needle.

3 Remove your fingers from the loops, slip the ends of the loops onto the left hand needle and knit them together with the original stitch through the backs of the loops. Pull gently on the loops on the right side to ease them through.

KNITTING IN STRANDS

Short strands of yarn can be worked into a knitted fabric. The fabric must be firmly knitted and, for the best results, the strands of either a heavier weight or a textured fluffy yarn. The result is secure enough to withstand reasonable wear-and-tear, but if fine yarn strands are worked into a chunky knitted fabric, they may ease out. This is an excellent technique for using up odd lengths of yarn, and the more varied the mix of yarns used within a project, the richer the final effect can be.

To make strands of an equal length, wrap yarn around a piece of card of the correct strand depth, beginning and ending on the same edge. Cut the yarn along this edge of the card.

1 Right-side facing, work to the position of the strand. Place the strand between the two needles, slip the next stitch, wrap the strand around the back of the slipped stitch and bring it forward between the two needles again. Slip the stitch back onto the left-hand needle. Insert the right-hand needle under the back of the strand, twist it clockwise and put it onto the left-hand needle. Work the strand loop and the next stitch on the left-hand needle together through the backs of the loops. Continue working along the row to the next strand position.

Shaping

Most three-dimensional shaping requires either an increase or a decrease in the number of stitches on a row. Any knitter who has ever glanced at a knitting manual before will know that there is a huge choice of both.

If the increases and decreases are to be used for subtle side shaping, then it should be noted that they are best worked two stitches in from the edge. Gathers, or increases to accommodate stitch patterns such as cables, should be evenly spaced along a row.

Increases and decreases can both be divided into stitches that slant to the left, stitches that slant to the right, or stitches with no bias in either direction.

If a right-slanting increase or decrease is used on the left-hand end of a row, then the stitch will slant along the same line as the edge of a knitted fabric, and vice versa for a left-slanting increase or decrease on a right-hand edge. Using increases and decreases in this way is common around necklines and when knitting complex shapes.

The term "fully fashioned" describes increases or decreases that slant towards the edge of a knitted fabric, instead of along the same line. This makes a distinct feature of the shaping and is often thought to be a indication of good design and technique.

INCREASES

There are two basic kinds of increases – those with holes and those without. It is important to select the correct increase to enhance the shaping, and to pair it with a complementary increase, if one is needed, on the other side of the project.

MAKE ONE RIGHT (M1R)

This increase slants to the right on the right side of the work.

On a knit row, work to the position of the increase. From back to front insert the left-hand needle into the strand of yarn between the two stitches. Knit into the front of this new stitch and continue working as before.

On a purl row, from front to back insert the left-hand needle into the strand of yarn between the two stitches and purl into the back of this new stitch.

MAKE ONE LEFT (M1L)

This increase slant to the left on the right side of the work.

On a knit row, work to the position of the increase. From front to back insert the left-hand needle into the strand of yarn between the two stitches. Knit into the back of this new stitch and continue working as before.

On a purl row, from back to front insert the left-hand needle into the strand of yarn between the two stitches and purl into the front of this new stitch.

INCREASE RIGHT (INCR)

This increase slants to the right on the right side of the work.

On a knit row, work to the position of the increase. Insert the right-hand needle into the back loop of the stitch below the next stitch on the left-hand needle and knit a new stitch, taking care to make the stitch loop the right length. Knit the next stitch and continue working as before.

On a purl row, the technique is exactly the same, but the back loop of the stitch below is at the front.

INCREASE LEFT (INCL)

This increase slant to the left on the right side of the work.

On a knit row, work to the position of the increase and knit the stitch. Insert the left-hand needle into the back loop of the stitch below the stitch just worked. Knit a new stitch, taking care to make the stitch loop the right length. Continue working as before.

On a purl row, the technique is exactly the same but the back loop of the stitch below is at the front.

WORK TWICE INTO THE SAME STITCH (INC)

This increase has a horizontal bar across the new stitch, but no bias.

On a knit row, work to the position of the increase. Knit into the back of the stitch then, without slipping the stitch off the left-hand needle, knit into the front of it. This can be repeated several times into the same stitch.

On a purl row, the technique is exactly the same, but purl into the back and front of the stitch.

YARNOVER

A yarnover is a loop of yarn wrapped around a needle and then worked as a stitch. This loop creates a small hole because it is not anchored to the stitches below.

On the next row the size of the hole can be reduced by working the stitch through the back of the loop. The size can be increased by wrapping the yarn twice around the needle and dropping one loop on the next row.

Yarnover is sometimes called "yarn forward" and is a staple of lace knitting, where it is often accompanied by a decrease. Decorative in themselves, yarnovers can also

be embroidered, fitted with eyelets, used to thread materials through, or reveal color behind. However, even if accompanied by a decrease, large numbers of yarnovers will affect the gauge (tension) and need to be swatched.

1 **On a knit row**, work to the yarnover. Bring the yarn to the front. Insert the right-hand needle into the next stitch and take the yarn under and around the tip of it to work the stitch. If the following stitch is knit, leave the yarn at the back; if it is purl, bring it to the front.

2 **On a purl row**, work to the position of the yarnover. Take the yarn over the right-hand needle. Insert the right-hand needle into the next stitch and take the yarn over and around the tip of it to work the stitch. If the following stitch is purl, leave the yarn at the front; if it is knit, take it to the back.

THUMB LOOP CAST ON

Thumb loop cast on creates one or more loops that can be worked as stitches. It is useful when shaping demands an abrupt change in width, and unlike cable cast on, it does not add an extra row of stitches. This cast on is often used to make the extra stitches to complete a buttonhole.

1 Work to the end of the row. Holding the yarn under your fingers against your palm, wrap the yarn around your thumb clockwise and slip the loop onto the needle. Work into the back of these new stitches on the next row.

DECREASES

There are many different decreases available to the knitter, all of which have a slightly different look. The most commonly used decreases are knit two stitches together (k2tog) and purl two stitches together (p2tog).

For k2tog, insert the right-hand needle knitwise through the second and then the first stitch on the left-hand needle and knit them together. This decrease slants to the right on a knit row. For p2tog, insert the right-hand needle purlwise through the first and then the second stitch on the left-hand needle and purl them together. This decrease slants to the left on a purl row.

As with increases, it is important to select the right decrease to enhance the shaping on a project, and to pair it with a complementary decrease, if one is needed, on the opposite edge.

SLIP, SLIP, KNIT TWO STITCHES TOGETHER (SSK)

This decrease slants to the left on a knit row. Use it on a right-hand side paired with knit two together on the left. The wrong-side equivalent is slip, slip, purl two together through the backs of the loops.

Work to the position of the decrease. Insert the right-hand needle into the next stitch and slip it knitwise onto the needle. Repeat with the next stitch. Insert the left-hand needle into both slipped stitches through the backs of the loops and knit the two stitches together, wrapping the yarn around the right-hand needle as usual.

SLIP, SLIP, PURL TWO STITCHES TOGETHER (SS P2TOG TBL)

This decrease slants to the left on a purl row. Use it on a left-hand side paired with purl two together on the right. The right-side equivalent is slip, slip, knit two together through the backs of the loops.

Work to the position of the decrease. Insert the right-hand needle into the next stitch and slip it knitwise onto the needle. Repeat with the next stitch. Transfer both stitches back to the left-hand needle and insert the right-hand needle into both slipped stitches through the backs of the loops and purl them together.

SLIP ONE, KNIT ONE, PASS THE SLIPPED STITCH OVER (SKPSSO)

This decrease slants to the left on a knit row. Use it on a right-hand side paired with knit two together on the left. The wrong-side equivalent is purl two together through the backs of the loops.

Work to the position of the decrease. Insert the right-hand needle into the next stitch and slip it knitwise onto the needle. Knit the next stitch, then pass the slipped stitch over the knit stitch and off the right-hand needle.

PURL TWO STITCHES TOGETHER THROUGH THE BACKS OF THE LOOPS (P2TOG TBL)

This decrease slants to the right on a purl row. Use it on a left-hand side paired with purl two together on the right. The right-side equivalent is slip one, knit one, pass the slipped stitch over.

Work to position of the decrease. From the right, insert the right-hand needle through the back loops of the next two stitches and purl them together.

KNIT ONE, PASS THE NEXT STITCH OVER (K1, PNSO)

This decrease slants to the right on a knit row. Use it on a left-hand side paired with slip one, knit one, pass the slipped stitch over on the right. The wrong-side equivalent is slip one, purl one, pass the slipped stitch over.

Work to the decrease. Knit one, pass it back to the left-hand needle, pass the next stitch over it and off the needle. Pass the knitted stitch back to the right-hand needle.

SLIP ONE, PURL ONE, PASS THE SLIPPED STITCH OVER (SPPSSO)

This decrease slants to the left on a purl row. Use it on a left-hand side paired with purl two together on the right. The right-side equivalent is knit one, pass the next stitch over.

Work to the decrease. Insert the right-hand needle into the next stitch and slip it purlwise. Purl the next stitch, then pass the slipped stitch over the purl stitch and off the needle.

EDGE STITCH DECREASES

Sometimes decreases have to occur on the very edge of a project. An effective decrease in these circumstances is slip one, knit two together (sk2tog), which slants to the left on a knit row. Use it on a right-hand side paired with knit two together on the left. Insert the needle into the first stitch and slip it knitwise onto the right-hand needle. Slip it purlwise back onto the left-hand needle and knit two stitches together through the backs of the loops.

If a number of stitches are to be decreased, then the stitches are bound (cast) off and one of the many techniques on pages 128–130 could be used. A neater finish is usually obtained by stopping one stitch short of the end on the previous row, then turning to proceed along the next row. Work the next stitch on the left-hand needle and pass the missed stitch over it. The rest of the row can then be worked or bound (cast) off as required.

If a series of unsightly holes appear when decreasing on the outer edges, then turn the work one stitch from the edge, as above. Before working the first stitch of the new row, make a yarnover and work one stitch. Then insert the left-hand needle into the worked stitch, the yarnover and slipped stitch through the backs of the loops and knit the three stitches together, wrapping the yarn around the right-hand needle as usual.

Here is a useful tip that is not a decrease, but is worked in a similar way. To avoid a saggy last stitch on a bound (cast) off row, slip the first stitch of the previous row. This works particularly well if the edge stitches are firmly knitted on every row.

SLIP TWO, PURL THREE STITCHES TOGETHER

(S2TOG, P3TOG)

This is a double decrease that makes the stitches on either side slant towards it. The right-side equivalent is slip two stitches together, knit one and pass the slipped stitches over

Work to the position of the decrease. Insert the right-hand needle into the next stitch on the left-hand needle and slip it knitwise onto the right-hand needle. Repeat this process with the next stitch. From the right, insert the left-hand needle into the front of the two stitches together, turning them around onto the left-hand needle. Insert the right-hand needle purlwise through the two slipped stitches and a third stitch and purl all three together.

SLIP TWO TOGETHER, KNIT ONE AND

PASS THE SLIPPED STITCHES OVER

(S2TOG, K1, PSSO)

This is a double decrease that makes the stitches on either side slant towards it. The wrong-side equivalent is slip two, purl three stitches together.

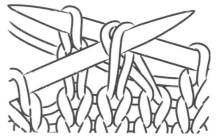

1 Work to the position of the decrease. Insert the right-hand needle into the second stitch and then the first one on the left-hand needle and slip them knitwise onto the right-hand needle. Knit the next stitch, then pass the slipped stitches over the knit stitch and off the right-hand needle.

YARNOVER DECREASES

A yarnover decrease involves reducing the number of stitches by one more than is required, but accompanying the decrease with a yarnover to make up the stitch count. For example, knit three together, yarnover, rather than knit two together. This creates a small hole next to the decrease and, although a triple decrease is more dense than a double decrease, the result is a looser line of decreases without affecting the gauge (tension). This is particularly useful for lacy fabric with solid lines of decreases along an selvedge, such as an armhole or neckline. On a right-hand side, work the decrease first and then the yarnover, and on a left-hand side, work the yarnover first and then the decrease. If the decrease on one edge is more prominent than the other, then work into the back of the loop on the subsequent rows to reduce the size of the hole.

Keep the decreases simple, pairing knit three together through the backs of the loops with knit three together on the right side of the work. On the wrong side, pair purl three together with purl three together through the backs of the loops. Working into the backs of the loops does produce a twisted stitch, but this can be avoided by slipping the stitches individually knitwise and transferring them back onto the left-hand needle before working them.

SHORT ROW SHAPING

Short row shaping involves working some stitches more often than others, creating a dart or a moulded semi-circular effect. This can be useful for collars and shoulder seams where binding (casting) off can be visible. It can also be used in decorative knitting to create geometric bands of color, contrast yarn textures, and stitch patterns. Shapes can be created that can then either be applied to a knitted fabric, or become part of a surface texture.

This technique involves two stages; the turning and the wrapping of the stitches and then, when that is completed, the hiding of the visible signs of the technique.

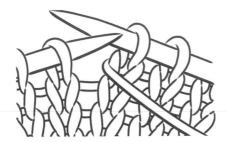

1 **To turn on a knit row**, work to the position of the turn. With the yarn at the back, slip the next stitch on the left-hand needle purlwise onto the right-hand needle. Bring the yarn forward between the needles.

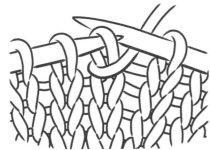

2 Slip the stitch back onto the left-hand needle and take the yarn to the back between the needles again. Turn the work around and work to the next short row turn.

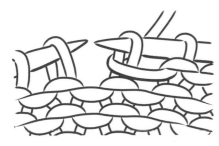

1 **To turn on a purl row**, work to the turn. Slip the next stitch on the left-hand needle purlwise onto the right-hand needle. Take the yarn back between the needles.

2 Slip the stitch back onto the left-hand needle and bring the yarn back to the front between the needles again. Turn the work around and work to the next short row turn.

To prevent the wrap loops and the slipped stitches showing, they need to be picked up and worked together; this is done when all the shaping is completed. After the last turn work right to the end of the row, picking up the loops as you go. If the shaping was worked on both sides of the project, pick up the loops on the other side on the next row of the work.

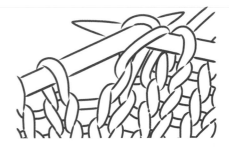

1 **On a knit row**, work to the position of the wrap loop. From the front, insert the right-hand needle under the wrap loop and through the slipped stitch on the left-hand needle. Knit the loop and the slipped stitch together so the wrap loop is no longer visible on the right side. Knit along the row to the next wrap loop and repeat the process.

2 **On a purl row**, work to the position of the wrap loop. From behind, insert the right-hand needle under the wrap loop and place it on the left-hand needle. Purl the loop and the slipped stitch together so the wrap loop is no longer visible on the right side. Purl along the row to the next wrap loop and repeat the process.

Knitted darts and gathers

An increase or decrease every second or third stitch across a row will give the effect of gathers. Pleats can be created by working bands of stitches together before binding (casting) them off.

Gathering up rows to create pintucks can be done by knitting stitches from previous rows with those on the working row. For a flatter finish, work the fold row (the halfway row of the pintuck) as a purl row.

Gussets can be created, for the thumb of a mitten for instance, by placing an increase either side of a stitch and then increasing above this stitch on subsequent rows, so that the space between the two original increases is increased by two stitches on each increase row.

Another way a pouch can be created is to work a number of stitches in the center of a row more frequently than others but, unlike a bobble, securing them to the surrounding knitting by wrapping the yarn round the edge stitches as an anchor.

PLEATS

Pleats are created by folding a section of a knitted fabric back on itself in one direction to make the return, and then again in the other direction to make the front. As you can imagine, the layers involved make it easier to execute pleats in fine yarns.

Each of the three sections of a pleat – the front, the return and the back – have the same number of stitches. To calculate how many stitches to cast on, work out how many stitches wide the pleat will be and multiply this by two, plus two stitches to create the fold lines. For each pleat, add this total to the number of stitches cast on. Once the principles of this technique have been mastered, knife, box and inverted pleats can also be created.

1 Work to the position of the first fold of the pleat. Either slip one stitch knitwise to mark the end of the front section or purl one to mark the end of the return, depending on which way the pleat folds. In this case a slip stitch comes first, then a purl stitch, because the pleat folds to the left. Work in this pattern until the pleat is the required depth.

This pleat is worked into a bound (cast) off row, but you can work to the pleat, pick up and knit together the stitches forming it, then work flat knitted fabric above it.

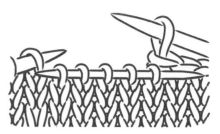

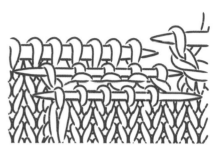

2 Bind (cast) off to the first pleat. Slip the front section stitches and the slipped stitch onto a cable needle.

3 Slip the stitches for the return, including the purl stitch, onto a second cable needle. Turn this needle and stitches so that the wrong side of the return is facing the wrong side of the front. Use a large safety pin to pin the fabric of the return and the front together just below the needles, taking care not to split the yarn. This just reduces the number of hands you will feel you will need later on.

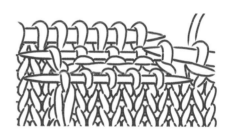

4 Slip the first stitch on the return onto the right-hand needle. Knit the first stitch on the back section and pass the two stitches on the right-hand needle over it one at a time.

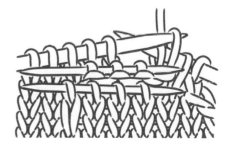

5 *Slip one stitch from the front section and one from the return onto the right-hand needle. Knit one stitch from the back section and pass each of the other three stitches on the right-hand needle over it. Repeat from * to the end of the pleat. Bind (cast) off along the row to the next pleat.

PINTUCKS

Pintucks are horizontal pleats of knitted fabric. They are created by picking up stitches from a lower row and knitting them together with the stitches on the working row. Pintucks can be of varying depths along a row, they can be knitted in a contrasting color, or be threaded with a length of cord to make them more prominent. For a softer effect, create a deeper pintuck with only a few inches at either end of the row knitted together with a lower row.

A picot pintuck can be created by working a row of yarnovers on the fold row. When the pintuck is completed the yarnovers will be folded in half, giving a gently scalloped edge.

However they are made, pintucks can create a bulky seam, and although a few selvedge stitches can be left flat and eased into the seam, the result is not always satisfactory, so make any pintucks part of the design.

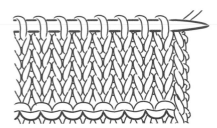

1 Work to the position of the pintuck. Mark the next row by working it with a slightly larger needle; this is not always necessary, but it will create larger stitch loops that are easier to pick up in Step 2. Continue to work a number of rows until the fold of the pintuck is reached. Work the next row using the same stitch as the previous row, or purl stitch if working a mixed stitch pattern. Work a number of rows equal to that between the marked row and the fold.

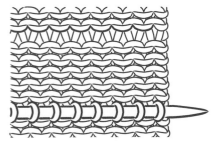

2 Before working the pintuck, and wrong-side facing, use a double-pointed needle to pick up the upper stitch loop of each stitch on the marked row. Then, right-side facing, work together across the row one stitch from the left-hand needle and one stitch from the double-pointed needle. As you become more experienced you will be able to

abandon the double-pointed needle and pick up the stitch loop on the marked row with the right-hand needle, transfer it to the left-hand needle and work the stitch and the loop together.

Selvedges

For three dimensional shapes with edges that will not be hidden within a seam, it is particularly important to take care with the edge stitches and the selvedge. It is good practice anyway to work the first and last stitches of each row more firmly than those in the middle of the row.

A popular selvedge is to slip the first stitch of every row, knitwise on a knit row and purlwise on a purl row. This creates a chain-stitch effect along the edge that is excellent when creating shapes, but if the edge is to be seamed, do not use mattress stitch on the edge stitch. As there is only one stitch every two rows, allow an extra stitch for seaming; the slipped stitches will reduce the seam bulk.

A simple alternative is to knit the first and last stitch of every row, whatever the stitch pattern. However, for invisible seaming on st st allow an extra stitch on each edge.

An I-cord type of selvedge is created by knitting into the back of the first stitch on right-side rows and slipping one or more stitches at the beginning and end of wrong-side rows. These edge stitches span two rows and the edge is less elastic, but very neat. On garter stitch, knit the first stitch through the back of the loop and slip the last stitch purlwise with the yarn at the front for a similar effect.

A yarnover selvedge produces a very satisfying result, makes seaming easier and retains its elasticity. On knit rows, make a yarnover, knit two stitches together, work to the end of the row and purl the last stitch through the back of the loop. On purl rows, make a yarnover, purl two stitches together through the backs of the loops and knit the last stitch through the back of the loop. This does create a twisted decrease stitch on the left-hand side, but the stitches can be turned by slipping them one at a time knitwise and transferring them back to the left-hand needle before working them together through the backs of the loops.

Three-dimensional yarn effects
SWATCH LIBRARY

Relief patterning, knitted-in shapes and surface texture can all add detail and interest to a knitted project. You can add ideas from this Library to a plain pattern, though remember that elements such as cables and ladders will alter the size of the finished project, so you will need to work swatches and make any necessary adjustments. Alternatively, if the pattern you are using already has some of the elements shown here, then use these ideas to embellish them further: for example, turn a plain bobble into a beaded one.

Bobbles

Quick and easy to create, bobbles↓ do not distort gauge (tension) and so, almost at a whim, can be used to enrich any knitting pattern in a variety of ways. All the bobbles shown here are based on the basic bobble from page 10, but these techniques can be adapted for any bobble, or can be combined to produce still more effects.

❶ TEXTURED BOBBLE
Knitting all the rows creates a bobble with a dense texture that will be slightly more prominent than one worked with alternate purl rows. In a similar way, a st st bobble contrasts well with a rev st st background.

❷ BEADED BOBBLE
On alternate rows and stitches beads↓ can be placed to create a bobble that will catch the light. This can be particularly successful when the bobble is worked within contrasting textures.

Abbreviations
PB = place bead using the slip stitch method. Here, 7 beads are threaded onto the yarn.

Row 1 (RS): K into front and back of st seven times
Row 2: [P1, PB] rep to last st, p1.
Row 3: Knit.
Row 4: [PB, p1] rep to last st, PB.
Row 5: Ssk, k3tog, k2tog.
Row 6: P3tog.

❸ BOBBLE IN ANOTHER YARN
Working a bobble in another yarn can add a contrasting texture or color, which is especially effective when the bobbles are grouped, or positioned at regular intervals.

To create the bobble, work 1 st on the previous row immediately below the proposed bobble in the second yarn. On the next row knit seven times into the front and back of this stitch to create the base of the bobble. Work the bobble in the second yarn and then continue in the main color.

This technique is also very useful when working bobbles in novelty yarns that can create unpredictably shaped bobbles. The two ends at the beginning and end of the bobble can be pulled and the bobble nudged into a perfect shape.

These bobbles are also good way of using up odd bits of yarn left over from other projects.

❹ TWO-COLOR BOBBLE
A bobble can also be created in two colors by working, in this case, the first two rows in one color and then continuing in a second. A variety of color combinations can be worked, but stranding yarns on a row can make the bobble rather stiff and less inclined to form a neat shape.

❺ EMBROIDERED BOBBLE
A bobble can also be embroidered↓ in colors chosen from other elements of the project.

❻ SINGLE-BEAD BOBBLE
Rather than knitting beads into a bobble, a bead, or beads, can be sewn on when the work has been completed. This gives more control over the position of the bead and it will stand slightly proud of the bobble.

❼ BOBBLES AS PART OF A MOTIF
Bobbles can be used in intarsia patterns to add texture; this works particularly well when the bobbles are part of the motif. Look for round elements of the right size and work a bobble instead. This flower has an embroidered bullion knot to represent the center.

❽ BIG BOBBLE
These bobbles are knitted separately and then sewn onto a project.

Cast on 8 sts using the thumb method. Work 16 rows in garter stitch, then make up the bobble.

Here, the bobbles are used to trim the edge of a piece of garter stitch knitted fabric that is worked in a contrasting color.

The bobble yarn is also threaded under the lower loops of the garter stitch fabric to decorate it further.

TECHNIQUES: Bobbles ♦ page 10　•　Slip stitch beading ♦ page 68　•　Embroidery ♦ page 94

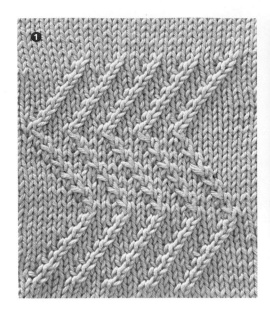

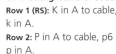

4 MIXED YARN CABLE

The additional yarn color adds definition to the cable, allowing it to be worked on either a st st or rev st st background. Simply knit the two yarns togther↓ for the cable.

A = background color
B = additional yarn color

Top Panel of 6 sts and repeat of 4 rows on a background of rev st st.
Row 1 (RS): K in A to cable, k6 in A and B, k in A.
Row 2: P in A to cable, p6 in A and B, p in A.
Row 3: K in A to cable, C6F in A and B, k in A.
Row 4: As row 2.
Rep rows 1–4 as required.

Bottom Panel of 6 sts and repeat of 4 rows on a background of st st.
Row 1 (RS): P in A to cable, k6 in A and B, p in A.
Row 2: K in A to cable, p6 in A and B, k in A.
Row 3: P in A to cable, C6F in A and B, p in A.
Row 4: As row 2.
Rep rows 1–4 as required.

Twists and crosses

These stitch techniques are quite subtle and so are best worked with a smooth yarn; a furry yarn can make them almost completely invisible on the background.

1 TWIST CHEVRON

Twist stitches↓ are defined enough to stand out on a st st background, particularly if a cotton yarn, which shows stitch patterns well, is used.

Panel of 23 sts and repeat of 24 rows on a background of st st.
Row 1 (RS): K6, T2F, [k3, T2F] rep to the end of the row.
Row 2 and every alt row: Purl.
Row 3: K5, T2F, [k3, T2F] rep three more times, k to end.
Row 5: K4, T2F, [k3, T2F] rep three more times, k to end.
Row 7: K3, T2F, [k3, T2F] rep three more times, k to end.
Row 9: K2, T2F, [k3, T2F] rep three more times, k to end.
Row 11: K1, T2F, [k3, T2F] rep three more times, k to end.
Row 13: K1, T2B, [k3, T2B] rep three more times, k to end.
Row 15: K2, T2B, [k3, T2B] rep three more times, k to end.
Row 17: K3, T2B, [k3, T2B] rep three more times, k to end.
Row 19: K4, T2B, [k3, T2B] rep three more times, k to end.
Row 21: K5, T2B, [k3, T2B] rep three more times, k to end.
Row 33: K6, T2B, [k3, T2B] rep to the end of the row.
Row 24: Purl.
Rep rows 1–24 as required.

2 Cross motif

On this swatch semi-abstract flower motifs are created with twisted stitches forming the stems and a bobble↓ or loop clusters↓ forming the head of the flower on a background of rev st st.

Establish the position of the knit stitches on the first row. Then twist the stitches on some knit rows and simply knit them on others to create meandering lines of twisted knit stitches across the surface of a knitted fabric.

When each stem reaches the required height, top it off with a bobble or a cluster of loops worked on the next row.

Cables

All the swatches shown are simple cable patterns↓, it is the way in which color and embellishment are used that make them so much more interesting.

3 TWO-COLOR OR TWO-YARN CABLE

This swatch is worked with both two colors and two yarns, but you could use just a different color to achieve a similar effect. A matching color, but different-textured, yarn will create a subtler look.

As the cable is defined by color or texture, it can be worked on a st st background. Use the intarsia technique to twist the yarns around each other at the back of the work to avoid holes when changing colors or yarns.

A = background color
B = cable color

Panel of 6 sts and repeat of 6 rows on a background of st st.
Row 1 (RS): K in A to cable, k6 in B, k in A.
Row 2: P in A to cable, p6 in B, p in A.
Row 3: K in A to cable, C6F in B, K in A.
Row 4: As row 2.
Rows 5–6: As rows 1–2.
Rep rows 1–6 as required.

TECHNIQUES: Twists and crosses ◆ page 11 • Bobbles ◆ page 10 • Loop clusters ◆ page 13 • Cables ◆ page 12
Mixing yarns ◆ page 40

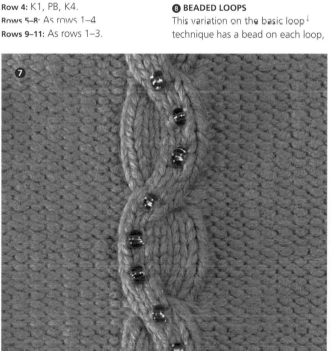

⑤ STRIPED CABLE

The difference between the color change on the rev st st background and on the st st cable makes the stripes more interesting.

A = first color
B = second color

Panel of 8 sts and repeat of 16 rows on a background of rev st st.
Row 1 (RS): P6 in A.
Row 2: K6 in A.
Rows 3–6: Rep rows 1–2 twice more.
Row 7: P6 in A.
Row 8: C4F in A.
Row 9: P6 in B.
Row 10: K6 in B.
Rows 11–14: Rep rows 1–2 twice more.
Row 15: P6 in B.
Row 16: C4F in B.
Rep rows 1–16 as required.

⑥ RIB CABLE

To harmonize the rib of a garment with the main body, run the cable into the rib pattern. Work out the pattern carefully to ensure that there are purl stitches either side of the cable; k2, p2 rib balances a cable better than single rib.

Panel of 6 sts and repeat of 6 rows on a background of k2, p2 rib.
Row 1 (RS) : [K2, p2] rep to cable, k6, [p2, k2] rep to the end of the row.
Row 2: [P2, k2] rep to cable, p6, [k2, p2] rep to the end of the row.
Row 3: [K2, p2] rep to cable, C6F, [p2, k2] rep to the end of the row.
Row 4: As row 2.
Rows 5–6: As rows 1–2.
Rep rows 1–6 as required.

⑦ BEADED CABLE

This technique works better on a wandering cable rather than a twisted one, as the beads define the wandering line but merely make a row on twists. Use the slip stitch↓ method to place the beads.

Abbreviations
C6FPB = slip 3 sts onto a cable needle and hold at front of work. K3, k1 from cable needle, place bead, k1 from cable needle.
C6BPB = slip 3 sts onto a cable needle and hold at back of work. K1, place bead, k1, k3 from cable needle.

Panel of 6 sts and repeat of 24 rows on a background of rev st st.
Row 1 (RS): P6.
Row 2: K6.
Row 3: P6.
Row 4: K1, PB, K4.
Rows 5–8: As rows 1–4.
Rows 9–11: As rows 1–3.

Row 12: C6FPB.
Rows 13–15: As rows 1–3.
Row 16: K4, PB, k1.
Rows 17–20: As rows 13–16.
Rows 21–23: As rows 1–3.
Row 24: C6BPB.
Rep rows 1–24 as required.

Loops and strands

Loop stitch offers a fabulous way of adding rich texture to knitting. The stitch is easy, if a little time-consuming, to work and can be used to create either all-over texture or to make an edging, border or band on a project. To create effective fur, just cut the loops.

⑧ BEADED LOOPS

This variation on the basic loop↓ technique has a bead on each loop, which gives weight to the fabric. Choose toning beads, as here, for a subtle look, or bright, contrasting ones for a more defined effect.

Work out how many beads are needed by dividing the total number of stitches to be worked in half. Thread the beads onto the yarn↓.

Row 1 (WS): Purl.
Row 2: Knit, making a loop in every stitch. Slide a bead down so that it sits on the yarn being wrapped around the fingers for every loop.
Rep rows 1–2 as required.

⑨ RANDOM CLUSTER LOOPS

As clusters of loops↓ are worked on the wrong side of the fabric, using seed (moss) stitch as a background allows them to be distributed randomly across the fabric rather than in rows. If a knitted fabric is to be reversible (for example, a scarf), the loops can be worked on both sides.

Row 1 (WS): [K1, p1, to position of loops, make cluster of loops] rep as required.
Rep this row as required.

TECHNIQUES: Slip stitch beading ▶ page 68 • Loop fur ▶ page 13 • Threading beads onto the yarn ▶ page 66 • Loop clusters ▶ page 13

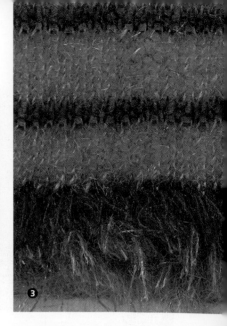

❶ LOOP BOBBLE

A perky variation on the basic bobble↓, this can be worked to complement loop knitting on another part of a project, or as a decorative detail in its own right.

Row 1 (RS): K to the position of the bobble, k twice into front and back of stitch.
Row 2: Purl.
Row 3: Knit, making a loop in every stitch.
Row 4: Purl.
Row 5: Slip 2 sts knitwise, k2tog, psso.

❷ MULTI-YARN LOOPS AND FUR

Mixing yarns↓ makes for thickly looped, but rather inflexible fabric. This technique is therefore best used on items such as bags that will benefit from the stiffness.

Here, DK cotton, DK wool and mohair yarn are worked together. The loops on the left of the swatch are cut to create fur. The st st fabric above the loops is worked with the wool and mohair yarns.

Row 1 (WS): Purl.
Row 2: Knit, making a loop with all three yarns in every st.
Rep rows 1–2 as required.

❸ STRIPED FUR

Make more of basic stripes by making them furry. This could be done all over a knitted fabric, or, as here, to make an edging that co-ordinates with the main fabric.

Work a stripe pattern in st st for the required number of rows. Keeping the pattern consistent, make a loop in every knit stitch for the required number of rows. Cut the loops to create fur.

❹ KNITTING-IN STRANDS

Strands of yarn can be knitted in↓ to a fabric to create three-dimensional texture. The strands are added on knit rows and can be applied in strips, as individual fringes, or thickly.
Left A vertical strip with strands knitted into three adjacent stitches on every knit row. The ends of the strands are deliberately left at different lengths.
Center Randomly placed strands with a bead threaded onto each end of each strand and the ends knotted to hold the beads in place.
Right All-over texture with a strand knitted into every stitch on every knit row. It can be difficult to work this stitch with short lengths of fiber and to get the ends completely even. Instead of trying, use longer lengths and trim them short and even when the work is completed.

Ladders

Usually ladders are the result of a dropped stitch, ghastly mistakes that can take time and patience to repair. However, when controlled by increasing↓ and then dropping a stitch they can add an interesting, "distressed" effect to a piece of knitted fabric. Bear in mind that the unravelling will affect the stitches two to three rows below the made stitch.

❺ ST ST LADDER

Worked on st st, ladders show up well. To avoid the stitches on either side becoming baggy and spoiling the effect, work them tightly.

Ladders can be placed at random, but you need to keep careful count of the stitches so that you drop the right one. Remember that ladders will affect the size of an item if there are a lot of them, so it is important to work a swatch.

This swatch is 30 sts by 40 rows and full instructions are given to help you understand how the stitches are counted.

Cast on 30 sts.
Starting with a knit row, work 4 rows st st.
Row 5 (RS): K6, M1, k to the end of the row.
Work 3 rows st st.
Row 9: K23, M1, k to the end of the row.
Work 5 rows st st.
Row 15: K17, M1, k to the end of the row.
Work 5 rows st st.
Row 21: K11, M1, k to the end of the row.
Row 22: Purl.
Row 23: K6, drop next st, k to the end of the row. (Row 5 st dropped.)
Work 5 rows st st.
Row 29: K17, drop next st, k to the end of the row.

TECHNIQUES: Bobbles ◈ page 10 • Mixing yarns ◈ page 40 • Knitting in strands ◈ page 14 • Increases ◈ page 14

Rep rows 1–2 until
4 sts remain.
Next row: Skpsso, k2tog.
Next row: K2tog.
Bind (cast) off.

8 FLOWER
This is made up of five separate knitted petals and a bobble↓. The petals are worked in garter stitch so that the flower will lie flat.

Cast on 6 sts using the thumb method.
Row 1 (RS) (base of petal): Knit.
Row 2: K1, inc, k to last 2 sts, inc, k1.
Rep rows 1–2 once more.
Knit 3 rows.
Row 8: As row 2.
Knit 6 rows.
Row 15: K1, skpsso, k to last 3 sts, k2tog, k1.
Row 16: Knit.
Rep rows 15–16 twice more.
Row 21: Skpsso, k2, k2tog.
Row 22: Knit.
Row 23: Skpsso, k2tog.
Bind (cast) off.

Make five petals. Sew the bases together to form a flower shape. Make a bobble↓ and sew it into the center of the flower.

9 LEAF
Worked in st st for a smooth surface, leaves can be attached to the back of a flower or used as separate items for appliqué↓. For a more interesting shape, this leaf is worked "on the bias."

Cast on 7 sts using the cable cast on method.
Row 1 (RS): Knit.
Row 2: P2tog, p5, cast on 2 sts.
Row 3: Knit.
Row 4: P8, cast on 1 st.
Row 5: Inc, k6, k2tog.
Row 6: P9, cast on 1 st.
Row 7: Inc, k7, cast on 1 st.
Row 9: K9, k2tog.
Row 10: P2tog, p8, cast on 1 st.
Row 11: K8, k2tog.
Row 12: P2tog, p7, cast on 1 st.
Row 13: K7, k2tog.
Row 14: Bind (cast) off 3 sts, p4.
Row 15: Inc, k2, k2tog.
Bind (cast) off.

10 HEART
For a neat selvedge, slip the first and last stitch on the purl rows purlwise and knit the first stitch on the knit rows through the back of the loop.

Abbreviations
M1L = make one left
M1R = make one right

Cast on 3 sts.
Work 4 rows of st st.
Row 5 (RS). K1, M1L, k1, M1R, k1.
Row 6 and every alt row: Purl.
Row 7: K2, M1L, k1, M1R, k2.
Row 9: K3, M1L, k1, M1R, k3.
Row 11: K4, M1L, k1, M1R, k4.
Row 13: K5, M1L, k1, M1R, k5.
Row 15: K6, M1L, k1, M1R, k6.
Row 17: K7, M1L, k1, M1R, k7.
Row 19: K8, M1L, k1, M1R, k8.
Row 20: P9, cast (bind) off 1st, p9.
Row 21: K9 turn and cont to work on these sts.
Row 22 and every alt row: Purl.
Row 23: K1, skpsso, k6. *(8 sts)*
Row 25: k1, skpsso, k5. *(7 sts)*
Row 27: K1, skpsso, k1, k2tog, k1. *(5 sts)*

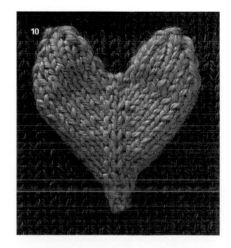

(Row 15 st dropped.)
Work 3 rows st st.
Row 33: K10, drop next st, k to end of the row. (Row 21 st dropped.)
Work 3 rows st st.
Row 37: K22, drop next st, k to end of the row. (Row 9 st dropped.)
Work 3 rows st st.
Bind (cast) off.

6 GARTER STITCH LADDER
This swatch uses the same pattern as the previous one, but every row is knitted. The effect is quite different, with the ladder being less visible, but the loops it makes standing proud of the surface of the fabric.

Flat shapes
Knitted shapes are a versatile form of decoration that can be applied to almost any knitted or other fabric. There are endless possibilities, but here are just a few popular shapes.

7 TRIANGLE
Working shaping↓ one stitch in from the edge of a shape gives a neat smooth edge, as on this simple triangle. Choose an increase and decrease that mirror one another.

Cast on 20 sts using the thumb method.
Row 1 (RS): Knit.
Row 2: K1, skpsso, k to last 3 sts, k2tog, k1.

TECHNIQUES: Shaping ◗ page 14 • Attach-later bobble ◗ page 11 • Appliqué ◗ page 101

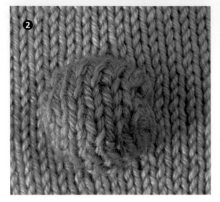

Row 28: Bind (cast) off the following stitch sequence, p2tog, k1, p2togtbl.
Rejoin yarn to rem sts with right-side facing.
Row 21: Knit. *(9 sts)*
Row 22 and every alt row: Purl.
Row 23: K6, k2tog, k1. *(8 sts)*
Row 25: K5, k2tog, k1. *(7 sts)*
Row 27: K1, skpsso, k1, k2tog, k1. *(5 sts)*
Row 28: Cast (bind) off the following stitch sequence, p2tog, k1, p2togtbl.

3-D shapes

Three-dimensional shapes can give a knitted fabric a feeling of novelty and fun. These shapes can be applied as part of an intarsia pattern in one or more colors, or they can be beaded or embroidered.

❶ PYRAMID

This is such a versatile shape and uses such a neat decrease↓; apply it to a knitted surface or use it to make a block from oddments of yarn. The shape can be enlarged by deciding on the width of one side (an odd number of stitches) and then multiplying this by four.

Abbreviations

S2tog, k1, psso = slip 2 sts together knitwise, k1, pass the 2 slipped sts over.

Note

It is easiest to use five dpn, one for each side and one to knit with.

Cast on 44 sts onto dpn using the thumb method. Divide the stitches between four needles, taking care not to twist the stitches.
Knit 2 rows.
Row 3: K4, [s2tog, k1, psso, k8] rep twice more, s2tog, k1, psso, k4. *(36 sts)*
Knit 2 rows.
Row 6: K3, [s2tog, k1, psso, k6] rep twice more, s2tog, k1, psso, k3. *(28 sts)*
Knit 2 rows.
Row 9: K2, [s2tog, k1, psso, k4] rep twice more, s2tog, k1, psso, k2. *(20 sts)*
Knit 2 rows.
Row 12: K1, [s2tog, k1, psso, k2] rep twice more, s2tog, k1, psso, k1. *(12 sts)*
Knit 2 rows.
Row 15: s2tog, k1, psso, rep three times more. *(4 sts)*
Thread the yarn through the remaining stitches and pull them up tight.

❷ DOME

This shape is created using short row shaping↓ and can be adapted to create any segment of a sphere. Each repeat is the equivalent of an eighth of a sphere, therefore repeating the pattern repeat eight times will create a sphere. The shape can be enlarged by deciding on the number of stitches from top to bottom of the sphere.

Approximately half of the stitches should always be be knitted and not be short row shaped, and the number of short rows should be the equivalent of approximately a quarter of the width of the row and an even number. This formula is only a rough guide, but as the stitch numbers increase it becomes more accurate.

Abbreviations

wrap = wrap the next st as for short row shaping.

Small dome

Cast on 10 sts using the thumb method.
Knit 1 row.
∗ P8, wrap and turn.
K6, wrap and turn.

P4, wrap and turn.
K2, wrap and turn.
P all the sts on the left-hand needle, picking up the wrapping loops as they appear.
K all the sts on the left-hand needle, picking up the wrapping loops as they appear.
Rep from ∗ three more times.

Larger dome

Cast on 20 sts using the thumb method.
Knit 1 row.
∗ P18, wrap and turn.
K16, wrap and turn.
P14, wrap and turn.
K12, wrap and turn.
P10, wrap and turn.
K8, wrap and turn.
P all the sts on the left-hand needle, picking up the wrapping loops as they appear.
K all the sts on the left-hand needle, picking up the wrapping loops as they appear.
Rep from ∗ three more times.

These domes can be stuffed with washable filling and sewn onto a knitted fabric.

TECHNIQUES: Decreases ◗ page 16 • Short row shaping ◗ page 18

Pleats

These may seem tricky to make, but work a sample swatch and you should find them easier than you might imagine. Pleats↓ offer a great way of adding shape and detail to an item, so do try them out.

❸ TWO-COLOR PLEAT

This technique adds a flash of color to the pleat that will be shown to best advantage in movement; for example, if the pleat is in a skirt and so opens up when walking.

This swatch is 50 sts by 36 rows and full instructions are given to help you understand how the color is placed. Use two dpn rather than cable needles. This pleat opens to the left.

A = background color
B = inner pleat color

Cast on 50 sts in A.
Row 1 (RS): K19A, p1A, k9B, p1B, k9B, k11A.
Row 2: P11A, p19B, p20A.
Rep rows 1–2 eleven more times, then row 1 once more. Break B and work in A.
Row 24: Purl
Row 25: K19, p1 onto 1st dpn; k9, p1 onto 2nd dpn; k20 onto right-hand needle.
Row 26: P10 from 1st dpn; p3tog ten times, taking one st from each of the needles, p10.
Row 27: Knit. *(30 sts)*
Work st st as required.
Bind (cast) off.

❹ BEADED PLEAT

A line of beads↓ on the leading edge of the pleat will catch the light and add swing to a knitted fabric. Count the numbers of rows in the pleat and thread half that number of beads onto the yarn before you start; here there are 15 beads.

This swatch is 25 sts by 40 rows and again, full instructions are given to help you understand the positioning of the beads. This pleat opens to the right.

Abbreviations

PB = place bead. Use the slip stitch beading method.

Cast on 25 sts.
Row 1 (RS): K10, p1, k4, PB, k9.
Row 2: Purl.
Rep rows 1–2 14 more times.
Row 31: K10, p1, k14.

Row 32: P10 onto 1st dpn; p5 onto 2nd dpn; p10 onto right-hand needle.
Row 33: K5 from 1st dpn, k3tog five times, taking one st from each of the needles, k5.
Work st st as required. *(15 sts)*

Pintucks

Producing straight, defined ridges across the width of a piece of knitted fabric, pintucks↓ are easy to work. Depending on the yarn, stitch and gauge (tension) used, they will affect the flexibility of the fabric and the size of the finished item, so you should always work a swatch.

❺ PINTUCKS AND BOBBLES

This swatch is worked in garter stitch, though the same principle could be applied to st st. The pintucks are quite large so that the bobbles↓ nestle into the top edge of them, rather than protruding beyond them.

Abbreviations

MB = make bobble. K twice into the front and back of the st, k 3 rows, sl 2 sts, k2tog, psso.

Knit to the position of the pintuck.
Next row (RS): [K to position of bobble, MB] rep to the end of the row.
Knit 9 rows.
Next row: Make pintuck, picking up the aligning sts on the back of the bobble row.

❻ BEADED SHORT PINTUCK

Short lengths of pintuck can be used to add shaping to an item. Highlight them with beads on the middle row; this technique can also be used on a full-length pintuck.

The beads are placed using the slip stitch method↓, so you will need a bead for every alternate stitch of the pintuck. For best effect ensure that the first and last stitch are beaded. Here, the pintuck is 9 stitches long so 5 beads are threaded onto the yarn.

The pintuck also needs to be an odd number of rows wide so that the beads sit centrally.

Work to the position of the bottom edge of the pintuck.
Work an odd number of rows, placing the beads on alternate stitches in the central row.
On the next row, knit to the position of the start of the pintuck. Pick up the required number of stitches for the pintuck in the usual way.

❼ STRIPED PINTUCKS

Color offers a way of further emphasizing pintucks. Consider working them as part of or as an alternative to a stripe pattern that is elsewhere in the design.

A = background color
B = pintuck color

Work st st in A to the position of the first pintuck, ending with a p row.
Work 6 rows of st st in B.
Next row: Make pintuck, picking up the aligning first loops of B on the back.
Work st st in A to position of next pintuck.

TECHNIQUES: Pleats ◗ page 19 • Slip stitch beading ◗ page 68 • Pintucks ◗ page 20 • Bobbles ◗ page 10

Cable and tail backpack

Colorful and full of fun, this textural backpack will delight all little girls, assuming no grown-up girls get their hands on it first. If childish fingers find the bobble button hard to negotiate, replace it with a shiny red plastic button.

Size
10¼ x 11½in (26 x 29cm)

Materials
Rowan hand knit cotton
1¾oz (50g) balls

Red A	1
Orange B	1
Pink C	1

15in (40cm) US 6 (4mm)
circular needle
1 pair of US 5 (3.75mm) needles
Cable needle

Knitter's sewing needle

Gauge (Tension)
21 stitches and 31 rows to 4in (10cm) over st st using US 6 (4mm) needles.

Abbreviations
C8FT = cable 8 front tail. Slip next 4 sts onto cable needle and hold at front of work, knit 2 sts from left-hand needle, slip on tail, knit tail loop with next st on left-hand needle keeping end of tail to the right, knit 1 st from left-hand needle, knit 4 sts from cable needle.

C8BT = cable 8 back tail. Slip next 2 sts onto cable needle, slip on tail, slip next 2 sts onto cable needle and hold at back of work, knit 4 sts from left-hand needle, knit 2 sts from cable needle, knit tail loop with next st on cable needle keeping end of tail to the left, knit 1 st from cable needle.

Sl2tog, k1, psso = slip 2 stitches together, knit one and pass the slipped stitches over.

MLB = make loop bobble. Knit into front and back of st, turn, p 2 sts, turn, k2 making a loop in each st, turn, p2tog.

ML = make loop.
See also page 157.

Tails (make 10)
Using the cable method and C, cast on 15 sts, bind (cast) off 15 sts. Store tails hanging by the last loop on a spare needle.

Bag
Using US 6 (4mm) circular needle and A, cast on 110 sts.
Knit 4 rounds in A.
Knit 3 rounds in B.
Round 8: In B, k43, C8FT, k9, C8BT, k42.
Rep rounds 1–8 twice more.
Break B and work in A.
Rounds 25–27: Knit.
Round 28: K26, Sl2tog, k1, psso, k53, Sl2tog, k1, psso, k25. (106 sts)
Rounds 29–30: Knit.
Round 31: K53, k1 in C, k52.
Round 32: K25, Sl2tog, k1, psso, k13, C8FT, k4, MLB in C, k4, C8BT, k13, Sl2tog, k1, psso, k24. (102 sts)
Rounds 33–35: Knit.
Round 36: K24, Sl2tog, k1, psso, k49, Sl2tog, k1, psso, k23. (98 sts)
Rounds 37–38: Knit.
Round 39: K49, k1 in C, k48.
Round 40: K23, Sl2tog, k1, psso, k11, C8FT, k4, MLB in C, k4, C8BT, k11, Sl2tog, k1, psso, k22. (94 sts)
Rounds 41–43: Knit.
Round 44: K22, Sl2tog, k1, psso, k45, Sl2tog, k1, psso, k21. (90 sts)
Rounds 45–46: Knit.
Round 47: K45, k1 in C, k44.
Round 48: K21, Sl2tog, k1, psso, k9, C8FT, k4, MLB in C, k4, C8BT, k9, Sl2tog, k1, psso, k20. (86 sts)
Rounds 49–51: Knit.
Round 52: K20, Sl2tog, k1, psso, k41, Sl2tog, k1, psso, k19. (82 sts)
Rounds 53–54: Knit.
Round 55: K41, k1 in C, k40.
Round 56: K19, Sl2tog, k1, psso, k7, C8FT, k4, MLB in C, k4, C8BT, k7, Sl2tog, k1, psso, k18. (78 sts)
Rounds 57–59: Knit.

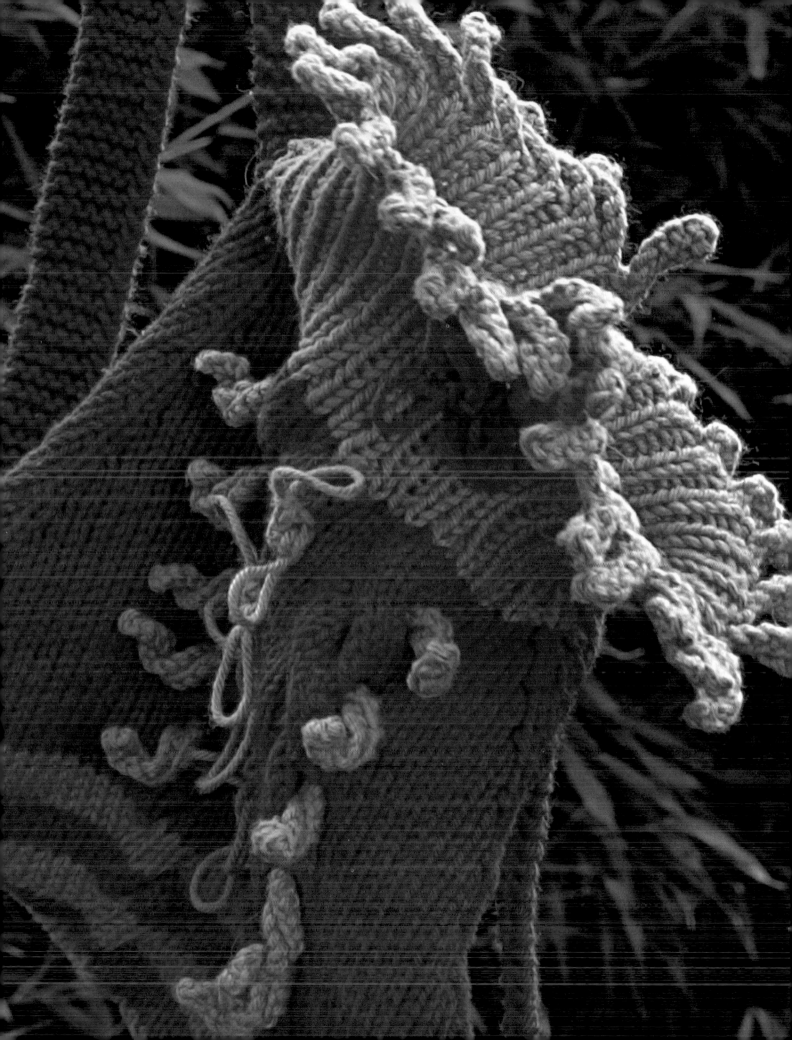

Round 60: K18, Sl2tog, k1, psso, k37, Sl2tog, k1, psso, k17. (74 *sts*)

Rounds 61–62: Knit.

Round 63: K37, k1 in C, k36.

Round 64: K17, Sl2tog, k1, psso, k5, C8FT, k4, MLB in C, k4, C8BT, k5, Sl2tog, k1, psso, k16. (70 *sts*)

Rounds 65–67: Knit.

Round 68: K16, Sl2tog, k1, psso, k33, Sl2tog, k1, psso, k15. (66 *sts*) Break A, join in C.

Round 69: Knit.

Round 70: (K1, p1) rep to the end of the round.

Rep round 70 seven more times.

Round 78: (K1, p1) rep fourteen more times, k1, bind (cast) off 5 sts, (k1, p1) rep to the end of the round.

Round 79: (K1, p1) rep fourteen more times, k1, cast on 5 sts, (k1, p1) rep to the end of the round.

Work 8 rounds in rib patt as set.

Picot bind (cast) off round: (Cast on 7 sts, bind (cast) off 9 sts, slip st on right-hand needle back onto left-hand needle) rep to the end of the round.

Straps (make 2)

Using US 5 (3.75mm) needles and A, cast on 6 sts.

Knit until strap measures approximately 17½in (45cm).

Bind (cast) off.

Button

Using US 5 (3.75mm) needles and A, cast on 5 sts.

Row 1 (WS): Purl.

Row 2: K1, (ML) rep twice more, k1.

Rep rows 1–2 three more times.

Row 9: Purl.

Cut yarn 4in (10cm) from sts and make square into attach-later bobble.

Finishing

Weave in loose ends on the WS. Press the bag, avoiding the cables and bobbles.

Using mattress stitch, sew up the bottom edge.

Sew one end of each strap to the bottom back corner of the bag. Sew the other end to the back on the last knit row, 2 sts in from the decrease.

Sew the attach-later bobble to the inside of the rib to align with the buttonhole.

TECHNIQUES: Picot bind (cast) off ◗ page 128 • Attach-later bobble ◗ page 11

Helix fur scarf

This scarf looks more complicated than it is, as none of the rows are more than nineteen stitches wide, and many are a lot less. The loop fur stitch disguises the reverse of the cable, but the scarf looks equally good, and uses less yarn, if the looped areas are replaced with rev st st.

Length
Unstretched 44in (112cm).

Materials
Rowan yorkshire tweed dk
   1¾oz (50g) balls
   Blue   5

1 pair of US 10 (6mm) needles
Cable needle

Stitch holder

Gauge (Tension)
20 stitches and 26 rows to 4in (10cm) over st st using US10 (6mm) needles.

Abbreviations
Cr6F3B = cross 6 front, 3 back. Slip next 6 sts on the left-hand needle onto a cable needle and hold at the front of the work, k3. Transfer the 3 sts on the far left of the cable needle back to the left-hand needle and hold the cable needle with the remaining 3 sts at the back of the work. K3 from the left-hand needle and then k3 from the cable needle.

M1L = make 1 left.

M1R = make 1 right.

ML = make loop.

Wrap st and turn = wrap the working yarn in a counterclockwise direction around the next stitch, slipping it to and from the right-hand needle as required and finishing at the front or back ready to work the next stitch. See also page 157.

Note Remember to pick up the wrapping loop around the stitch and work it together with the stitch either knitwise or purlwise as the stitch dictates and as they appear.

Shaped end

Using the thumb method, cast on 5 sts.

Row 1: K1tbl, k to the end of the row.
Row 2: Sl2 purlwise, k1, sl2 purlwise. Rep rows 1–2 once more.
Row 5: K1tbl, k1, M1L, k1, M1R, k2. (7 sts)
Row 6: Sl2 purlwise, k3, sl2 purlwise.
Row 7: K1tbl, k to the end of the row.
Row 8: Sl2 purlwise, k3, sl2 purlwise.
Row 9: K1tbl, k2, M1L, k1, M1R, k3. (9 sts)
Row 10: Sl2 purlwise, k5, sl2 purlwise.
Row 11: K1tbl, k to the end of the row.
Row 12: Sl2 purlwise, k5, sl2 purlwise.
Row 13: K1tbl, k3, M1L, k1, M1R, k4. (11 sts)
Row 14: Sl2 purlwise, k7, sl2 purlwise.
Row 15: K1tbl, k to the end of the row.
Row 16: Sl2 purlwise, k7, sl2 purlwise.
Row 17: K1tbl, k4, M1L, k1, M1R, k5. (13 sts)
Row 18: Sl2 purlwise, (ML) rep twice more, p3, (ML) rep twice more, sl2 purlwise.
Row 19: K1tbl, k1, p3, k3, p3, k2.
Row 20: Sl2 purlwise, (ML) rep twice more, p3, (ML) rep twice more, sl2 purlwise.
Row 21: K1tbl, k1, p3, k1, M1L, k1, M1R, k1 p3, k2. (15 sts)
Row 22: Sl2 purlwise, (ML) rep twice more, p5, (ML) rep twice more, sl2 purlwise.
Row 23: K1tbl, k1, p3, k5, p3, k2.
Row 24: Sl2 purlwise, (ML) rep twice more, p5, (ML) rep twice more, sl2 purlwise.
Row 25: K1tbl, k1, p3, k2, M1L, k1, M1R, k2, p3, k2. (17 sts)

Row 26: Sl2 purlwise, (ML) rep twice more, p7, (ML) rep twice more, sl2 purlwise.
Row 27: K1tbl, k1, p3, k7, p3, k2.
Row 28: Sl2 purlwise, (ML) rep twice more, p7, (ML) rep twice more, sl2 purlwise.
Row 29: K1tbl, k1, p3, k3, M1L, k1, M1R, k3, p3, k2. (19 sts)
Row 30: Sl2 purlwise, (ML) rep twice more, p3, (ML) rep twice more, p3, (ML) rep twice more, sl2 purlwise.
Row 31: K1tbl, k1, p3, k3, p3, k3, p3, k2.
Row 32: Sl2 purlwise, (ML) rep twice more, p3, (ML) rep twice more, p3, (ML) rep twice more, sl2 purlwise.
Row 33: K1tbl, k1, p3, Cr6F3B, p3, k2.
Row 34: Sl2 purlwise, (ML) rep twice more, p9, (ML) rep twice more, sl2 purlwise.

Cable and helix pattern

Row 35: K1tbl, k1, p3, k2, p1, k3, p1 k2, p2, wrap st and turn. (16 sts worked)
Row 36: (ML) rep once more, p2, k1, p3, k1, p2, (ML) rep twice more, sl2 purlwise.
Row 37: K1tbl, k1, p3, k2, p1, k3, p1 k2, wrap st and turn. (14 sts worked)
Row 38: P2, k1, p3, k1, p2, (ML) rep twice more, sl2 purlwise.
Row 39: K1tbl, k1, p3, k1, wrap st and turn. (6 sts worked)
Row 40: P1, (ML) rep twice more, sl2 purlwise.
Row 41: K1tbl, k1, wrap st and turn. (2 sts worked)
Row 42: Sl2 purlwise.
Row 43: K1tbl, k1, p3, k2, wrap st and turn. (7 sts worked)
Row 44: P2, (ML) rep twice more, sl2 purlwise.
Row 45: K1tbl, k1, p3, wrap st and turn. (5 sts worked)

Row 46: (ML) rep twice more, sl2 purlwise.
Row 47: K1tbl, k1, p1, wrap st and turn. (3 sts worked)
Row 48: ML, sl2 purlwise.
Row 49: K1tbl, wrap st and turn. (1 st worked)
Row 50: Sl1 purlwise.
Row 51: K1tbl, k1, p3, k2, p1, p3, wrap st and turn. (11 sts worked)
Row 52: P3, k1, p2, (ML) rep twice more, sl2 purlwise.
Row 53: K1tbl, k1, p3, k2, p1, wrap st and turn. (8 sts worked)
Row 54: K1, p2, (ML) rep twice more, sl2 purlwise.
Row 55: K1tbl, k1, p3, wrap st and turn. (5 sts worked)
Row 56: (ML) rep twice more, sl2 purlwise.
Row 57: K1tbl, k1, wrap st and turn. (2 sts worked)
Row 58: Sl2 purlwise.
Row 59: K1tbl, k1, p3, k1, wrap st and turn. (6 sts worked)
Row 60: P1, (ML) rep twice more, sl2 purlwise.
Row 61: K1tbl, k1, p1, wrap st and turn. (3 sts worked)
Row 62: ML, sl2 purlwise.
Row 63: K1tbl, wrap st and turn. (1 st worked)
Row 64: Sl1 purlwise.
Row 65: K1tbl, k1, p3, k2, p1, k3, p1, wrap st and turn. (12 sts worked)
Row 66: K1, p3, k1, p2, (ML) rep twice more, sl2 purlwise.
Row 67: K1tbl, k1, p3, k2, wrap st and turn. (7 sts worked)
Row 68: P2, (ML) rep twice more, sl2 purlwise.
Row 69: K1tbl, k1, p2, wrap st and turn. (4 sts worked)
Row 70: (ML) rep once more, sl2 purlwise.

TECHNIQUES: Increases ◗ page 14 • Short row shaping ◗ page 18 • Cables ◗ page 12• Kitchener stitch ◗ page 130

Row 71: K1tbl, k1, wrap st and turn.
(2 sts worked)

Row 72: Sl2 purlwise.

Row 73: K1tbl, k1, p3, k2, p1, k3, p1, k2, p3, k2. *(all 19 sts worked)*

Row 74: Sl2 purlwise, (ML) rep twice more, p2, k1, p3, k1, p2, (ML) rep twice more, sl2 purlwise.

Row 75: K1tbl, k1, p3, Cr6F3B, p3, k2.

Row 76: Sl2 purlwise, (ML) rep twice more, p2, k1, p3, k1, p2, (ML) rep twice more, sl2 purlwise.

Rep the cable and helix pattern until the length worked is half the desired length of the scarf and a full rep has been completed; approximately 22in (56cm) long.

Cut the yarn and transfer the stitches onto a stitch holder.

Make one more scarf piece in the same way, but finish on row 73 of the patt repeat.

Finishing

Press the scarf pieces lightly, working from the center of the helix out.

Cut the loops to make fur and trim them as necessary.

Using Kitchener stitch, join the two sections together.

Pyramid block sweater

This baggy cropped sweater looks good over a longer T-shirt, or revealing a slender midriff, and is the perfect sweater for lounging around the house in.

The pyramid block is slightly different from that described on page 26, thanks to Margaret Roberts who devised a flatter decrease for it.

The pyramid edging on this sweater could be applied to any favorite pattern and can be made from yarn odds and ends for a multicolored look.

Sizes

One size
Knitted measurements
Chest in (cm)   44in (112cm)
Length in (cm)   18in (48cm)

Materials

Rowan handknit dk cotton
        1¾oz (50g) balls
        Ecru   15

1 set of 5 US 6 (4mm) dp needles
1 pair of US 6 (4mm) needles
F/5 (4mm) crochet hook
Cable needle

Gauge (Tension)

20 stitches and 28 rows to 4in (10cm) over st st repeat using US 6 (4mm) needles.

Abbreviations

slstdec = slip stitch decrease. Slip 1 stitch, slip the next stitch onto a cable needle and hold at the front of the work, transfer the slipped stitch on the right-hand needle to the left-hand needle and k2tog using the left point of the cable needle. Pass the right st on the cable needle over the left and transfer the remaining st on the cable needle onto the right-hand needle. See also page 157.

Pyramid strip (make 2)

Using US 6 (4mm) dp needles and the crochet invisible cast on method, cast on 68 sts.

Divide the sts between four needles, taking care not to twist the sts.

Row 1: Knit.

Row 2: K7, (slstdec, k14) rep twice more, slstdec, k7. (60 sts)

Row 3: K7, (sl1, k14) rep twice more, sl1, k7.

Row 4: K6, (slstdec, k12) rep twice more, slstdec, k6. (52 sts)

Row 5: K6, (sl1, k12) rep twice more, sl1, k6.

Row 6: K5, (slstdec, k10) rep twice more, slstdec, k5. (44 sts)

Row 7: K5, (sl1, k10) rep twice more, sl1, k5.

Row 8: K5, (k1tbl, k10) rep twice more, k1tbl, k5.

Row 9: K4, (slstdec, k8) rep twice more, slstdec, k4. (36 sts)

Row 10: K4, (sl1, k8) rep twice more, sl1, k4.

Row 11: K4, (k1tbl, k8) rep twice more, k1tbl, k4.

Row 12: K3, (slstdec, k6) rep twice more, slstdec, k3. (28 sts)

Row 13: K3, (sl1, k6) rep twice more, sl1, k3.

Row 14: K3, (k1tbl, k6) rep twice more, k1tbl, k3.

Row 15: K2, (slstdec, k4) rep twice more, slstdec, k2. (20 sts)

Row 16: K2, (sl1, k4) rep twice more, sl1, k2.

Row 17: K2, (k1tbl, k4) rep twice more, k1tbl, k2.

Row 18: K1, (slstdec, k2) rep twice more, slstdec, k1. (12 sts)

Row 19: K1, (sl1, k2) rep twice more, sl1, k1.

Row 20: (Slstdec) rep three more times. (4 sts)

Cut the yarn, thread through the remaining stitches and pull up tight. Make 13 more pyramids. Press each pyramid.

Unpick the crochet invisible cast on along one edge of each of two pyramid blocks and put the loops onto US 6 (4mm) needles.

Use a crochet hook and some yarn to tambour stitch (chain stitch) through the loops, joining the two pyramids together.

Unpicking edges as required, rep for all 14 pyramids to create two rows of seven pyramids.

Bind (cast) off the loops on the lower edge using the back stitch bind (cast) off.

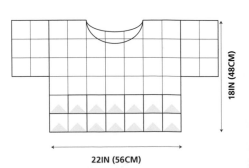

22IN (56CM)

TECHNIQUES: Crochet invisible cast on ▸ page 127 • Pyramid swatch ▸ page 26 • Chain stitch ▸ page 104 • Back stitch bind (cast) off ▸ page 129

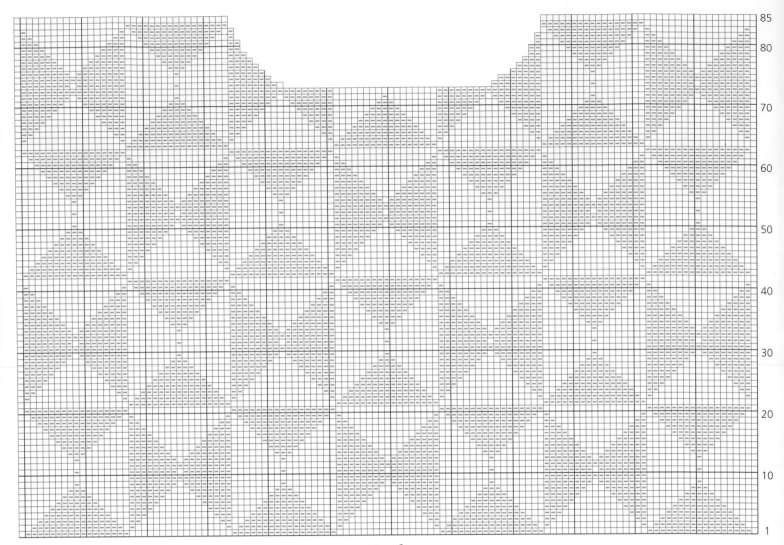

Back

Key

☐ K on RS, p on WS.

⊟ P on RS, K on WS.

Back

Cast on 1 st, using US 6 (4mm)
needles, unpick and put the 121 st
loops on the upper edge of 1 strip of
7 by 2 pyramids, add 1 st using the
backward thumb method.
Work following Back chart.
Bind (cast) off.

Front

Cast on 1 st, using US 6 (4mm) needles,
unpick and put the upper edge of rem
pyramid strip as for Back, add 1 st
using the backward thumb method.
Work following Front chart.
Bind (cast) off.

Right sleeve

Using US 6 (4mm) needles and the
thumb cast on method, cast on 104
sts.
Row 1: Foll the chart for the Back for
103 sts, k1.
Row 2: P1, foll the chart for the Back
for 103 sts.
Cont foll the chart for the Back as set
until row 42.
Row 43: Knit.
Bind (cast) off.

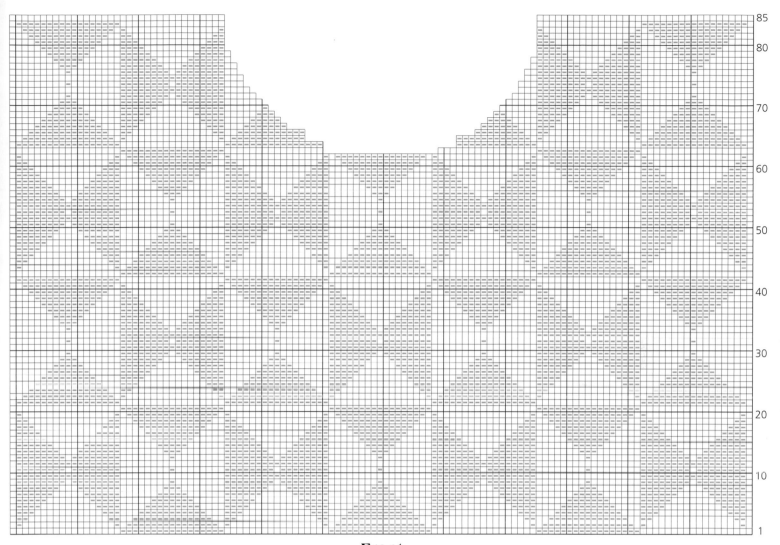

Front

Left sleeve

Using US 6 (4mm) needles and the thumb cast on method, cast on 104 sts.

Row 1: Foll the chart for the Front for 103 sts, k1.

Row 2: P1, foll the chart for the Front for 103 sts.

Cont foll the chart for the Front as set until row 42.

Row 43: Knit.

Bind (cast) off.

Finishing

Press the edges carefully.

Join left shoulder seam.

Starting with the right shoulder, using US 6 (4mm) needles, pick up 13 sts down the right back decreases, 33 sts across the back and 13 sts up the left back decreases, 27 sts down the left front decreases, 18 sts across the front and 27 sts up the right front decreases.

Bind (cast) off using the I-cord bind (cast) off method and 2 extra stitches. Join the right shoulder seam. Attach the sleeves so three pattern blocks fall either side of the shoulder seam. Sew up the side and sleeve seams.

TECHNIQUES: I-cord bind (cast) off ◆ page 129

yarn plus

AT SOME POINT ALL KNITTERS WILL HAVE STOOD in front of a display of yarns in a vast range of colors, textures, finishes, weights and fibers, and regretted that they can choose only one with which to knit their next project. But why? With a little care, different yarns can be combined in a single knitted fabric.

Whether you simply knit the yarns together, or use one of the decorative knitting stitches in the techniques section to combine them, there are a lot of ideas in the swatch library to consider.

Despite the range of yarns available, sometimes you still can't find exactly what you are looking for. In these circumstances, a little imagination can get great results. All sorts of materials will knit up well, but the only way to find out is to work a swatch. Here, you will find advice on knitting with different materials, and a selection of knitted swatches with some ideas as to how you might use them.

Yarn plus
SWATCH LIBRARY

Yarns of different weights, fibers and finishes can be used together to great effect, though some caution is needed. If the item will need washing then the yarns should be compatible, though careful handwashing can overcome many potential problems. If you are unsure, then knit a swatch and wash it before starting the project.

The other main issue springs from different yarns knitting up to different sizes. This can be overcome by increasing or decreasing the number of stitches as required, or it can be exploited as a feature.

And why stop with yarn? There are many other materials that can be knitted up, often with surprising and stunning results.

Mixing yarns

Different weights or textures of yarn can be used to highlight a border or edging, to add shaping or just as a decorative device. Yarns can also be mixed↓ by simply knitting them together; mohair yarns work well as their light weight adds texture rather than bulk.

Always knit a swatch before starting a mixed yarn project to check that the effect you are hoping for can be produced, as the results can be unpredictable.

❶ TWO-YARNS, SAME NUMBER OF STITCHES

Yarns of similar weights can be used in a single piece of knitting without too much distortion. However, if the yarns are of very different weights, then the areas knitted in the finer yarn will be a different size to those knitted in the thicker yarn. On unfitted items, such as scarves and bags, this can be used to produce natural shaping.

Here, stripes of double-knitting yarn and mohair yarn, both worked for the same number of rows, create a fabric of varying weight and width. The thicker yarn also highlights the fragility of the mohair.

❷ TWO YARNS, DIFFERENT NUMBER OF STITCHES

Here, the fawn yarn is worked first, then the number of stitches is increased evenly across the work as the blue yarn is brought in, so both sections of the knitted fabric are the same width.

This method requires careful, accurate swatching for every different combination of yarns, but when perfected it can produce great results.

❸ MIXED YARN STRIPES

Introducing a very fine yarn into areas of a piece of knitted fabric can be done with confidence, as it will rarely make any difference to the width of the knitted fabric. However, the areas where the yarns are combined will tend to be stiffer.

Here, a fine mohair yarn is used to blend cotton stripes together. Part of the swatch is knitted with just the cotton yarns so that you can see the effect clearly.

A = lime green cotton
B = yellow cotton
C = green mohair

Work in st st throughout.
2 rows B.
7 rows B and C together.
10 rows A and C together.
4 rows A.
4 rows B.
4 rows A.
2 rows A and C together.
5 rows B and C together.
4 rows A and C together.
Cont in A.

❹ TWO-COLOR AND TWO-YARN SHADING

A second yarn can be used to affect the color of a knitted fabric in places. This does not have to be a specific motif, a shading effect can highlight shaping or other decorative elements.

In this swatch a medium-weight mohair yarn is knitted in with the background blue yarn on the right-hand side of the swatch.

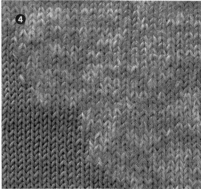

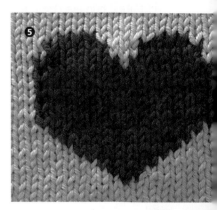

⑤ TWO-COLOR AND TWO-YARN MOTIF

Add further interest to an intarsia design by combining yarns within it for a more textural look. This heart motif is worked in a combination of mid-pink cotton and dark pink fine mohair on a background of green cotton. Work to the position of the motif then follow the chart to place it

◻ Background green

◼ Mixed pink yarns

⑥ NOVELTY AND MIXED YARN STRIPES

To use a particular thick yarn within a knitted fabric, but avoid distortion, combine other yarns to bring them up to the same thickness to work the other parts of

the fabric. In this swatch the first rows are knitted in a multi-colored, bulky novelty yarn. The next 4 rows are knitted in two chunky yarns combined. The next 6 rows are knitted in a chunky, a DK-weight and a mohair yarn combined. The last rows are knitted in the novelty yarn again.

⑦ DIFFERENT-SIZE NEEDLES

Rather than using different weights of yarn to shape a knitted item, you can use different-size needles instead. This swatch is knitted in the same yarn throughout, but the needle size changes at regular intervals to produce an elegant flare that would work well as a cuff or as an edging on a skirt or smock.

This swatch is worked in st st, with the first rows worked on US 6 (4mm) needles. The next 10 rows are worked on US 8 (5mm) needles. The next 10 rows on US 10½ (6.5mm) and the last 10 rows on US 11 (8mm) needles.

⑧ NOVELTY YARN FUR

There is a wide range of novelty yarns on the market and they can produce some very interesting effects. However, a little caution is best observed as some of them may produce a brash or over-stated fabric. Consider using them as a

cuff or collar detail, or as a band within the knitted fabric.

Here, the main part of the fabric is worked in chunky cream yarn in st st. The green edging is worked in a fur yarn in rev st st. The latter stitch often works well with textural yarns, as the loops show up the texture better than the flat face of st st does.

⑨ DIP-STITCH FLOWERS

A simple, but pretty flower motif is easily worked in dip stitch ↓. A yarn of a very different weight and texture can be used to make the flowers with no affect on the knitted fabric.

Pass the dipped loop over the next stitch before knitting it. Once the fabric is complete, work a bullion knot ↓ over the stitches the dip stitches came out of.

Panel of 10 sts and 10 rows
Row 1 (RS): Knit.
Row 2 and every alt row: Purl.
Row 3: K1, dip to st 5 on row 2, k6, dip to st 6 on row 2, k1.
Row 5: K2, dip to st 5 on row 2, k4, dip to st 6 on row 2, k2.
Row 7: K3, dip to st 5 on row 2, k2, dip to st 6 on row 2, k3.
Row 9: K4, dip to st 5 on row 2, dip to st 6 on row 2, k4.
Row 10: Purl.

⑩ DIP-STITCH STRIPES

Dip stitch can be used to blend the edges of stripes in two different colored yarns – and here, two different stitch patterns – together. Keep the dips quite short and space them to complement the horizontal stripes.

A = blue
B = yellow

Work the required number of rows in st st in A, ending with a k row. Knit 3 rows in B.
Next row: K in B to first dip stitch [dip down 6 rows and pull up A, knit loop and next st together, k to next dip stitch] rep to the end of the row.
Knit the required number of rows in B.
Repeat the process, pulling up loops of B into a stripe of A.

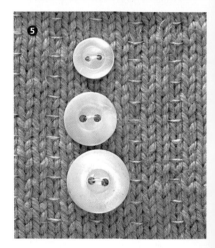

❶ KNOTTED CLUSTERS

Make even more of a feature of clusters↓ by binding them in a contrasting color and yarn. Here, blue embroidery thread is used to bind clusters of stitches worked in a green tweed yarn.

Groups of five stitches are clustered together, with spaces of five stitches between clusters. Each cluster is tightly bound to draw the stitches in. The binding thread is not woven into the back of the knitted fabric, rather it is firmly knotted on the front and the ends trimmed short to add extra interest.

❷ BEADED CLUSTERS

The beads need to fit snugly onto the second yarn to prevent them from moving around on the clusters. Thread the beads↓ onto the second yarn before working the stitch and catch it into the back of the knitted fabric between clusters.

For this swatch groups of three stitches are clustered together, with a space of three stitches between clusters. There are three rows between cluster rows, with the next row of clusters worked over the stitches that formed the spaces on the previous cluster row. Alternate rows of clusters are beaded.

❸ CHUNKY CLUSTERS

A thick yarn will make the clusters more pronounced, and if the groups of stitches are not bound tightly, the gauge (tension) of the fabric will not alter. However, the drape will be affected.

This swatch has the same stitch pattern as Beaded Clusters. The working yarn is bound loosely five times around the groups of stitches.

❹ COLORFUL WEAVING

Weaving↓ is quick and simple to work and the result can be very decorative, making it perfect for large areas of knitted fabric. It will

make the fabric stiff, however, and you need to be careful not to pull the weaving yarn tight or the gauge (tension) will be affected. Consider using all-over weaving on projects such as bags, which can benefit from a firmer fabric.

Here, every alternate stitch on every row is woven, with the weaving staggered by one stitch on alternate rows. Three different yarns are used to make stripes of weaving on a plain background, each stripe consisting of five woven rows.

❺ BUTTON WEAVING

Thread decorative elements such as beads↓, or in this case buttons, onto the weaving yarn before you start. Slide them down the yarn as you work until you reach the required position. Then, with the weaving yarn in front, slide the element down to sit in front of the stitch and continue weaving. The elements cannot be too heavy or they will pull on the yarn and hang down from the knitted fabric.

In this swatch three pearl buttons are threaded onto fine white crochet yarn. Every alternate stitch on every knit row is woven, keeping the woven stitches in vertical columns. The buttons are placed centrally above one another.

❻ WEAVING ON STRIPES

A simple stripe pattern can be made far more interesting by incorporating weaving. The effect can be as subtle or as vibrant as you wish, depending on the colors chosen.

The background stripe pattern for this swatch is six rows dark green, four rows lime green; the weaving is in purple to provide a strong contrast. On the dark stripes, every alternate stitch on every row is woven, keeping the woven stitches in vertical columns. On the lime stripes, every fourth stitch is woven.

❼ MIXED YARN COUCHING

Couching↓ offers a way of incorporating a multitude of different yarns into a knitted fabric. They can be of entirely different weights, though fine, silky yarns have a tendency to slide within the couching stitches and may be visually overwhelmed by them.

A simple stripe pattern using three different weights and types of purple yarn is couched onto a plain blue background for this swatch. Every third stitch on every knit row is couched over a strand of yarn.

❽ STAGGERED COUCHING

The positioning of the couching stitches can be varied along the

rows to add interest to the finished result. Plan the design on graph paper before you start and then work a swatch to ensure that what you envisioned translates effectively.

Here, every fifth stitch on every knit row is couched over a strand of contrast yarn. The couching stitches are moved on by one on every row to produce diagonal lines of couched stitches.

TECHNIQUES: Cluster stitch ◗ page 41 • Threading beads onto the yarn ◗ page 66 • Weaving ◗ page 41 • Couching ◗ page 41

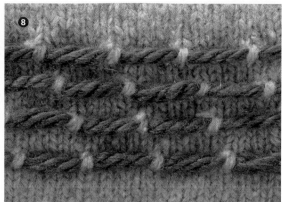

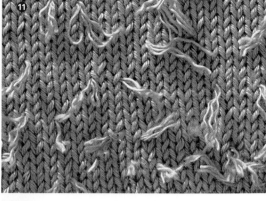

Untwisting yarns

This technique cannot be used on all types of yarn, as some will simply disintegrate when untwisted.

However, when the yarn does allow it, untwisting can be very useful. For example, if you are making a cardigan in a thick yarn and would like matching buttons, simply reduce the thickness of the yarn by a ply or more and work squares to cover buttons with.

If you want a specific color – to work part of a motif maybe – that is not available in the weight you need, then untwisting a heavier yarn that is the right shade can provide the solution.

❾ WORKING WITH DIFFERENT PLYS OF THE SAME YARN

These three swatches are all made from the same yarn, but two have taken advantage of untwisting.

Top 6 ply
This swatch shows the yarn at full weight worked in st st on US 8 (5mm) needles.

Center 3 ply
Here, the yarn is untwisted and three plys are worked in st st on US 3 (3.25mm) needles.

Bottom 1 ply
Not many yarns have single plys that are strong enough to be knitted alone, but here 1 ply is worked in st st on US 0 (2mm) needles.

❿ COMBINING 1 PLY

For this st st swatch a single ply of the blue yarn was used to balance the very fine purple mohair yarn. The first rows are worked in 1 ply of the blue yarn. The next 10 rows are worked in the mohair and the last rows are worked in both yarns combined.

⓫ DISTRESSED COTTON

Short lengths of untwisted yarn can be used in conjunction with the yarn at full weight to achieve a "distressed" effect using the knitting-in method↓.

Here, the short lengths are 3 plys thick, of varying sizes and are knitted in randomly, but more densely towards the bottom of the swatch.

Ribbons and fabric

As alternatives to yarn, ribbons and fabrics↓ are an obvious choice. Ribbons knit up well, and are easy to use. Organza ribbon works particularly well, as it compresses easily within the stitch and is usually double-sided, so you do not need to worry about the back showing.

Fabric↓ needs to be cut up into strips but also produce effective results. Frayed edges can be particularly interesting, though you must tear the fabrics along the grain rather than cutting them on the bias to achieve this. Do remember that you will need a lot of ribbon or fabric to knit even quite a small project. Ribbon can be mixed with yarn in a knitted fabric, though the restrictions of mixing yarns↓ will apply.

⓬ GARTER STITCH RIBBON

This garter stitch swatch is knitted from double-sided satin ribbon 2in (5cm) wide. The lush texture and thick fabric would make for a glamorous evening bag.

⓭ REV ST ST RIBBON

Here, 1-in (2-cm) wide checked organza ribbon is worked in rev st st. Small designs, such as this one, tend to work better as they remain at least partly visible, whereas larger patterns will get lost in the stitches.

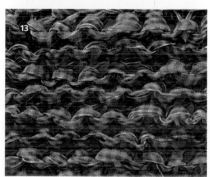

TECHNIQUES: Knitting in strands ♦ page 14 • Ribbon and fabric tape ♦ page 42 • Fabric ♦ page 42 • Mixing yarns ♦ page 40

➏ EMBROIDERY YARN CABLE AND BOBBLES

These yarns are easy to handle and work, being approximately the weight of double knitting yarn.

A = background color
B = cable color
C = bobble color

Panel of 14 sts and repeat of 6 rows on a background of st st.
Row 1 (RS): K4 in A, k6 in B, k4 in A.
Row 2: P1 in C, p3 in A, p6 in B, p3 in A, p1 in C.
Row 3: MB in C k3 A, C6F in B, k3 in A, MB in C.
Row 4: As row 2.
Rows 5–6: As rows 1–2.
Rep rows 1–6.

➐ EMBROIDERY YARN FAIR ISLE

Small Fair Isle designs and intarsia motifs are perfect for embroidery yarns, as they do not require a large amount of yarn and the range of colors available makes it easy to achieve an interesting result. If worked on a background of DK-weight yarn, there should be no fabric distortion.

A= green
B = light pink
C = dark pink

Multiple of 4 sts + 2 and repeat of 6 rows.
Cast on the required number of sts in A.
Row 1 (RS): [K2A, k2B] rep to last 2 sts, k2A.
Row 2: [P2A, p2B] rep to last 2 sts, p2A.

➊ VERTICAL RIBBON STRIPE

The intarsia technique is used to create a vertical stripe of narrow organza ribbon two stitches wide within a piece of st st. The ribbon needs to be carefully selected and a swatch must be worked to ensure that the ribbon and yarn balance one another if this technique is to be used in a project.

➋ RIBBON BAND

Ribbon can also be knitted into the knitted fabric using elongated stitch. In this example, ¼ in (6 mm) organza ribbon is used because its stiffness helps the stitches to hold their shape, but it does make the last and first rows of knitting yarn difficult to keep neat.

Work several rows of st st using the knitting yarn, ending with a wrong-side row. Cut the yarn.

Work the next row in elongated stitch with the ribbon as the working yarn. Insert the right-hand needle into the first stitch on the left-hand needle and wrap the ribbon three times around the right-hand needle before drawing it through the stitch. Repeat this on every stitch across the row.

On the next row, rejoin the knitting yarn and purl across the row, inserting the right-hand needle into the first loop on the left-hand

needle, purl and drop the first loop and then the other two loops when the stitch has been completed.

➌ RIBBON AND COTTON STRIPES

Here, stripes of narrow satin ribbon contrast well with the matte finish of the cotton yarn in a garter stitch swatch. Ribbon can be bulky if carried up the side of the knitting, so unless it is very narrow it is better to start a new length for each stripe. Secure cut ends by tucking them into the back of a stitch and sewing them in place with a needle and thread.

➍ FRAYED FABRIC

Scissors are used to start each cut on this chambray fabric↓, but then the strips are torn to give straight, but frayed edges. Be careful as you come towards the end of each strip and do not tear too far. Garter stitch shows off the frayed edges well

Embroidery threads and yarns

Knitters have often envied the range of colors available to embroiderers: the delight of being able to choose the perfect lilac from a selection of shades, all in the same weight and finish. There is no reason why knitters should not use

embroidery threads and yarns↓ though, due to the quantities they are sold in, small projects, or details such as intarsia motifs or covered buttons, are certainly advisable.

➎ EMBROIDERY THREAD STRIPES

This st st swatch is worked entirely in embroidery threads. The first two stripes are in subtly varying shades of green, the third in a coordinating taupe and the last in a variegated green thread. Embroidery thread does split easily, so care needs to be taken when working with it.

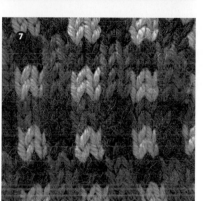

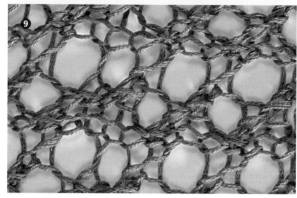

Row 3: [K2C, k2B] rep to last 2 sts, k2C.
Row 4: [P2C, p2B] rep to last 2 sts, p2C.
Row 5: [K2A, k2C] rep to last 2 sts, k2A.
Row 6: [P2A, p2C] rep to last 2 sts, p2A.
Row 7: [K2B, k2C] rep to last 2 sts, k2B.
Row 6: [P2B, p2C] rep to last 2 sts, p2B.
Rep rows 1–6 as required.

❽ MOHAIR AND THREAD SPOTS AND BOBBLES
Yarn can be combined with embroidery thread, but the distortion problems associated with mixing yarns↓ do apply.

Here, a fine mohair yarn overcomes the problem and offsets the satin finish of the thread at the same time. The spots are placed randomly, while the bobbles↓ are worked on a single row.

Abbreviations
MB = make bobble. K into the front and back of the st twice, p 1 row, k 1 row, p 1 row, sl 2 sts, k2tog, psso.

A = background color
B = thread color

Spots
Row 1: Work in A to position of spot, 1 st in B, cont in A.
Row 2: Work in A to st before spot, 3 sts in B, cont in A.
Row 3: Work in A to position of row 1, 1 st in B, cont in A.

Bobbles
Row 1: Work in A to position of bobble, 1B, cont in A.
Row 2: Work in A to position of bobble, MB in B, cont in A.

❾ LACE
Embroidery thread makes silky lace that drapes beautifully, though a single skein does not go far. Work a swatch before starting a project to check that what you have in mind is practical.

Multiple of 3 sts + 2 and repeat of 4 rows
Row 1: K2, [yf, k2tog, k1] rep to the end of the row.
Row 2: Purl.
Row 3: [K1, yf, k2tog] rep to last 2 sts, k2.
Row 4: Purl.
Rep rows 1–4 as required.

Loose fibers
Popular with crafters of all persuasions, loose fibers can be bought in packs in a huge range of colors and a variety of finishes. Use them to add texture and color to a knitted fabric, though the restrictions on washing and mixing yarns↓ should be born in mind.

You can also use short sections of yarn as fibers, or untwist lengths of yarn: it does not matter how strong they are as they will not be taking any strain. In addition, look around the house and try using any other materials that seem suitable.

❿ KNITTED IN FIBERS
One way to incorporate short lengths of fiber is to simply mix them with the working yarn.

Here, pieces of untwisted yarn are knitted into some rows and the ends left long on the front of the work.

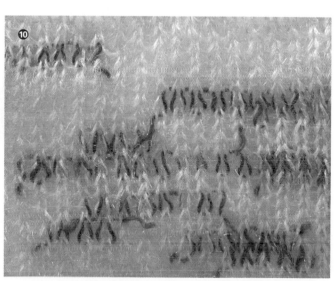

TECHNIQUES: Mixing yarns ◆ page 40 • Bobble ◆ page 10

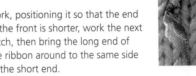

1 METALLIC STRAND
Here, a long length of metal strip unravelled from a scouring pad is knitted into the fabric. Catch the strip in on the right side of the knitted fabric at random intervals, using the stranding technique usually used on the wrong side of Fair Isle. The strip should not be stranded too tightly or it will distort the gauge (tension) of the fabric.

2 CAUGHT-IN FIBERS
This swatch uses exactly the same technique as the previous one, but short lengths of fibers are knitted into the background fabric at random. Each length of fiber is caught in on every stitch.

3 KNOTS AND BOWS
A variation on the weaving↓ technique is used on this swatch to add lengths of ribbon that can be tied into knots or bows. The ribbons can be added on knit or purl rows.

Work to the position of the knot, lay the ribbon across the work, positioning it so that the end at the front is shorter, work the next stitch, then bring the long end of the ribbon around to the same side as the short end.

Complete the row, then tie the ribbon as required.

4 COUCHING
Bundles of fine mohair yarn work well as loose fibers, though they can be a little difficult to handle. The trick is to get one end of the bundle anchored, then it is much easier to control the rest of it.

Here, bundles of different lengths are couched↓ onto a smooth knitted fabric. Once the work is complete, the ends of the bundles are trimmed.

5 WOVEN-IN FIBERS
The weaving technique is used in this swatch to incorporate short lengths of a contrast yarn into a knitted background fabric. The lengths are woven in at random during the knitting (though this could be planned out in advance), and the ends left long on the front of the fabric.

Unusual materials
If you look around the house there are all sorts of things that can be knitted, though some of them may not be very practical. However, use your imagination, experiment a little and see what you achieve.

Here are some examples of unusual knitting materials, and some ideas for using them.

6 STRING
Ordinary household string↓ knits up easily and makes excellent bath mitts and mats. It comes in smooth finishes and rough ones, like the one shown here, so swatch a few and decide which you prefer.

7 COLORED STRING
As well as the widely available green garden string, look out for other colors: this pink string came from a gift store. Do wash a swatch to check for color fastness before knitting a bath mitt and staining yourself.

8 GIFT RIBBON
This is excellent for knitting as it comes on large spools. If you are a really dedicated knitter, consider knitting your own gift bags or wrap and fastening the parcels with matching gift ribbon↓.

9 PAPER STRING
This is stiffer than ordinary string and so a little harder to work. It is usually sold for decoratively tying parcels, and would also make good gift bags.

TECHNIQUES: Weaving ◗ page 41 • Couching ◗ page 41 • String and raffia ◗ page 42 • Paper string and gift ribbon ◗ page 42

⑩ SPARKLE GIFT STRING
Rev st st makes the most of this tinsel string, which could be knitted up into the most wonderful Christmas decorations.

⑪ SCOURING PAD
An unravelled scouring pad knits up interestingly, though it is a little scratchy to work with. It is naturally curly, so do not try to pull it tight as you work; the curliness gives an interesting texture. Another candidate for a keen knitter to turn into Christmas decorations?

⑫ RAFFIA
This is not the easiest material to knit with, as it generally comes in quite short lengths and does split easily. However, make a decorative feature of the knots and consider knitting a unique raffia↓ sun hat.

⑬ WIRE STRIPES
Soft 28-gauge craft wire↓ is easier to knit with than you might think and is available in a range of colors from good craft stores.

 The trick with working with wire is not to try and pull it tight with each stitch: allow it to find its own way a little and accept the uneven nature of the stitches as part of the effect. Knitted wire jewellery is popular and can be stunning.

⑭ WIRE AND SEQUINS
As you can see through knitted wire, items can be attached to the back and still be visible: the effect is as though they are caught in a net.

 These flower sequins are threaded onto the wire before starting work and then just pushed up to the stitch on the purl rows of the st st.

⑮ WIRE EDGE
Wire can be incorporated into a knitted fabric to allow it to be bent into a specific shape. This is not an advisable technique for an item that needs frequent laundering, but does work well for knitted jewellery or bags.

 In this swatch the first rows are knitted and the wire is combined with the yarn in the first row after the cast on only. The wire is completely invisible on the right side of the fabric.

⑯ LEATHER EDGE
Leather↓ thong is fairly easy to work with, though it creates a stiff fabric. Try using it as an edging to give structure to a collar, cuff or the top edge of a bag.

 Here, the leather thong is cast on using the thumb loop method and two rows of st st are worked to produce a decorative edge. The rest of the swatch is worked in a yarn of a similar weight to the thong to avoid distortion.

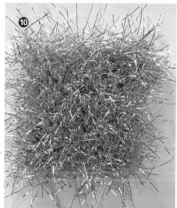
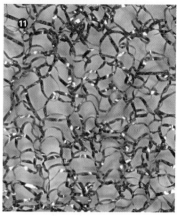

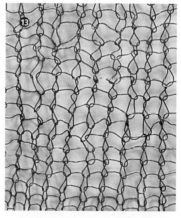

TECHNIQUES: String and raffia ◗ page 42 • Wire ◗ page 43 • Leather ◗ page 43

Denim afghan

This afghan just gets better with age. The dyes fade and the edges of the knitted fabric strips fray and soften. In this case the denim fabric was bought especially for the project, but given a large, fast-growing family it won't take long to find well-worn pieces that were destined to be thrown away.

Size

56 x 64in (140 x 160cm)

Materials

Jaeger aqua cotton 1¾oz (50g) balls
Red A   3

Rowan denim 1¾oz (50g) balls
Blue B   16

Denim fabric 60in (150cm) wide
Blue C   3yds (3m)
Cut 1½yds (1.5m) into a ¼in (6mm) strip using the technique described on page 43.

1 pair of US 5 (3.75mm) needles
1 pair of US 6 (4mm) needles
1 pair of US 10½ (7mm) needles
Cable needle

¼ in (6mm) piping cord
3yds (3m)
Medium weight batting (wadding)
1½yds (1.5m)

Rotary cutter
Knitter's sewing needle
Sewing needle and thread
Chalk pencil
Red buttonhole thread
Sewing machine

Gauge (Tension)

19 stitches and 33 rows to 4in (10cm) after washing, over st st with denim yarn using US 6 (4mm) needles.
9 stitches and 20 rows to 4in (10cm) over garter stitch with denim fabric using US 10½ (7mm) needles.

Note Denim yarn shrinks by about a fifth over its length, so it is important to wash the gauge (tension) swatch to get an accurate stitch count.

Abbreviations

C4F = cable 4 forward.
ML = make loop.
C4B = cable 4 back.
T3B = twist 3 back. Slip the next st onto a cable needle and hold at the back of the work, k2 from the left-hand needle, p st from the cable needle. The knit sts move to the right across the work.
T3F = twist 3 forward. Slip the next 2 sts onto a cable needle and hold at the front of the work, p1 from the left-hand needle, k sts from the cable needle. The knit sts move to the left across the work.
See also page 157.

Pintuck 1

Using US 5 (3.75mm) needles, the thumb method and A, cast on 308 sts.
Work 13 rows in st st ending with a RS row.
Bind (cast) off using the tubular cast off method into the upper st loops of row 4.

Panel 1

Using US 6 (4mm) needles, the thumb method and B, cast on 70 sts.

Row 1: K1tbl, k13, p3, k2, p14, k4, p14, k2, p3, k14.

Row 2 and every alt row: Sl2 purlwise, work the stitches as they come, knitting the k sts and purling the p sts, to last 2 sts, sl2 purlwise. Rep the rows 1–2 once more.

Row 5: K1tbl, k7, C4F, (ML) rep once more, p3, k2, p4, (ML) rep five more times, p4 k4, p4, (ML) rep five more times, p4, k2, p3, (ML) rep once more, C4B, k8.

Patt repeat

Row 7: K1tbl, k11, (ML) rep once more, p3, k2, p4, (ML) rep five more times, p4 C4F, p4, (ML) rep five more times, p4, k2, p3, (ML) rep once more, K12.

Row 9: K1tbl, k7, C4F, (ML) rep once more, p3, T3F, p3, (ML) rep five more times, p3, T3B, T3F, p3, (ML) rep five more times, p3, T3B, p3, (ML) rep once more, C4B, k8.

Row 11: K1tbl, k11, (ML) rep once more, p4, T3F, p3, (ML) rep three more times, p3, T3B, p2, T3F, p3, (ML) rep three more times, p3, T3B, p4, (ML) rep once more, k12.

Row 13: K1tbl, k7, C4F, (ML) rep once more, p5, T3F, p8, T3B, p4, T3F, p8, T3B, p5, (ML) rep once more, C4B, k8.

Row 15: K1tbl, k11, (ML) rep once more, p6, T3F, p6, T3B, p6, T3F, p6, T3B, p6, (ML) rep once more, k12.

Row 17: K1tbl, k7, C4F, (ML) rep once more, p7, T3F, p4, T3B, p8, T3F, p4, T3B, p7, (ML) rep once more, C4B, k8.

Row 19: K1tbl, k11, (ML) rep once more, p8, T3F, p2, T3B, p10, T3F, p2, T3B, p8, (ML) rep once more, k12.

Row 21: K1tbl, k7, C4F, (ML) rep once more, p9, T3F, T3B, p12, T3F, T3B, p9, (ML) rep once more, C4B, k8.

Row 23: K1tbl, k11, (ML) rep once more, p10, C4F, p14, C4B, p10, (ML) rep once more, k12.

Row 25: K1tbl, k7, C4F, (ML) rep once more, p9, T3B, T3F, p12, T3B, T3BF, p9, (ML) rep once more, C4B, k8.

Row 27: K1tbl, k11, (ML) rep once more, p8, T3B, p2, T3F, p10, T3B, p2, T3F, p8, (ML) rep once more, k12.

Row 29: K1tbl, k7, C4F, (ML) rep once more, p7, T3B, p4, T3F, p8, T3B, p4, T3F, p7, (ML) rep once more, C4B, k8.

Row 31: K1tbl, k11, (ML) rep once more, p6, T3B, p6, T3F, p6, T3B, p6, T3F, p6, (ML) rep once more, k12.

Row 33: K1tbl, k7, C4F, (ML) rep once more, p5, T3B, p8, T3F, p4, T3B, p8, T3F, p5, (ML) rep once more, C4B, k8.

Row 35: K1tbl, k11, (ML) rep once more, p4, T3B, p3, (ML) rep three more times, p3, T3F, p2, T3B, p3, (ML) rep three more times, p3, T3F, p4, (ML) rep once more, k12.

Row 37: K1tbl, k7, C4F, (ML) rep once more, p3, T3B, p3, (ML) rep five more times, p3, T3F, T3B, p3, (ML) rep five more times, p3, T3F, p3, (ML) rep once more, C4B, k8.

Row 38: Sl2 purlwise, work the stitches as they come, knitting the k sts and purling the p sts, to last 2 sts, sl2 purlwise.

Rep patt repeat rows 7–38 until the work measures 62¼in (158cm) from the cast on edge (this should be thirteen more times.)

Rep rows 7–8 once more.
Rep rows 5–6 once more.
Rep rows 1–4 once more.
Bind (cast) off.

Panel 2

Using US 10½ (7mm) needles, the cable method and C, cast on 70 sts. Knit in garter stitch until the work measures 54in (140 cm) from the cast on edge ending with a WS row. Bind (cast) off.

Pintuck 2

Using US 9 (3.75mm) needles, the thumb method and A, cast on 308 sts.

Work 13 rows in st st ending with a RS row.

Work a pintuck into the upper st loops of row 4.

Work 4 rows in st st ending with a WS row.

Bind (cast) off.

Panel 3

Using US 6 (4mm) needles, the thumb method and B, cast on 34 sts.

Row 1: K1tbl, k to the end of the row.

Row 2: Sl2 purlwise, p to last 2 sts, sl2 purlwise.

Rep rows 1–2 twice more.

Patt repeat

Row 7: K1tbl, k12, (ML) rep seven more times, k13.

Row 8: Sl2 purlwise, p to last 2 sts, sl2 purlwise.

Rep rows 7–8 until the work measures 62¼in (158cm) from the cast on edge.

Bind (cast) off.

Panel 4

Cut the batting (wadding) to 56 x 32in (140 x 80cm).

Cut the denim fabric to 60 x 36in (150 x 90cm).

Wrong-side facing, fold the denim fabric in half with the batting (wadding) in the center.

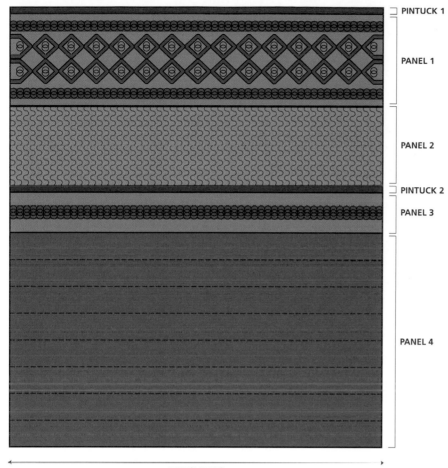

PINTUCK 1
PANEL 1
PANEL 2
PINTUCK 2
PANEL 3
PANEL 4

64IN (160CM)

56IN (140CM)

Piecing diagram

Fold in, pin and baste (tack) the raw edges, using the batting (wadding) as a guide to a finished size of 56 x 32in (140 x 80cm).

Working from the folded edge of the denim upwards, chalk parallel lines 4in (10cm) apart and baste (tack) along them.

Machine sew along the parallel lines using red buttonhole thread.

Slip stitch around the folded in edges of the panel.

Remove all basting (tacking) and chalk marks.

Finishing

Weave in loose ends on the WS.

Wash the panels that are worked in denim yarn.

Press all the panel pieces avoiding the loop fur and the cables.

Thread the piping cord through the pintucks and sew the ends of the pintucks closed.

With the cast on panel edges to the right and using whip stitch, sew together the panels and pintucks following the piecing diagram.

Organza blind

Knitting is a good way of using up odd lengths of fabric. Here, organza fabric has been combined with yarn to create a blind, which can either be made into a Roman blind or used as a decorative panel.

Size

24 x 42in (60 x 105cm)

Materials

Rowan cotton tape 1¾oz (50g) balls
    White A   1

Rowan R2 braid 1¾oz (50g) balls
    Cream B   1

Jaeger trinity 1¾oz (50g) balls
    Cream C   1
Rowan cotton braid 1¾oz (50g) balls
    Cream D   1

Rowan cotton glace 1¾oz (50g) balls
    White E   1

Jaeger fur 1¾oz (50g) balls
    Cream F   1

Organza 44in (112cm) wide
    Ivory G   1½yds (1.5m)
Cut into a ¼in (6mm) strip using the technique described on page 43.

30in (80cm) US 10½ (6.5mm)
    circular needle
30in (80cm) US 13 (9mm)
    circular needle
30in (80cm) US 8 (5mm)
    circular needle
Crochet hook

1in (2.5cm) long glass oval beads
    Clear   28
1in (2.5cm) glass disc beads
    Clear   18

½in (12mm) glass round beads
    Clear   36

3 x ⁵⁄₁₆ in (8mm) wooden dowel
    24in (60cm) long

1 x ½ in (12mm) wooden dowel
    24in (60cm) long

For a roman blind

11 metal curtain rings
¼in (6mm) cord
    17ft (5m)
Cut the cord into two lengths
108in (270cm) and 84in (210cm)

Rotary cutter
Sewing needle and thread
Hacksaw

Gauge (Tension)

9 stitches and 13 rows to 4in (10cm) over st st with organza using 30in (80cm) US 13 (9mm) circular needle. (The swatch was slightly stretched and flattened across its width.)

Note Some allowances have been made for the differing yarn weights by increasing and decreasing the stitch counts, but the nature of the blind is that lighter weight yarn should be worked on larger needles and heavier weight yarns on smaller needles to create the desired texture. Because one yarn weight affects another, the selvedges won't be perfectly square.

Abbreviations

Sl2tog, k1, psso = slip 2 stitches together, knit one and pass the slipped stitches over.
See also page 157.

To customize the pattern

Read through the pattern. Measure the window you wish to make a blind for and check the yarn quantities given. Divide the window into 4 sections, each between 12–18in (30–45cm) deep. These are the positions for the pintucks, which can be used to make a Roman blind or to support the width of the panel. Work swatches of each yarn on various needles and work out how many stitches are required for the width of the window. Decide on a sequence of yarns and increase and decrease the stitches as necessary.
To bead the bottom edge, the number of cast on stitches needs to be a repeat of 5 +1. To bead with oval beads, the stitch count needs to be divisible by 3.

First blind section

Using US 10½ (6.5mm) circular needle, the crochet invisible cast on and A, cast on 86 sts.
Row 1: K1, purl to last st, k1.
Row 2: K1, purl to last st, k1.
Cut A leaving a 3in (7.5cm) tail.
Change to US 13 (9 mm) needles and B.
Row 3: K1, (k2tog) rep to last st, k1. (44 sts)
Row 4: Knit.
Cut B leaving a 3in (7.5cm) tail.
Change to US 10½ (6.5mm) needles and C.

Row 5: K1, (M1, k1) rep to last st, k1. *(86 sts)*

Rows 6–8: K1, purl to last st, k1.

Cut C leaving a 3in (7.5cm) tail.

Change to D.

Rows 9–11: Knit.

Row 12: K1, purl to last st, k1.

Cut D leaving a 3in (7.5cm) tail.

Change to E.

Rows 13–14: K1, purl to last st, k1.

Rows 15–17: Knit.

Row 18: K1, purl to last st, k1.

Cut E leaving a 3in (7.5cm) tail.

Change to F.

Rows 19–20: K1, purl to last st, k1.

Cut F leaving a 3in (7.5cm) tail.

Change to A

Row 21: Knit.

Row 22: (K27, k2tog) rep once more, k28. *(84 sts)*

Row 23: (Sl2tog, k1, psso, extend the new stitch loop and thread with an oval bead and slip onto the right-hand needle) rep twenty-seven more times. *(28 sts)*

Row 24: K1, (thumb loop cast on 2 sts, p1) rep to last st, thumb loop cast on 2 sts, k1. *(82 sts)*

Row 25: (K16, M1) rep three more times, k18. *(86 sts)*

Row 26: K1, purl to last st, k1.

Cut A leaving a 3in (7.5cm) tail.

Change to US 8 (5mm) needles and E.

Row 27: K1, (M1, k2, M1, k1) rep to last st, M1, k1. *(143 sts)*

Pintuck

Row 28-29: Knit

Row 30: K1, purl to last st, k1.

Row 31: Knit.

Rep rows 30-31 five more times.

Row 42: K1, purl to last st, k1.

Row 43: (Pick up the upper loop of the st on row 28 immediately below the working st and put on the left-hand

needle, k2tog) rep to the end of
the row.

Row 44: K1, purl to last st, k1.

Second blind section

Cut E leaving a 3in (7.5cm) tail.
Change to US 10½ (6.5mm) needles
and F.

Row 45: K1, (k2tog, k1, k2tog) rep to
last 2 sts, k2tog. (*86 sts*)

Row 46: Knit.
Cut F leaving a 3in (7.5cm) tail.
Change to D.

Row 47: Knit

Rows 48–50: K1, purl to last st, k1.

Row 51: Knit.

Row 52: K1, purl to last st, k1.
Cut D leaving a 3in (7.5cm) tail.
Change to C.

Row 53: K1, (k28, M1) rep once
more, k29. (*88 sts*)

Rows 54–56: K1, purl to last st, k1.
Cut C leaving a 3in (7.5cm) tail.
Change to US 13 (9 mm) needles
and B.

Row 57: (K2tog) rep to the end of the
row. (*44 sts*)

Row 58: Knit.
Cut B leaving a 3in (7.5cm) tail.
Change to G.

Row 59: K1, (M1, k2, M1, k1) rep to
last st, M1, k1. (*73 sts*)

Rows 60–66: Work in st st.
Cut G leaving a 3in (7.5cm) tail.
Change to US 8 (5mm) needles
and E.

Row 67: K2, (M1, k1) rep to last st,
k1. (*143 sts*)
Rep rows 28–44.

Third blind section

Cut E leaving a 3in (7.5cm) tail.
Change to US 10½ (6.5mm) needles
and F.

Row 85: K1, (k2tog, k1, k2tog) rep to
last 2 sts, k2tog. (*86 sts*)

Row 86: Knit.
Cut F leaving a 3in (7.5cm) tail.
Change to US 13 (9 mm) needles
and G.

Row 87: K4, (k2tog, k4) rep to last 4
sts, k4. (*73 sts*)

Rows 88–116: Work in st st.
Cut G leaving a 3in (7.5cm) tail.
Change to US 8 (5mm) needles
and E.

Rows 117: K2, (M1, k1) rep to last st,
k1. (*143 sts*)
Rep rows 28–44.

Fourth blind section

Rep the Third Blind Section.
Cut E leaving a 3in (7.5cm) tail.
Change to US 10½ (6.5mm) needles
and F.

Row 135: K1, (k2tog, k1, k2tog) rep
to last 2 sts, k2tog. (*86 sts*)

Row 136: Knit.
Cut F leaving a 3in (7.5cm) tail.
Change to B.

Rows 137–154: Work in st st.
Bind (cast) off using the tubular cast
off method into row 137.

Finishing

Unpick the crochet invisible cast on
and put the loops onto a US 10½
(6.5mm) needle. Bind (cast) off the
stitches using beads and stem stitch
bind (cast) off as folls.

Right-side facing, secure a length of
A six times the width of the project to
the left-hand corner.

*Insert the tapestry needle into the
second st knitwise. Thread on one
round bead, one disc bead and one
round bead. Return the needle through
the disc bead and the first round bead
and pull tight. Thread the needle
through the first st purlwise and drop
the first st off the needle. Bind (cast) off
4 sts.*

Rep from * to * sixteen more times.
Bead and bind (cast) off the last st.

Weave in loose yarn ends on
the WS. Stitch loose fabric and tape
ends on the WS.

Insert the thinner dowel into the
pintucks and the thicker dowel into
the tubular bind (cast) off. Sew up
the ends of the pintucks using
whip stitch.

Roman blind

Wrong-side up, lay the blind flat on a
large surface. Securely sew a metal
ring to each of the three pintucks, 4in
(10cm) in from each edge. Attach rings
to the tubular bind (cast) off at 4in
(10cm) intervals across its width,
Attach the longer cord to the ring on
the lower pintuck on the opposite side
to where the blind will be pulled from.
Thread the cord through the rings on
the pintucks above and through all the
rings along the tubular bind (cast) off.

Then attach the shorter cord to
the other ring on the lower pintuck
and thread it through the rings on the
pintucks above, including the one on
the tubular bind (cast) off.

Draw both cords together
so there is no slack as they pass
through the rings, and knot them
together. When the two cords are
pulled together, the pintucks should
be drawn up together. To hold the
blind in an open position the cords
have to be secured to a cleat
attached to the window frame
or wall.

TECHNIQUES: Fabric ◗ page 42   •   Tubular bind (cast) off ◗ page 128   •   Stem stitch bind (cast) off ◗ page 129

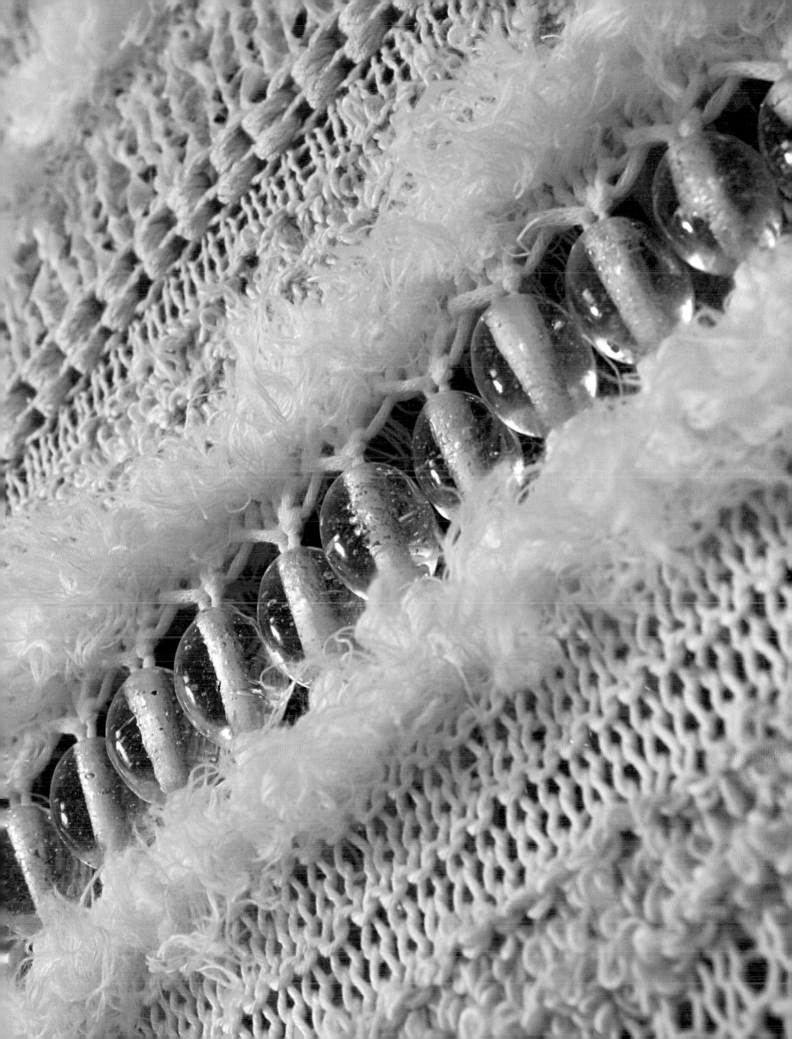

Striped bolster

Cables worked on a st st background "grow" out of the knitted fabric and are subtler than cables worked on rev st st. Similarly, stripes shaded and softened by mixing yarns make for calm color changes rather than harsh divisions. Worked together, these techniques are used to make this delicately colorful and gently textured bolster, with large pearl buttons picking up the yarn colors.

Materials

Rowan wool cotton 1¾oz (50g) balls

Grey A	2
Light blue C	2
Mauve E	1

Rowan kidsilk haze 1oz (25g) balls

Blue (B)	1
Mauve (D)	1

1 pair US 6 (4mm) needles
Cable needle

14 large mother-of-pearl buttons
2 7in (18cm) diameter circles of
    gray velvet
Needle and gray sewing thread
15¾in (40cm) long bolster pad with
    circumference of 25in (64cm)

Gauge (Tension)

24 stitches and 34 rows to 4in (10cm) over st st using US 6 (4mm) needles.

Abbreviations

MB = k1, p1 twice into next st, turn work, p4, turn work, k4, turn work, p4, turn work, slip 2 sts, k2tog, pass slipped sts over.

C8F = cable 8 front.

C6F = cable 6 front.

C6B = cable 6 back.

C8B = cable 8 back.

PB = place button. Use the slip stitch method.

See also page 157.

Note When working with two yarns, MB in wool cotton yarn only.

To make

Using A, cast on 112 sts.
Work chart to row 33, following color and button instructions below.
Rep chart rows 2–33 following color and button instructions below until row 228 is completed.
Bind (cast) off.

Color and button instructions

Rows 1–6: A

Rows 7–10: A and B

Rows 11–16: B and C

Rows 17–26: C. 2 buttons threaded onto yarn.

Rows 27–32: C and D

Rows 33–35: D and E

Rows 36–43: A and D

Rows 44–58: A. 2 buttons threaded onto yarn.

Rows 59–62: A and B

Key

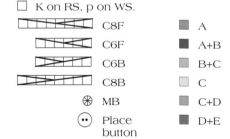

☐	K on RS, p on WS.
⬛ C8F	⬛ A
⬛ C6F	⬛ A+B
⬛ C6B	⬛ B+C
⬛ C8B	⬛ C
✳ MB	⬛ C+D
⊙ Place button	⬛ D+E

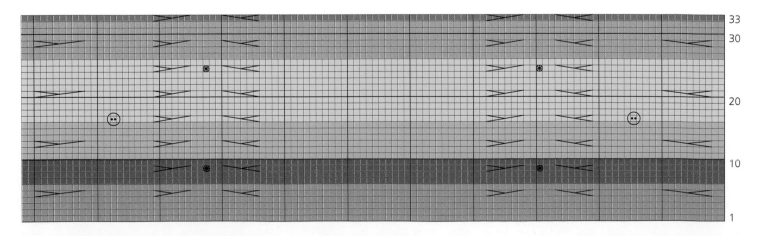

Rows 63–66: B and E

Rows 67–68: B and C

Rows 69–70: B and E

Rows 71–75: B and C

Rows 76–80: C

Rows 81–86: C and D. 2 buttons threaded onto C.

Rows 87–100: A and D

Rows 101–107: C and D

Rows 108–110: D and E

Rows 111–114: B and E. 2 buttons threaded onto E.

Rows 115–119: B and C

Rows 120–137: C

Rows 138–143: B and C

Rows 144–156: A and B. 2 buttons threaded onto A.

Rows 157–160: B and E

Rows 161–166: D and E

Rows 167–182: A and D. 2 buttons threaded onto A.

Rows 183–184: D and E

Rows 185–197: C and D

Rows 198–205: C

Rows 206–215: B and C. 2 buttons threaded onto C.

Rows 216–224: A and B

Rows 225–228: A

Finishing

Do not press the knitted fabric. Right-sides facing, pin the two short ends together. Using mattress stitch, sew 2in (5cm) of the pinned edges together at each end. Turn the work wrong-side out and pin a circle of velvet into each end of the bolster, easing the knitted fabric to fit the circles. Using the needle and sewing thread, sew the circles to the knitted fabric, taking a seam of ¼in (0.5cm) on the velvet and two stitches on the knitting. Turn the bolster right-side out and slip the pad into it. Using mattress stitch, sew up the opening.

Caterpillar baby snuggler

The natural shaping created by the alternating bands of different yarns gives this otherwise simple pattern its caterpillar effect. Use the snuggler to keep a baby warm when out and about in a stroller, or as an extra layer when taking a nap.

Size
24½ x 15in (62 x 38cm)

Materials
Rowan polar 3½oz (100g) balls
    Green A   4

Rowanspun dk 1¾oz (50g) hank
    Green B   1

1 pair each of US 11 (8mm) and
    US 10½ (6.5mm) knitting needles

Knitter's sewing needle
3 wooden toggles

Gauge (Tension)
13 sts to and 22 rows to 4in (10cm) on polar over garter stitch using US 11 (8mm) needles.

Abbreviations
M1R = make 1 right.
M1L = make 1 left.
See also page 157.

To make
Stripe patt is 10 rows A on US 11 (8mm) needles, 8 rows B on US 10½ (6.5mm) needles.
Keep stripe patt correct throughout until otherwise stated.

Using thumb method and US 11 (8mm) needles, cast on 32 sts in A.
Row 1 and every alt row (WS): Knit.
Row 2: K8, M1L, k1, M1R, k14, M1L, k1, M1R, k8. (*36 sts*)
Row 4: K9, M1L, k1, M1R, k16, M1L, k1, M1R, k9. (*40 sts*)
Row 6: K10, M1L, k1, M1R, k18, M1L, k1, M1R, k10. (*44 sts*)
Cont in increase patt as set (on every alt row knit 1 more st before the first and after the last increase and 2 more sts in the central panel), to row 36. (*104 sts*)
Knit 72 straight rows in stripe patt. Break B and cont in A on US 11 (8mm) needles.

Left-hand side and buttonhole band
Row 109: K52, slip rem 52 sts on stitch holder and work sts on needles only.
Using the thumb method, cast on 4 sts. (*56 sts*)
Row 110: (K1, p1) rep three more times, k48.
Row 111: K48, (p1, k1) rep three more times.
Rep rows 110–111 four more times.
Rep row 110 once more.
Row 121: K48, p1, k1, p1, k1, yo, k2tog, p1, k1.
Keeping seed (moss) patt correct, rep rows 110–121.
Rep rows 110–111 twice more.

Row 138: (K1, p1) rep to the end of the row.
Work 8 rows seed (moss) stitch.
Row 147: Seed (moss) to last 4 sts, yo, k2tog, p1, k1.
Work 3 rows seed (moss) stitch.
Bind (cast) off in seed (moss) stitch.

Right-hand side and button band
Cast on 4 sts, knit 52 sts from stitch holder. (*56 sts*)
Next row: K48, (p1, k1) rep three more times.
Next row: (K1, p1) rep three more times, k48.
Rep these last 2 rows thirteen more times.
Next row: (K1, p1) rep to the end of the row.
Work 12 rows seed (moss) stitch.
Bind (cast) off in seed (moss) stitch.

Finishing
Weave in ends on the WS of the work.
    Lightly press the snuggler. Using mattress stitch, join the back seam. Sew 3 wooden toggles onto the buttonband to align with the buttonholes.

knitting in

A KNITTED FABRIC CAN BE DECORATED WITH color, pattern, texture, and by adding other items to it. Beads are the most popular items, and there are a various techniques in this chapter for adding them.

Beads are widely available in a vast range of colors, finishes and sizes, so you should always be able to find something to suit, and they do add an instant glamor to the plainest knitted project.

The slip stitch method is the most commonly used beading technique, but there are others, so do try using them, especially to bead areas you haven't considered before, such as edges or buttonholes.

Do not limit yourself to beads, however. Almost any item of suitable scale that is not too heavy can be knitted into a fabric, and here you will find advice and techniques for doing so.

There are dozens of swatches in the Library to inspire you, showing many different ways of using the knitting in techniques.

Knitting in
TECHNIQUES

Knitting in beads

Beading offers a way of adding color, texture and luxurious detail to any knitted project. Depending on the beads you use, the effect can be subtle, or brilliant and bold.

Almost any yarn can be beaded, but if a large number of beads are to be used then some yarns with little or no ply, or textured yarns, can lose their character and strength as the beads pass along them. A solution is to use two balls of yarn, one threaded with beads, and the Fair Isle stranding or weaving technique to work beaded sections from the beaded ball of yarn. This does produce a denser fabric, but this may be of benefit to some beading techniques.

TYPES OF BEADS

The beads should not be too heavy for the yarn and must have a hole large enough for double-thickness yarn to pass through. This means in bead-sizing terms about a size 6, but always take a needle (see Threading Beads onto the Yarn, opposite), and a length of the yarn to the store and check whether or not the hole is big enough. This is also an excellent opportunity to see how the yarn and the bead look together. The range of beads is almost as varied as the range of yarns, so you are bound to find something.

Wooden beads are light and strong, but if dyed they may fade with washing and the varnish, if there is one, may flake. Wooden beads, even when varnished, have a matte, dulled look that will suit a project with a homespun or ethnic look.

Plastic beads are light and durable and can be found in a variety of colors and shapes, sometimes simulating materials such as glass, metal, or ceramic. The only cautionary note is that they can melt, and sometimes at surprisingly low temperatures.

Bone beads tend to come only in a cream color, in limited shapes and are very expensive. However, if you are planning to use the bead as a main feature of the project, they are worth considering.

Glass beads can be bought in a vast range of colors and a variety of shapes. They will add a glamorous note to a project, and although they can shatter this should only be considered a problem if they are applied so densely that they have very little knitted fabric around them to cushion them.

Metal beads often give a project vintage charm but, like metal buttons, they will tarnish. It is often recommended that they are removed before washing, though this is completely impractical if they are knitted into the fabric.

Ceramic beads do not wash well: even if they survive the laundry once, their future is not assured.

With the perfect bead chosen, it is time to swatch. For most bead techniques the fabric should be fairly firm or beads may slip to the wrong side, although beaded lace should not be discounted. Also, the weight of the beads may drag a loosely knitted garment out of shape. Now is the time to find out.

THREADING BEADS ONTO THE YARN

Most patterns specify the number of beads to be threaded on to each ball of yarn. If not, thread up half a ball with more beads than you will need, then count the number used after completing half a ball and add the remaining beads required from the other end of the ball. This also reduces the wear on the yarn caused by large numbers of beads sliding along it. If you have threaded on too few beads and it is too onerous to unwind the ball and thread more beads on from the other end, then break the yarn.

Fold a length of sewing cotton in half and thread both ends through a sewing needle. Thread the end of the yarn through the loop in the sewing cotton and fold it back on itself. Thread beads along the needle, down the sewing cotton and onto the yarn until you have the number of beads on the yarn that your pattern requires.

BEADING SEQUENCE

When threading beads onto yarn to follow a charted design, first thread on the bead closest to the top left-hand corner of the chart. Follow the row along to the right-hand side, threading on the correct beads as they appear on the chart. Follow the next row from right to left, threading on the correct beads. Continue until you reach the bottom right-hand corner of the chart. This ensures that when you work the chart, following from bottom right to top left, the beads will be on the yarn in the correct order.

Edge beading techniques

A quick way to decorate a cast on or bound (cast) off edge is with beads. In addition to its decorative qualities, the right bead will help to create a firm edge, the weight will reduce curl on a st st edge, or it will highlight the knit stitch on a ribbed edge.

Edges with more than one row of beads can be weighty and cumbersome, and make the rest of the knitting awkward. The weight can also easily distort the shape of a project. For an edge with a cascade or cluster of beads, it is better to use the Invisible Cast On on page 126 and when the piece is finished, go back and pick up the stitches, and use one of the sewn bound (cast) offs on page 129.

BEADED CABLE CAST ON

This cast on is both decorative and sturdy with very little stretch. The curl of the fabric brings the beads up level with the first row of stitches.

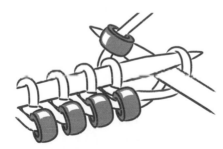

1 Thread beads onto the yarn. Place a slip knot on the left-hand needle. Position a bead behind the knot. Insert the right-hand needle into the loop. * Knit, drawing the bead through with the loop. Put the loop onto the left-hand needle and slide the bead to the front so it sits against the knot. Slide a bead up the yarn, insert the right-hand needle between the last stitch and the slip knot and repeat from *.

BEADED THUMB CAST ON

This cast on has the advantage of the standard thumb cast on in that it is elastic, but when beaded it also allows the beads to hang slightly below the cast on edge.

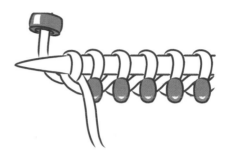

1 Thread the beads onto the yarn and push them beyond the position for the slip knot, which will be the first stitch. Work the cast on with the beads on the length of yarn coming from the ball, and leaving the tail without any beads. Before each new stitch, push one bead up against the last stitch then work as usual.

There are several variations of this cast on, including having beads on the tail and pushing them up to the last stitch, and a frill with beads on both sections of the yarn.

BEADED BIND (CAST) OFF

This helps to create a firm bound (cast) off edge that will splay slightly if larger beads are used. It is perfect for preventing the rolling of the edge on a st st bind (cast) off. Using the Beading on Individual Stitches technique on page 68 also works well for a bound (cast) off edge.

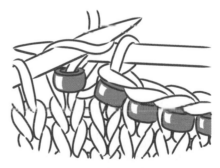

1 Cut the yarn to four times the width of the row from the last stitch. Thread the yarn with sufficient beads to work the row, minus two. Work one stitch. * Push a bead up against the back of the knitted fabric, work the next stitch and draw the bead through the stitch with the loop. Pass the first stitch on the right-hand needle over the last one. Repeat from * to the last stitch. Work the last stitch without a bead and bind (cast) it off.

Adding beads to a knitted fabric

There are two ways to describe the process of adding beads to knitted fabric – beaded knitting and bead knitting. The difference may seem subtle, but the two terms actually mean two completely different things.

Beaded knitting is the scattering of beads over a knitted fabric, which can be done in variety of ways. The first four techniques on these pages are all for beaded knitting and you should choose the one that suits the size and shape of the beads and the bead pattern and stitch you want to use.

The beads can be applied sparingly, with just a few over a large area of knitting, or they can be knitted in quite densely. They can also be used to highlight a knitted detail or to make a motif.

Bead knitting is illustrated with the close beading technique. This is where the yarn becomes merely a vehicle holding the bead fabric together and is itself almost totally obscured by beads hanging with the holes up and down the fabric. As the beads lie very close together, the size of bead is paramount: they should closely match the width and height of the stitch or the fabric will be distorted.

This is a technique that requires a lot of attention to detail when stringing the beads, and some practice to achieve a smooth knitting action.

SLIP STITCH BEADING

This is the most common method of beaded knitting. It is quick and easy to do and simple to chart. However, beads cannot be positioned on adjoining stitches or directly above one another, which limits design options a little.

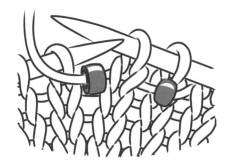

1 **On a knit row**, work to the position of a bead. Bring the yarn to the front of the work and slide a bead along it, so that it is close to the last stitch but lies in front of the next stitch on the row.

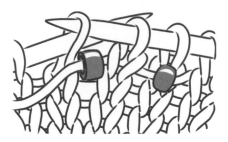

2 Slip the next stitch purlwise, leaving the bead in front of the slipped stitch. Take the yarn to the back of the work and knit the next stitch firmly. Knit to the position of the next bead and repeat the process. On the next row, work the slipped stitches firmly.

3 **On a purl row**, work to the position of a bead. Take the yarn to the back of the work and slide a bead along to lie in front of the next stitch on the row. Slip the next stitch purlwise, then bring the yarn forward and purl to the position of the next bead. On the next row, work the slipped stitches firmly.

BEADING ON INDIVIDUAL STITCHES

This is a good method of adding the occasional bead or a forgotten bead in a bead sequence. However, its appearance differs from that of slip stitch beading in that the bead holes lie up and down the knitting and the bead does not stand proud of the knitted surface. The bead is equally visible on the right and wrong sides.

1 At the position of the bead, thread the stitch through the bead using either a crochet hook or a needle and thread. Return the loop to the left-hand needle and knit or purl the stitch as usual.

BEADING WITH A SECOND YARN

If you wish to use tiny beads, it is possible to thread them onto a fine yarn or thread and work the project with both the fine and main yarn. If a contrasting or complementary color is chosen, the fine yarn can be a feature of the work, as well as carrying the beads, though the restrictions of mixing yarns would apply. If a matching color is used, however, the fine yarn can be almost invisible.

1 When you reach the position of a bead, leave the main yarn at the back of the work. Bring the fine yarn to the front and slide a bead down to the stitch. Work the stitch in the main yarn, then take the fine yarn to the back of the work. Continue working in both yarns until you reach the next stitch to be beaded.

BEADING BETWEEN STITCHES

This is a useful method of beading on garter stitch without any slipped stitches distorting the regular undulations of the stitch pattern. Beads can only be added on alternate rows and the yarn is very visible.

This method can also be used to produce bead knitting if rev st st is used and beads are positioned between every bead and on every row. On knit rows, position the beads as described below, and on purl rows, simply slide a bead up the yarn to sit next to the last stitch, then purl the next stitch.

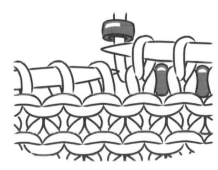

1 With the yarn on the right side, work to the position of a bead. Slide a bead along the yarn, up tight against the last stitch, and work the next stitch.

CLOSE BEADING

This is the most commonly used form of bead knitting. It produces a twisted stitch and every stitch on both the knit and the purl rows carries a bead, which is positioned on top of the stitch loop.

This can be an awkward stitch to master because it is important to keep the beads on the front of the stitch loop, and they will show an inclination to slip through the stitch if given the opportunity. A tighter gauge (tension) does help the fabric, but not, unfortunately, the frustration level of the knitter. Having said this, once you have got to grips with the stitch, the resulting beaded fabric has a drape and glamor that is hard to beat.

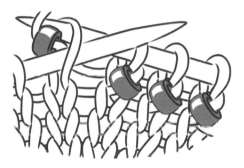

1 On a knit row, slide a bead along the yarn so that when the yarn is wrapped round the needle the bead can be drawn through the stitch with the stitch loop. Knit the stitch, but knit into the back of it, not into the front, and draw both the loop and the bead through. Pull gently to tighten the stitch, ensuring that the bead is sitting on the front of the loop.

2 On a purl row, depending on your gauge (tension) and size of bead, the row can be worked in one of two ways.

Either purl into the back of the stitch and draw the loop and bead through to produce a firmer fabric.

If you have a firm tension already, purl through the front of the stitch and draw the bead through. This is easier to work, but sometimes the beads fall through to the back of the knitted fabric.

KNITTING IN SEQUINS

Knitting in sequins need not be any more difficult than beads, but they are more delicate. Today's sequins are often made of thin plastic, so heat can be a disaster. The slip stitch method can be used, but care should taken to position the sequins flat against the fabric and to work the stitch after the slipped stitch firmly.

Sequins can also be added by drawing them through with a new stitch loop, as in Close Beading, but the the stitch has to be worked from the front and only worked through the back of the stitch on the next row. On st st this simple approach is the best, and it also seems to help them to lie flat.

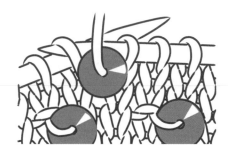

1 On a knit row, right-side facing, knit to the position of the sequin, bring the yarn forward between the needles and slide the sequin flat against the previous stitches. Purl the next stitch firmly, take the yarn to the back and knit along the row.

On a purl row, wrong-side facing, purl to one stitch short of the the position of the sequin, knit one, position the sequin as before, and purl to the end of the row.

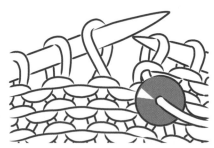

2 On a purl row, right-side facing, purl to the position of the sequin and slide the sequin up to the right-hand needle. Purl the next stitch firmly through the back of the loop, then purl along the row.

On a knit row, wrong-side facing, knit to one stitch short of the position of the sequin, knit one through the back of the loop, position the sequin, knit one through the back of the loop and continue along the row.

Knitting in objects

Given the right fixtures and fittings, almost anything can be knitted in. Arm yourself with a craft drill or an Archimedes screw drill and a range of glues, and look around for bits of wood, shell, stone or metal to adorn your knits.

Some of your new treasures will already have holes in them, or you will be able to see a way of knitting them in – using couching for instance. However, some items will need a little help to hang comfortably and face in the right direction.

The place to look is a craft store with a good beading and notions (haberdashery) section.

EYELETS

These are commonly used in sewing projects, but can also be found in all kinds of shapes and colors for scrapbooking and card making. Each brand and size also has a setting tool that is given a sharp tap with a hammer to fix the eyelet in place. Eyelets look great on knitted fabric, but choose the size carefully and ensure that it will have a firm grip on the fabric, even if it slightly distorts the stitches around it. Eyelets are added after the project is completed, so they can be used to brighten a disappointing result.

SPLIT RINGS

Split rings are a small coil of wire that objects can be threaded onto. They can be found in a variety of sizes in beading stores. The object needs to have a hole that is close enough to the edge to pass the ring through, and then the ring can be threaded onto yarn.

JUMP RINGS

These are very similar to split rings, but are a single ring of wire with aligned ends. These should be pried apart with a pair of pliers so the ends move left and right of the circle. An object with a hole can then be threaded on and the two ends closed again with the pliers. Jump rings are not as strong as split rings, but they do not put as much strain on the hole in the object. Jump rings can also be used to turn an object with a front to back hole so that it will hang flat against a knitted fabric.

EARRING BACKS

Earring backs provide a flat surface on which you can glue an object that does not have a hole. These backs are usually made of stainless steel, but if you can find them in silver it is much easier to curl the posts with pliers to create a loop to thread onto yarn. Choose a back with the largest gluing surface that will remain hidden behind your chosen object, as the glue will be the weakest point.

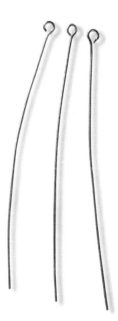

PINS

Pins can be found with a head like a nail, or a loop like those shown left. This pin can have an object threaded onto it and the end without the loop manipulated using pliers into another loop or a decorative twist. The yarn can then be threaded through the loop. These pins can also be used to wrap an object that has no hole. If the object narrows or has a waist, then the wire can be coiled around the narrow area, with the wider area above to prevent it slipping out of the wire coil. Otherwise the wire has to be wrapped around in two directions at right angles to each other. This may need some experimentation, but you will quickly see what will work.

CRIMPS

Crimps are flexible metal beads that can be threaded onto yarn or other fixtures and squashed flat using pliers, gripping whatever is threaded through them. Crimps are used to secure objects or beads near the end of lengths of yarn where knotting or gluing would not be secure.

Choose the size carefully because it has to be large enough to prevent the object sliding over it and to grip what is within it, but still be sympathetic with its surroundings. Having said that, crimps can be decorative in their own right, and for a more dramatic statement, large copper plumbing fixtures can serve a similar purpose.

WIRE

Wire can be threaded through holes, wrapped around objects and used to link an object to a fixture. A hardware store will supply wire, but it will not have the flexibility of craft wire and will not come in a choice of colors. It might be worth investing in a pair of pin-nose pliers if the work is fiddly, as those from the garage may be a bit awkward to use. A pair of old scissors can usually be used to cut wire.

Choose a silver wire or a coated silver wire if you intend to bend or wrap it back on itself, as these are the most supple. Choose the gauge carefully: the store assistant should be able to advise you.

A disadvantage of wire is that the ends can be destructive. Fold them back and twist them together underneath the object. A spot of glue can dull cut ends.

DRILLING AND GLUING

Not all materials can have a hole drilled in them: glass and ceramic can shatter dangerously, so mosaic tiles have to be glued to a fitting. Metal and stone require specialist drills and cooling agents and metal will leave a rough edge that will snag. However, most other things, especially organic items such as shell or wood, can be drilled.

You will need a small vice or sticky putty to hold the object in place. There are specialist craft drills on the market, but read the safety instructions carefully and buy more bits than you think you will need. A hand drill can be easier to use and control. With either drill, gently does it; slow and steady will produce less failures. And always wear gloves, safety glasses and a mask to protect you from dust and any object that might shatter.

Items that cannot be drilled can be glued, either to the fixtures shown left, or perhaps to other objects such as sequins or ribbon. It is best to avoid water-based glues and superglues that are brittle when hard. The most useful all-round glue is epoxy adhesive. Toothpicks or match sticks are excellent for mixing it and make it easier to apply the glue exactly where you want it and nowhere else.

However, the only sure way to find out which adhesive will work is to experiment. Always ensure you have enough of your new-found treasure to try, and maybe try again. Remember to read any safety instructions and work in a well ventilated room.

Knitting in
SWATCH LIBRARY

Most of us will have tried knitting beads into a project, and the range of colors, sizes and bead materials available certainly does make them an interesting and creative option. However, there are many ways of using beads above and beyond just knitting them into the fabric.

And why stop at beads? Any item of a suitable scale that has a hole in it can be used, and items without holes can have jewellery findings attached to them, making them perfect for knitting in.

Always work a swatch when experimenting with knitting in to check that the item looks as good as you hoped, that it is not too heavy for the stitches and that it can, if necessary, be laundered.

Edge beading

Beading the edge of a project is very effective way of adding a touch of individuality. These swatches are knitted to demonstrate the techniques and give you an idea of how they will look, but there is no reason why the beads should be just one color, or the cast on yarn the same as the main yarn.

❶ BEADED CABLE CAST ON

This cast on↓ is particularly decorative, with long strands of yarn visible, and when the fabric is flat, the bead hangs right on the edge. However, as with all cable cast ons, the edge is not very elastic.

Here, each cast on stitch is beaded, but alternate beaded stitches will create a subtle beaded picot edge.

Experiment with matching the bead sequence to the stitch pattern you wish to use.

❷ BEADED THUMB CAST ON

With this cast on↓ the beads sit slightly above the edge and are proud of the fabric. The edge is not as elastic as it will be if it is not beaded, but it is still more elastic than beaded cable cast on.

Every stitch on this cast on row has been beaded, but this need not be the case. For a dramatic start to an edge of a project, bead the following rows, too.

❸ BEADED FRILL

The beads used here are slightly wider than a stitch, so when they are positioned on every stitch using the thumb cast on method, they produce a pronounced frill.

Cast on twice as many stitches as required for the body of the work, using the beaded thumb cast on method and placing a bead on every stitch.

Next row: [K2tog] rep to the end of the row.

Work in chosen stitch pattern.

❹ BEADED BIND (CAST) OFF

The beads on this bind (cast) off↓ appear on the top edge above the bound (cast) off stitches and do not affect the elasticity of the edge.

In this swatch each stitch is beaded, but alternate beaded stitches will produce a picot edge.

❺ BEADED FACING

If the cast on and the bind (cast) off are beaded, then the obvious complement is to bead the selvedges and facings of a project.

Choose the beads carefully as they will take a lot of wear-and-tear, especially around buttonholes. The beads don't all need to be the same color or size and, even if they aren't always on display, they will shine when they are.

Beaded selvedge

Beads can be added to the selvedges, and help to produce a neat, presentable edge without using other selvedge techniques. The selvedge is a particularly good place to vary the size of the beads, as they will not distort the stitches around them. This swatch is worked in st st.

To produce a bead that sits on the front of the edge stitch, work the following.

Row 1 (WS): P to the last st, p1tbl.
Row 2: Slide the bead to the base of the yarn and k to the end of the row.

To produce a bead that sits slightly to the back of the edge stitch, work the following.

Row 1 (WS): P to the end of the row.
Row 2: Slide the bead to the base of the yarn, k1tbl and k to the end of the row.

Slightly larger beads should be used for this if the effect is not to become too subtle.

Beaded buttonhole

This little detail won't always be visible, it will mean working a larger buttonhole to accommodate the button, and it may be slightly fiddlier to use, but you will know it is there. Worked in a contrasting color, it will sparkle provocatively at the keen observer.

To make a buttonhole on st st.
Row 1 (RS): K to the position of the buttonhole and bind (cast) off using the beaded bind (cast) off method. Close bead 1 st after the bind (cast) off and k to the end of the row.
Row 2: P to the position of the bound (cast) off sts, use the thumb loop method to cast on the sts, passing the yarn to between your thumb and the needle before the last stitch is cast on, and p to the end of the row.
Row 3: K to just above the buttonhole, close bead into the front of the cast on sts and k to the end of the row.
Note Beading the cast on makes the buttonhole stronger. The thumb loop cast on makes the buttonhole look closed rather than gaping, as it would with a cable cast on.

Slip stitch beading method

If commercial patterns are to be believed, this is the most popular beading method. Certainly for objects and beads that can't pass through a stitch for close beading, or are too wide and will pull the

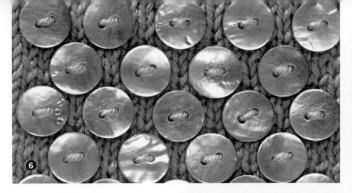

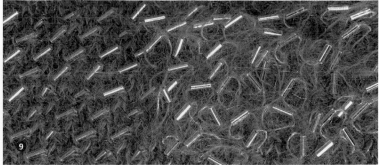

fabric out if worked between the stitches, it is the perfect solution. It is also quick and easy to work and does not distort the stitches. However, the beads or objects will hang slightly low and only alternate stitches and rows can be worked.

⑥ SLIP STITCH BUTTONS
Buttons are ideal for the slip stitch beading method↓ because either one or two stitches can be slipped to accommodate the distance between the holes, and the button itself will hide any sagging or long strands of yarn.

Here, there are an odd number of stitches between each button to allow the next row to be centered above two buttons in the row below. These buttons are ½in (12mm) in diameter.

Abbreviations
PB = place button by bringing the yarn forward, sliding the button up the yarn, slipping the next stitch and taking the yarn back between the needles.

Row 1 (RS): K1, [PB, k3] rep to the end of the row.
Work 3 rows in st st.
Row 5: K3, [PB on the st between the two buttons on the previous button row, k3] rep to the end of the row.
The number of stitches and rows between buttons will vary depending on the gauge (tension) and the size of the button. A rough count can be made by placing the buttons in position on a gauge (tension) swatch and noting the number of stitches around them.

⑦ SLIP STITCH BUTTONS AND BEADS
The technique used is the same as that in the swatch above, but beads are also used. These buttons are ½in (12mm) in diameter.

Thread a button then a bead onto the yarn, and then pass the yarn through the second hole of the button. Repeat until all the buttons

have been threaded on. If there is a lot of friction on the yarn, thread the buttons and beads onto short separate lengths and use the beading with a second yarn↓ method of working.

Work to the position of the first button and place it by bringing the yarn forward, sliding the button and bead down the yarn, slipping the next stitch and taking the yarn back between the needles. Work to the next button position.

Beading on individual stitches

This beading technique is quite slow and stops the flow of the work while an individual bead↓ is positioned. However, it does have some advantages: it allows forgotten beads to be positioned at the last minute and bead colors that are only used occasionally can be worked as required. It also avoids complicated threading sequences and allows you to thread large or cumbersome beads onto elongated stitches.

⑧ LONG BEADS
Work st st to the bottom of the row of beads, ending with a WS row.
Next row (RS): K to the position of the first bead. [Insert the right-hand needle into the next st on the left-hand needle. Wrap the yarn around the right-hand needle six

times, draw it through and drop the st off the needle]. Rep once for each bead. K to the end of the row.
Next row: P to the elongated sts and drop all but one loop for each st. Transfer the elongated sts onto one stitch holder and the rem sts onto another stitch holder.

Turn, and work the rem sts on the needle in st st as set until a strip has been worked that equals the length of the elongated sts, ending with a WS row. Cut the yarn and transfer these sts onto another stitch holder.

Rejoin the yarn, starting on the WS, onto the sts to the right of the beads and work in st st the same number of rows as those just worked on the left of the beads.

Knit to the end of these sts. Use a crochet hook to loop each of the elongated sts through a bead. Transfer the sts on the stitch holder and the elongated stitches onto the spare needle. Knit across the elongated sts and the sts to the left of the beads.

Beading with a second yarn

Beading with a second yarn↓ allows the use of small beads that would normally be unavailable to knitters, or would require a gauge (tension) that would limit the projects in which they can be used.

⑨ BUGLE BEADS AND FLUFFY YARN
Small bugle beads are threaded onto a fine, fluffy yarn using a beading needle and a length of sewing cotton↓.

Left The bugle beads lie at an angle and slightly proud of the fabric.
For every second stitch the beaded yarn is brought to the front and the stitch is worked with the background yarn only before the beaded yarn is taken to the back and worked with the background yarn again.

Right The beaded yarn and the background yarn are worked together, but every second stitch is worked in looped fur with the beaded yarn only.

⑩ BEAD WEAVING
The weaving technique↓ is used to secure a second yarn threaded with seed beads to the knitted fabric. This will inevitably catch and is not practical for a project that will receive constant wear.
This swatch is worked in st st using the main color only (without the beaded thread), except for the first and last stitches of every row.

Thread the beads onto the embroidery thread.
Multiple of 6 sts + 2sts
Row 1 (RS): K1 [beaded thread yf, k3, beaded thread yb, k3] rep to last st, k1.
Row 2: P1 [p3, beaded thread yf, p3, beaded thread yb] rep to last st, p1.
Rep rows 1–2 as required.

TECHNIQUES: Slip stitch beading ◗ page 68 • Beading with a second yarn ◗ page 69 • Beading on individual stitches ◗ page 68
Threading beads onto the yarn ◗ page 66 • Weaving ◗ page 41

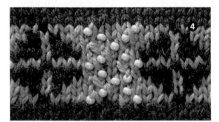

Beading between stitches

This technique produces a dense tapestry of beads if beads are positioned between every stitch↓. If charting a design, remember to position the beads on the grid line between two stitches, and make the knitted fabric as interesting as the beads because it will show.

❶ RANDOM BEADS

A selection of beads of similar colors and sizes are threaded onto the yarn and worked as they come on a background of garter stitch.

The background of this swatch is one color so that you can see how the beads are positioned, but as the beads are only placed every second row, the following row

could be worked in one or more colors with the bead yarn stranded across the back. Alternatively, different colored yarns could be threaded with beads and worked in the same random fashion.

❷ BEADING ON ST ST

The beads are positioned on the purl row of st st between each stitch. On the right side the beads can be seen through columns of knit stitches. It is subtle, but it is also intriguing.

Close beading

This technique beads every stitch↓ on every row. The beads do not hang low and remain on top of the stitch. It is perfect for charting and working solid blocks of beading, and if the twisted stitch is accepted as a feature, it is very versatile.

❸ MOTIF BEADING

The preferred choice for most commercial patterns is slip stitch beading↓. However, close beading can be substituted in every case and creates an interesting texture.

This plain heart motif is close beaded at regular intervals, and then stripes of duplicate stitch↓ are added later.

❹ FAIR ISLE BEADING

True Fair Isle traditionally has only a maximum of two colors per row, but that tradition is often broken. To avoid the dense mass of stranded threads at the back of a Fair Isle, particularly one with more than two colors, substitute beads for one of the colors.

Stranding beads

Most of the beading techniques described in the techniques section can be adapted to hold more than one bead, as can the stranding yarn technique used in color knitting.

However, the longer the strand of yarn holding the beads, the more likely it is to stretch and not hang in the correct place.

❺ STRANDED PANELS

The width of the panels is very much dependent on the gauge (tension), as the edges, and the beads, tend to sag if it is loose or if care is not taken with it.

This swatch is worked in fingering weight yarn in st st, with 3 panels that are 3 stitches wide.

Thread the beads onto the yarn. Work to the bottom of the vertical panels, ending with a WS row.

Next row (RS): K to the position of right panel, [bind (cast) off 3 sts for the base of the first panel, k3] rep twice more, then k to the end of the row.

Next row: P to the position of the first bound (cast) off st, [slide 4 beads tight against the base of the last st on the right-hand needle, p3] rep twice more, then k to the end of the row.

Next row: K to the position of the beads, [slide 4 beads tight against the base of the last st on the right-hand needle, k3] rep twice more, then k to the end of the row. Cont in the patt set to the top of the vertical panels, ending with a RS row.

Next row: P to the position of the beads, [cast on 3 sts using the

thumb loop method, p3] rep twice more, then p to the end of the row. Cont to work in st st.

The number of beads required to span the gap created by the bound (cast) off sts will vary depending on the size of the beads and the gauge (tension).

Try threading the beads so that one color is at the front on the knit row and one color is at the back on the purl row.

As always, this swatch is simplified for clarity, but experiment with other stitch patterns and more than one color of bead.

❻ STRANDED EDGE

The technique for this is similar to that of Stranded Panels, but beads are threaded onto the tail of a thumb cast on and slipped up to the needle in long groups, each group being twice as long as the gap between the cast on stitches. A further 6 rows are worked as described above.

The curl of this edge is created by the st st pattern worked in a tight gauge (tension).

Hanging beads

All these swatches involve beads that fall free over a knitted fabric. The anchor point can be determined, but how they will fall will be slightly different each time the project moves.

In each swatch a single row of beads is worked, but do not forget to consider groups of hanging beads, varying the colors of the beads and the yarn, and using different stitch patterns.

TECHNIQUES: Beading between stitches ◆ page 69 • Close beading ◆ page 69 • Slip stitch beading ◆ page 68 • Duplicate stitch ◆ page 97

Knitting with sequins

Sequins come in all shapes and sizes and one method of knitting them in does not always suit all.

⑪ SEQUIN PANEL

This shows a variety of different effects possible with sequins.

Top Thread a sequin, then a bead onto the yarn, and then pass the yarn back through the hole of the sequin. Repeat until all the sequins are threaded on, then place them using the slip stitch method. There is a lot of friction on the yarn so they will not be easy to slide along. If possible, thread the sequins onto short separate lengths and use the beading with a second yarn↓ method of working.

Middle Square sequins are positioned using the close beading method in a checkerboard fashion on every second row so they overlap. The method twists the sequins, giving a random effect. The corners become caught in the fibers of the fabric anyway, so a virtue is made of this problem.

Row 1 (RS): K1, [PS through the back of the st, k3] rep to the end of the row.
Row 2: Purl.
Row 3: K2, [PS through the front of the st, k3] rep to the end of the row.
Row 4: [P to the position of sequin, p1tbl] rep to the end of the row.
Rep rows 1–4 as required.

Bottom These round sequins are positioned immediately above each other, 4 rows apart so that they do not overlap, using the method described in Slip Stitch Buttons on page 73.

⑫ COUCHED SEQUINS

Sequins can be added individually as work progresses by threading the next stitch through the hole before working it, but for these sequins a feature is made of the larger hole by couching↓ them in position.

Work to the position of the sequin. Put the sequin on the right-hand needle, draw the loop through the next st on the left-hand needle and slide the sequin onto the loop. Then, without dropping the original st off the needle, put the loop on

❼ RINGS OF BEADS

This ring of beads contains only enough beads to create a tight cluster that hangs as one strand. This is approximately four beads if they are round and their width equals their depth.

Thread alternate colors of beads onto the yarn. Work st st to the position of the bead ring row.
Next row (RS): [Work to the position of the bead ring, yf, slide beads up to the base of the last st on the right-hand needle, yb, ktbl] rep to the end of the row.

❽ OUTSIZED BEADS

These beads are large and made of glass, so they are not light. A tight gauge (tension) will help to stop the bead pulling the fabric, but a better solution is to wrap the stitch holding the bead.

Thread beads onto the yarn. Work st st to the bead row.
Next row (RS): [Work to the position of the first bead, sl1, yf, position the bead, sl the st back, yb, k1tbl] rep to the end of the row.
Knit 6 rows to create the garter stitch band before resuming st st. The garter stitch band conceals the wrapped stitch, and it is decorative in itself.

❾ RAISED BAND OF BEADING WITH HANGING BEADS

This is worked in exactly the same way as the previous swatch, but a red round bead, a blue bugle bead and a red round bead are threaded onto the yarn instead of one large bead. For the second beaded row,

alternate blue and red round beads are threaded onto the yarn, and for the last row of beading, red round beads are threaded onto the yarn.

Work as for first bead row of previous swatch, swapping three beads for the one large bead.
Next row: K1, [slide 1 bead tight against the base of the last st on the right-hand needle, k1] rep to the end of the row.
Next row: K1, close bead each st along the row knitwise tbl to the last st, k1.
Cont work in st st, starting with a p row.

❿ BEADED LOOPS

A bracelet of looped beads inspired this swatch, which has the beads worked on the edge of a knitted fabric. Of course, the beads do not have to be on an edge, but could be in a band across the middle of a project, as a vertical strip, or as single stitches.

Thread beads onto the yarn.
Cast on using the thumb method.
Work 2 rows of k1, p1 rib.
Row 3 (RS): [K1, yf, slide 7 beads to the base of the right-hand needle, p1tbl, k1] rep to the end of the row.
Row 4: [P1, purl into the loop of the st below the next st and place it onto the left-hand needle, p2tog] rep to the end of the row.
Rep the last two rows twice more. Alternatively, row 4 can be just purled to give a flatter edge.

the left-hand needle and k2tog There is an odd number of stitches between each sequin, and the sequins are couched on the center stitch so each one hangs between two sequins on the previous row. The number of rows and stitches between sequins will vary depending on the size of the sequin and the gauge (tension) of a knitted fabric.

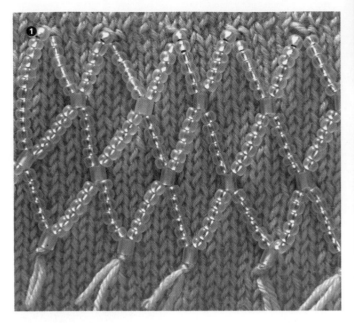

Bead jewellery techniques and fixtures in knitting

Bead jewellery books are a rich source of inspiration once you have mastered loop stitch↓ and understood some of the principles behind the threading of beads.

The knitting need not be secondary to the beading. These swatches are worked on st st so the images can act as a guide to the bead sequences, but do experiment with stitch patterns.

❶ LATTICE BEADING

This pattern would look good on a background of bobbles or colored stripes.

Abbreviations

ML = see looped fur, and make the loop length about a third longer than the full depth of the lattice.

Work to the top of the lattice in the stitch pattern of your choice, ending with a WS row.
Next row (RS): [K3, ML] rep to the end of the row.
Work to the end of the project and bind (cast) off.
∗ Using a beading needle and a length of sewing cotton knotted around the end of each loop, thread 6 beads onto each loop. Then thread two adjacent loops through a larger bead to create a triangle. Thread 6 beads onto each loop again, but this time miss the

first loop and thread the two adjacent loops through a larger bead to form a diamond. Thread sufficient beads onto the missed edge loop to make it hang straight and join it with a large bead onto the next row (here, 11 beads). Rep from ∗ to the depth required, ending with a larger bead. Tie and trim off the ends. Sew through the knot a few times with sewing cotton to hold it secure.

The number of beads on a loop will vary depending on the beads used and the gauge (tension) of a knitted fabric.

❷ BEAD FRINGING

This fringing could be used as an edging, to highlight a pocket or as part of an intarsia design. The ends are secured using crimps, which are small rings of soft metal. They grip beading thread or wire and prevent the beads falling off the ends when they cannot be secured any other way. They are readily available from beading outlets in variety of sizes.

This example shows a single row of fringes one stitch apart so that they can be seen, but they can also be grouped over several rows and varied in length. Remember, the longer the fringe, the more difficult it is to control how it will hang.

Abbreviations

ML = see looped fur and make the loop length a little longer than the depth of the fringe.

Work to the top of the fringe in the stitch pattern of your choice, ending with a WS row.
Next row (RS): [K1, ML] rep to the end of the row.
Work to the end of the project and bind (cast) off.
∗ Using a beading needle and a length of sewing cotton knotted around the end of each loop, thread beads and a crimp bead onto the loop. Close the crimp using pliers. Trim and tidy the ends.

An alternative way to create a fringe is to knit a longer loop and cut it. Thread the beads onto the length of yarn then, skipping the first bead, pass the yarn back through the holes of the other beads. Weave in the ends on the back of the work.

The holes in the beads have to be large enough to accommodate three strands of yarn and a needle.

❸ WIRED OBJECTS

In this example a looped head pin used in beading is wound around an agate in a cross fashion. Starting at the back with the end without a loop, bend the pin around and across the top. At the back, use a pair of pliers to twist the pin at right angles, then bend it around the front to the back again. Bend it again at right angles to come up behind the stone.

This can also be done using craft wire, which is available in a variety of colors, but the top loop would have to be created by gripping the end with pliers and twisting the wire around the nose of the jaws.

These stones are quite small and light in weight, but several of them,

or larger stones, may stretch a knitted fabric.

Thread the yarn with sufficient small pearl beads for one row, and then the loops of the wired stones. Work to the position of the beading and close bead the row with pearls.
Next row (RS): Work the row, positioning the wired stones at regular intervals using the slip stitch method↓.The wired stones are added a row after the pearls as the slip stitch method makes the pin loops hang a bit lower than the other stitches in the row.

❹ END SPACER PANEL

End spacers come in a variety of shapes and styles and are designed to be attached to the ends of strings of beads and space them out.

Here, one is used to space elongated stitches. The swatch is worked in st st. The number of loops on the end spacer dictates the panel width.

Work to the bottom of the panel, ending with a WS row.
Next row (RS): K to the right of the panel, [insert the right-hand needle into the next st on the left-hand needle. Wrap the yarn around the needle eight times, draw through and drop the st off the needle]. Rep once for each loop in the end spacer. K to the end of the row.
Next row: P to to the elongated sts and drop all but one loop for each st. Transfer the elongated sts onto one stitch holder and the rem sts onto another.
Turn, and work the rem sts in st st as set until a strip has been worked

TECHNIQUES: Looped fur ↓ page 13 • Slip stitch beading ↓ page 68

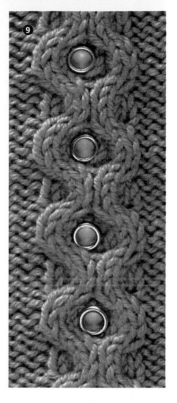

that equals the length of the elongated sts, ending with a WS row. Cut the yarn and transfer the sts onto a stitch holder.

Rejoin the yarn, starting with the WS, onto the sts to the right of the panel and work in st st the same number of rows as those just worked to the left of the panel.

Knit to the end of the strip. Use a crochet hook to loop the elongated sts through the end spacer. Transfer the sts on the stitch holder and the elongated sts onto the spare needle, starting with the sts to the left of the panel and ending with the elongated st furthest to the right.

Knit the elongated sts and the sts to the left of the panel.

❺ OPENWORK PANEL

The idea behind this panel is that a necklace closure is worked into the fabric, then a choice of beads or broaches can be attached and changed on a whim.

Work to the bottom of the panel, ending with a WS row.
Next row (RS): K to the bottom apex, k2tog, put the rem sts of that row onto a stitch holder.
Next row: Sl1 purlwise, p to the end of the row.

Next row: K to the last 2 sts, k2tog. Rep the last 2 rows until the panel is half as wide as required, ending with a WS row.
Next row: K to the last st, M1L, k1.
Next row: Sl1 purlwise, p to the end of the row.
Rep the last 2 rows until there are the same number of sts as before the decreasing, ending with a RS row. Transfer the sts onto a stitch holder and cut the yarn.
Thread the necklace closure onto the yarn.
Transfer the sts from the left of the panel onto a needle and rejoin, starting with a RS row.
Next row: Ssk, k to the end of the row.
Next row: P to the last st, sl1 purlwise.
Rep the last 2 rows until the same number of sts have been decreased as on the right, ending with a WS row.
Next row: K1, M1R, k to the end of the row.
Next row: P to the last st, sl1 purlwise.
Rep the last 2 rows until there are the same number of sts as before the decreasing, ending with a RS row. Transfer the sts from the stitch holder onto a third needle so the cut yarn end is at the tip.
Next row: P, place the necklace closure, purl across the sts from the stitch holder.

❻ DRILLED SHELLS

These shells are gently drilled using an Archimedes screw. A head pin is threaded through the hole from back to front and, using a pair of pliers, twisted into a series of tight loops. The loops are threaded onto the yarn and the slip stitch beading↓ method is then used to attach them to a knitted fabric.

❼ KNITTED IN MOSAIC TILES

Loops are twisted into the posts of earring backs using pliers. These backs are glued to the reverse of acrylic mosaic tiles. The loops are threaded onto the yarn. The slip stitch beading↓ method is then used to attach them to a knitted fabric one row higher than the design would dictate, to allow them to drop slightly into position.

Knitting in unusual objects

This library shows only a small fraction of the things that could be placed in a knitted fabric, but it should inspire you to try out your own ideas.

❽ EYELETS ON A GARTER STITCH BAND

These novelty eyelets are marketed for scrapbooking. They are less substantial than those available for dressmaking and should be laundered carefully.

Work a st st fabric, ending with a WS row.
Knit 2 rows.
Next row (RS): Knit to the position of the eyelet, yo, k2tog. Cont to the next eyelet.
Knit 3 rows.
Cont in st st patt set.
Position and secure the eyelets through the yarnovers. Matching yarn is woven along the back, brought from back to front through each eyelet, threaded with a bead and taken back through the same eyelet to the back of the fabric

❾ METAL EYELETS IN A CABLE PATTERN

These eyelets are commonly used in dressmaking, but are used here to create a focal point in a popular cable↓ pattern.

Panel of 12 sts with 3 sts rev st st on either side and 12 rows.
Row 1 (RS): P3, k12, p3.
Row 2: K3, p12, k3.

Row 3. P3, C6B, C6F, p3.
Row 4: P3, k12, p3.
Row 5: K3, p12, k3.
Rep rows 4–5 once more.
Row 9: P3, C6F, C6B, p3.
Row 10: P12.
Row 11: P3, k12, p3.
Row 12: K3, p12, k3.
Rep rows 1–12 as required.
Then, prise a hole between the stitches and, following the instructions supplied with the them, secure an eyelet. Choosing the size of the eyelet carefully, and not creating a hole using a yarnover, means that the eyelet fits snugly into the cable.

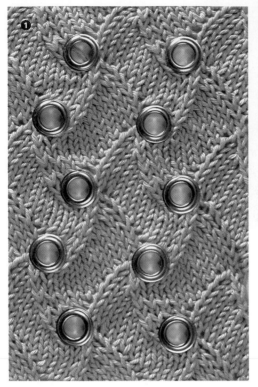

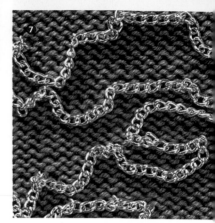

❶ EYELETS ON A TRAVELLING VINE PATTERN

It is worth looking through stitch pattern books for patterns with regular yarnovers↓ – or other focal points – that can be emphasized with eyelets.

This travelling vine pattern is a good example, because the yarnovers are supported on either side by dense knitting.

Multiple of 8 sts + 2 and 14 rows.

Row 1 (RS): K1, [yo, k6, k2tog] rep to the last st, k1.
Row 2: P1, [p2tog, p5, yo, p1] rep to the last st, p1.
Row 3: K1, [k2, yo, k4, k2tog] rep to the last st, k1.
Row 4: P1, [p2tog, p3, yo, p3] rep to the last st, p1.
Row 5: K1, [k4, yo, k2, k2tog] rep to the last st, k1.
Row 6: P1, [p2tog, p1, yo, p5] rep to the last st, p1.
Row 7: K1, [k6, yo, k1, k2tog] rep to the last st, k1.
Row 8: P1, [yo, p6, p2togtbl] rep to the last st, p1.
Row 9: K1, [ssk, k5, yo, k1] rep to the last st, k1.
Row 10: P1, [p2, yo, p4, p2togtbl] rep to the last st, p1.
Row 11: K1, [ssk, k3, yo, k3] rep to the last st, k1.

Row 12: P1, [p4, yo, p2, p2togtbl] rep to the last st, p1.
Row 13: K1, [ssk, k1, yo, k5] rep to the last st, k1.
Row 14: P1, [p6, yo, p2togtbl] rep to the last st, p1.
Rep rows 1–14 as required.
Position and secure the eyelets through the yarnovers at the intersection points.

❷ EYELETS THREADED WITH RIBBON

These are dressmaker's eyelets, which tend to have a slightly wider shank compared to the visible ring than those used for stationery.

Repeat of 4 sts and 6 rows.

Work a st st fabric, ending with a WS row.
Row 1 (RS): [K1, yo, k2tog] rep to the end of the row.
Row 2: [P1, p1tbl, k1] rep to the end of the row.
Row 3: [K2tog, yo, k1] rep to the end of the row.
Row 4: [P1, p1tbl, k1] rep to the end of the row.
Rep rows 1–2 once more.
Cont in st st pattern set.
Position and secure the eyelets through the yarnovers.

❸ COUCHED TUBING

Couching↓ is a technique that will be familiar to you for securing loose fibers to a knitted fabric. However, it can also be used to attach objects such as tubing. Its only limitation is that it can be difficult to secure the ends of the tubing and prevent it sliding out.

❹ BALL CHAIN KNITTED BETWEEN THE STITCHES OF RIB

Ball chain has the advantage of being both very flexible and available in a variety of sizes. Here, lengths of a ball chain measuring ⅛ in (3 mm) in diameter are worked into knitted fabric.

Cast on the required number of sts using the thumb method.
Row 1: [K1, yf, position a length of ball chain between the yarn and the next st on the left-hand needle, p1, yb] rep to the end of the row.
Row 2: K1, p1, following the pattern set.
Rep the last two rows as required.

In this swatch the lengths of ball chain are knitted in halfway along their length and cut using wire cutters to create the shape shown.

❺ BALL CHAIN ON STRIPE PATTERN

This pattern may not be good for projects that will require regular washing, but the articulation of the ball chain means it hangs slightly proud and adds a three-dimensional element to the project.

Work a st st fabric, ending with a WS row.
Work 2 rows st st in a contrasting color yarn.
Next row (RS): K2, [couch the ball chain between two of the links, k3] rep to the end of the row.
To create the dips in the chain, attach it to the knitted fabric slightly further along its length than the distance along the fabric.

In this swatch it is attached every seven links, but this will vary depending on the gauge (tension) and the size of the ball chain. Of course, the ball chain could be couched at random intervals.

❻ CHAIN EDGE

Couching a chain near a lower edge of a project can help it to hang straight, but there is a fine balance

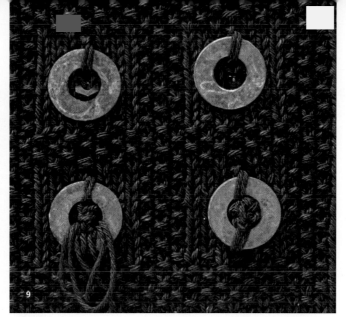

Next row: K to position of the top of the washer and couch the washer in place, k to the end of the row.

Washer and bead (top right)
Follow the pattern for Washer and Nut, above, but place a bead at PB.

Washer and loop (bottom left)
Row 1 (RS): K to position of the base of the washer and couch the washer in place, k to the end of the row.
Work 4 rows.
Row 5 (center of the washer): K to the position above the couched washer, ML, k to the end of the row.
Work 3 rows.
Row 9: K to position to the top of the washer and couch the washer in place, k to the end of the row.

Washer and bobble (bottom right)
Follow the pattern for Washer and Loop, above, but MB at ML.

⑩ FEATHER EDGE
Highly impractical on any level, but glamorous enough to be worth the inconvenience. Do not wash, do not handle roughly, but do enjoy – your cat certainly will.

Using sewing cotton and a sharp needle, thread the cotton through the quill of each feather, choosing the thickest part the needle will pass through. Trim the ends carefully so as not to split the quills.

Cast on and work a few rows, then using the beading with a second yarn method↓, place a feather every 3rd stitch.

---

between this and stretching a project uncontrollably.

Cast on using the thumb method. Knit 6 rows of garter st.
Next row: K and couch in the chain regularly along the row.

⑦ ALL-OVER CHAIN TEXTURE
This idea gives you that feeling of slight unpredictability you get with variegated yarn. For the best effect work quite densely, but this will add to the overall weight of a knitted fabric, so make sure that it is well supported. This swatch is worked in rev st st.

Thread the yarn randomly through the links of the chain. On the right side only, slide the chain up the yarn at irregular intervals and knit the next stitch firmly to hold the link of chain close to the knitted fabric.

⑧ RINGED CABLE
A brass ring used by plumbers is inserted into the work instead of a cable repeat. This pattern is easily adapted for any cable↓ pattern

elongated sts = wrap the yarn twice around the needle before drawing it through the st.

Panel of 4 sts with 3 sts rev st st on either side and 14 rows.
Row 1 (RS): P3, k4, p3.
Row 2: K3, p4, k3.
Row 3: P3, C4F, p3.
Row 4: P3, k4, p3.
Row 5: K3, p4, k3.
Rep rows 4–5 once more.
Row 9: P3, k4, p3.
Row 10: K3, k4 elongated sts, p3.
Row 11: P3, transfer 1 loop from the next 4 sts onto a crochet hook and pass a brass ring over the sts, slip onto the left-hand needle, k4, p3.
Row 12: P3, k4, p3.
Row 13: K3, p4, k3.
Rep rows 12–13 once more.
Row 14: K3, p4, k3.
Rep rows 1–14 as required.

⑨ WASHERS, NUTS AND BEADS
Metal objects do add a lot of weight to a project and may stretch the work, they are also best laundered in a cotton bag to protect the washing machine. However, they do look so good, especially on this denim yarn.

The washers used in these swatches are aluminium and 1in (2.5 cm) in diameter. The number of stitches between couching stitches (which are in the centers of the washers) will vary depending on the washer and the gauge (tension).

Abbreviations
couch = put the object on the right-hand needle, draw the loop through the next st on the left-hand needle, and slide the object onto the loop. Then, without dropping the original st off the needle, put the loop on the left-hand needle and k2tog through the loop and the original st.

---

elongated sts = wrap the yarn twice around the needle before drawing it through the st.
PB = Place the nut or bead. Thread it onto an elongated st loop. Knit into the top of the loop.
ML = Make loop; this creates a cluster of loops with a bobble at the base. [Slip 1, bring the yarn forward, slip st back, make loop of yarn, purl the st but do not drop the st off the needle, place the stitch loop on the left-hand needle]. Rep twice more. Knit all three loops and the original st together.
MB = make bobble. Knit into the front, back, front, and back of the next st and turn the work Purl 4 sts, turn, skpsso, k2tog, turn, purl 2 sts, turn, k2tog.
All the panels are worked on st st.

Washer and nut (top left)
Place a nut at PB.
Work to the position one row below the center of the washer and make an elongated st.
Next row (center of the washer) (RS): K to the elongated st, drop 1 loop, PB, k to the end of the row.
Work 3 rows.

Beaded fingerless mittens

Worn with casual style or dressed up for a night out, these mittens are fabulous accessories for any wardrobe. There is no need to get worried about the careful threading of bead sequences, because the pearl and cut glass beads are added using a variation on the individual beading technique. The beading information is given separately to the knitting pattern, so why not look through the swatch libraries and embellish the mittens with your own design or choice of beads.

Size
Hand circumference 7½in (19cm)

Materials
Anchor stranded embroidery
    cotton skein
    Gray A   1
    Split into 2 lengths of 3 strands

Rowan kidsilk haze 1oz (25g) balls
    Mauve B   2

1 set of 5 US 0 (2mm) dp needles

Size 10 beads ⅓oz (9g) pack
    Gray   1 (472 beads)

3mm beads
    Pearl   96

4mm cut glass beads
    Fuchsia   14

Gauge (Tension)
52 stitches and 56 rows to 4in (10cm) over st st using US 0 (2mm) needles.

Abbreviations
K1tblPB = knit 1 tbl, place bead. Attach gray bead using the close beading technique.
See also page 157.

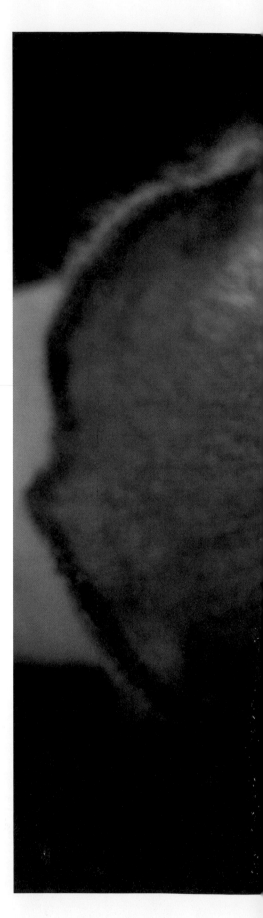

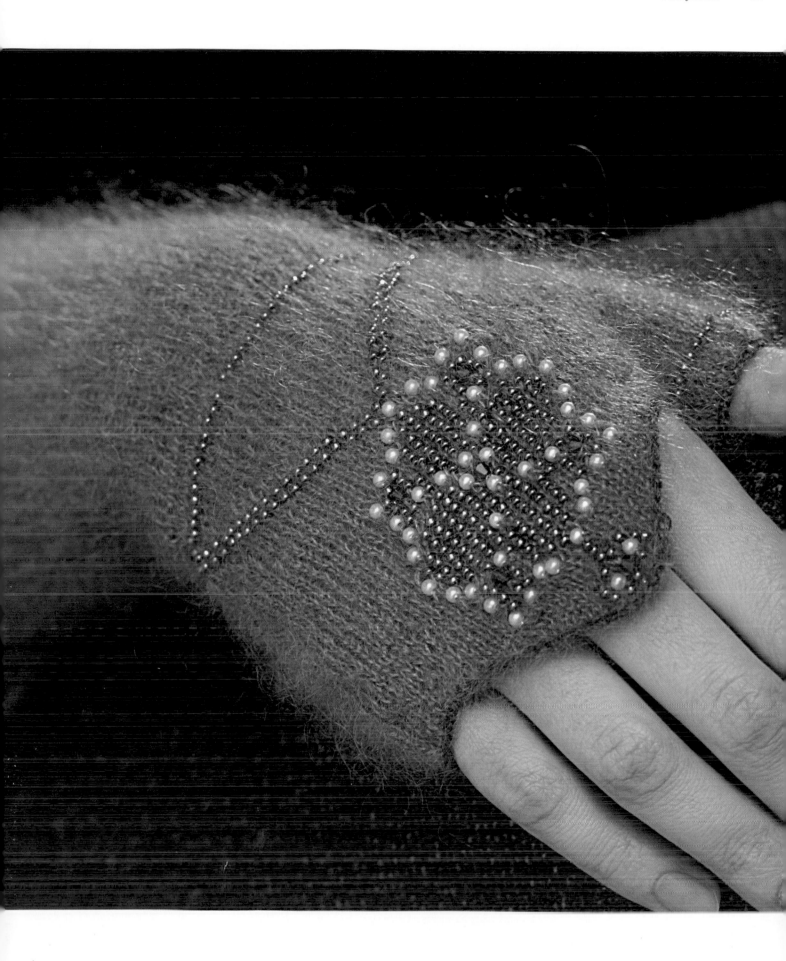

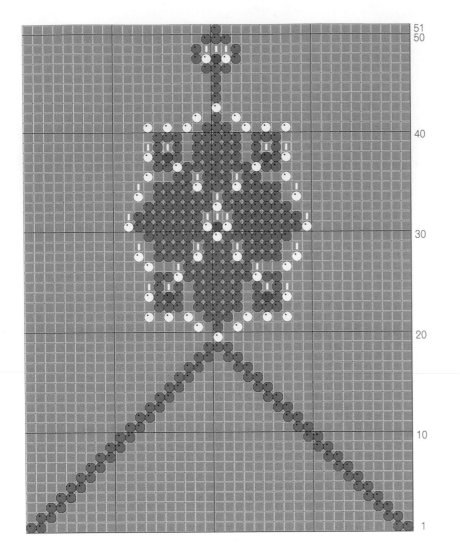

Key

■ Yarn B, k on RS, p on WS.

● Place gray bead

☉ Place pearl bead. Knit the st, thread the bead onto the new st loop using the individual beading technique, return the st to the right-hand needle and adjust its size.

● Place fuchsia bead. Knit the st, thread the bead onto the new st loop using the individual beading technique, return the st to the right-hand needle and adjust its size.

Ⅰ Slip st

Left mitten

Arm

Using the thumb method and A, cast on 160 sts.

Divide the sts evenly between four needles and join, taking care not to twist the sts.

Rounds 1–4: Knit.

Change to B.

Rounds 5–14: Knit.

Round 15: [K2tog] rep to the end of the round. *(80 sts)*

Round 16: [K1, p1] rep to the end of the round.

Cont in rib patt set until the work measures 7in (18cm).

Next round: K40, M1, k40. *(81 sts)*

Thumb gusset

Thread the gray beads onto B.

Next round: K40, M1L, k1, M1R, k40. *(83 sts)*

Next round: K1tblPB to end of round. Work chart from position indicated.

Chart round 1: K40, M1L, k3, M1R, k1, first st of chart, k39 foll first line of chart. *(85 sts)*

Chart round 2: Knit.

Chart round 3: K40, M1L, k5, M1R, k40. *(87 sts)*

Chart round 4: Knit.

Chart round 5: K40, M1L, k7, M1R, k40. *(89 sts)*

Chart round 6: Knit.

Chart round 7: K40, M1L, k9, M1R, k40. *(91 sts)*

Chart rounds 8–9: Knit.

Chart round 10: K40, M1L, k11, M1R, k40. *(93 sts)*

Chart rounds 11–12: Knit.

Chart round 13: K40, M1L, k13, M1R, k40. *(95 sts)*

Chart rounds 14–15: Knit.

Chart round 16: K40, M1L, k15, M1R, k40. *(97 sts)*

Chart rounds 17–18: Knit.

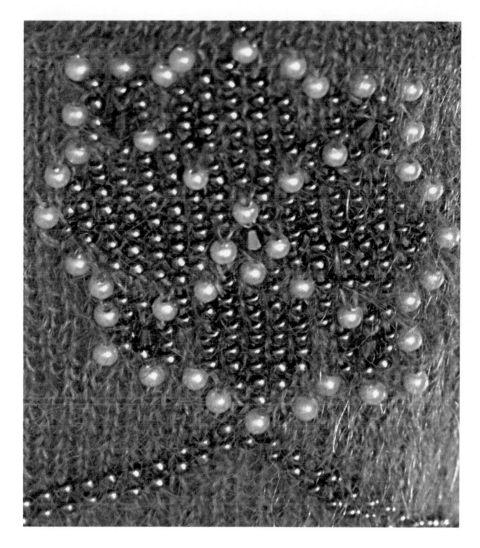

Rep the last 2 rows until 2 sts rem.

Next row: Using B, k2tog.

Cut the yarn and draw it through the last st loop.

Thumb

Transfer the sts from the stitch holder onto 3 dp needles. Starting with the st that would have been knitted next if the sts hadn't been transferred and using B, knit the sts on the needles. Evenly pick up 5 sts from the base of the hand. *(32 sts)*

Rounds 1–5: Knit.

Round 6: (k1tblPB) rep thirteen more times, individually bead 1 pearl bead, 1 cut glass bead and 1 pearl bead, (k1tblPB) to the end of the round.

Rounds 7–12: Knit.

Bind (cast) off using A.

Right mitten

Work as for Left Mitten to chart row 1.

Chart round 1: K1, first st of chart, k39 foll first line of chart, M1L, k3, M1R, k1, k39. *(85 sts)*

Cont working chart and mitten as for Left Mitten until row 39.

Chart round 40: K26, cut B and join in A, leaving a tail 8 in (20 cm) long, k1, bind (cast) off 59 sts.

Chart round 41: Bind (cast) off 1 st. Rejoin B and cont to the last 2 sts of the round, and using the intarsia technique and the tail left of A, k1, pnso. *(26 sts)*

Cont working chart and mitten as for Left Mitten until the end of the pattern.

Finishing

Weave in ends. Do not press the mittens because the beads may shatter.

Chart round 19: K40, M1L, k17, M1R, k40. *(99 sts)*

Chart rounds 20–21: Knit.

Chart round 22: K40, M1L, k19, M1R, k40. *(101 sts)*

Chart rounds 23–24: Knit.

Chart round 25: K40, M1L, k21, M1R, k40. *(103 sts)*

Chart rounds 26–27: Knit.

Chart round 28: K40, M1L, k23, M1R, k40. *(105 sts)*

Chart rounds 29–31: Knit.

Chart round 32: K40, M1L, k25, M1R, k40. *(107 sts)*

Chart round 33: K40, place the next 27 sts onto a stitch holder, cast on 1 st, k40. *(81 sts)*

Hand

Chart rounds 34–39: Knit.

Chart round 40: K73, cut B and join in A, leaving a tail 8in (20cm) long, k1, bind (cast) off 7 sts.

Chart round 41: Bind (cast) off 48 sts. Rejoin B and cont to the last 2 sts of the round, and using the intarsia technique and the tail left of A, k1, pnso. *(26 sts)*

Work on 2 needles only.

Next row (WS): Sl 1 st purlwise, p1, psso, using B, work to the last 2 sts, using A, p1, pnso.

Next row (RS): Sl 1 st knitwise tbl, k1, psso, using B, work to the last 2 sts, using A, k1, pnso.

Button bag

The pattern for this gorgeous little evening bag may look rather complicated, but it is actually a simple decrease repeat on either side of a central panel – it is written out in full here to help you keep track of the stitch count. The corsage is simplicity itself to make, and adds an elegant finishing touch.

Size
7 x 7¾in (20 x 18cm)

Materials
Jaeger siena 4 ply cotton
    1¾oz (50g) balls
      Dark pink A   1
      Light pink B   1

1 pair of US 2 (2.75mm) needles
2 cable needles

10 oval pearl buttons with 2 holes
1 round pearl button with 2 holes
Sewing needle and thread
Knitter's sewing needle

Gauge (Tension)
28 stitches and 44 rows to 4in (10cm) over st st using US 2 (2.75mm) needles.

Abbreviations
PB = place button. Use the slip stitch technique.
See also page 157.

Front
Using the cable cast on method and A, cast on 77 sts.
Thread 10 oval buttons onto B.
Row 1 (RS): K26A, k25B, k26A.
Row 2: P26A, seed (moss) 25B, p26A.
Row 3: K19A, sl1, k6A, seed (moss) 25B, k6A, sl1, K19A.
Rep rows 2–3 once more.
Rep row 2 once more.
Row 7: K1A, skpsso, K16A, sl1, k6A, seed (moss) 12B, PB, seed (moss) 12B, k6A, sl1, k16A, k2tog, k1A. *(75 sts)*
Row 8: P25A, seed (moss) 25B, p25A.
Row 9: K18A, sl1, k6A, seed (moss) 25B, k6A, sl1, K18A.
Rep rows 8–9 twice more.
Row 14: P1A, p2tog, p22A, seed (moss) 12B, PB, seed (moss) 12B, p22A, p2togtbl, p1A. *(73 sts)*
Row 15: K17A, sl1, k6A, seed (moss) 25B, k6A, sl1, K17A.
Row 16: P24A, seed (moss) 25B, p24A.
Rep rows 15–16 twice more.
Row 21: K1A, skpsso, K14A, sl1, k6A, seed (moss) 12B, PB, seed (moss) 12B, k6A, sl1, k14A, k2tog, k1A. *(71 sts)*
Row 22: P23A, seed (moss) 25B, p23A.
Row 23: K16A, sl1, k6A, seed (moss) 25B, k6A, sl1, K16A.
Rep rows 22–23 twice more.
Row 28: P1A, p2tog, p20A, seed (moss) 12B, PB, seed (moss) 12B, p20A, p2togtbl, p1A. *(69 sts)*
Row 29: K15A, sl1, k6A, seed (moss) 25B, k6A, sl1, K15A.

Row 30: P22A, seed (moss) 25B, p22A.
Rep rows 29–30 twice more.
Row 35: K1A, skpsso, K12A, sl1, k6A, seed (moss) 12B, PB, seed (moss) 12B, k6A, sl1, k12A, k2tog, k1A. *(67 sts)*
Row 36: P21A, seed (moss) 25B, p21A.
Row 37: K14A, sl1, k6A, seed (moss) 25B, k6A, sl1, K14A.
Rep rows 36–37 twice more.
Row 42: P1A, p2tog, p18A, seed (moss) 12B, PB, seed (moss) 12B, p18A, p2togtbl, p1A. *(65 sts)*
Row 43: K13A, sl1, k6A, seed (moss) 25B, k6A, sl1, K13A.
Row 44: P20A, seed (moss) 25B, p20A.
Rep rows 43–44 twice more.
Row 49: K1A, skpsso, K10A, sl1, k6A, seed (moss) 12B, PB, seed (moss) 12B, k6A, sl1, k10A, k2tog, k1A. *(63 sts)*
Row 50: P19A, seed (moss) 25B, p19A.
Row 51: K12A, sl1, k6A, seed (moss) 25B, k6A, sl1, K12A.
Rep rows 50–51 twice more.
Row 56: P1A, p2tog, p16A, seed (moss) 12B, PB, seed (moss) 12B, p16A, p2togtbl, p1A. *(61 sts)*
Row 57: K11A, sl1, k6A, seed (moss) 25B, k6A, sl1, K11A.
Row 58: P18A, seed (moss) 25B, p18A.
Rep rows 57–58 twice more.
Row 63: K1A, skpsso, K8A, sl1, k6A, seed (moss) 12B, PB, seed (moss) 12B, k6A, sl1, k8A, k2tog, k1A. *(59 sts)*
Row 64: P17A, seed (moss) 25B, p17A.

Row 65: K10A, sl1, k6A, seed (moss) 25B, k6A, sl1, K10A.

Rep rows 64–65 twice more.

Row 70: P1A, p2tog, p14A, seed (moss) 12B, PB, seed (moss) 12B, p14A, p2togtbl, p1A. *(57 sts)*

Row 71: K9A, sl1, k6A, seed (moss) 25B, k6A, sl1, K9A.

Row 72: P16A, seed (moss) 25B, p16A.

Rep rows 71–72 twice more.

Row 77: K4A, k6A onto 1st cable needle, k6A onto 2nd cable needle, turn 2nd cable needle round to form pleat, (k3tog (1 st from each cable needle and 1 st from left-hand needle)) rep five more times, seed (moss) 13B, k6A onto 1st cable needle, k6A onto 2nd cable needle, turn 1st cable needle round to form pleat, (k3tog (1 st from each cable needle and 1 st from left-hand needle)) rep five more times, k4A. *(33 sts)*

Break B.

Keeping patt correct, seed (moss) 11 rows.

Row 89: Seed (moss) 5 sts, bind (cast) off 23 sts, seed (moss) to end.

Row 90: Seed (moss) 5 sts, cast on 23 sts, seed (moss) 5 sts.

Keeping patt correct, seed (moss) 14 rows.

Bind (cast) off.

Back

Using the cable cast on method and A, cast on 53 sts.

Starting with a k row, work 6 rows st st.

Row 7 (RS): K1, skpsso, k to last 3 sts, k2tog, k1.

Work 6 rows st st.

Row 14: P1, p2tog, p to last 3 sts, p2togtbl, p1.

Rep these 14 rows four more times.

Work 7 rows st st.

Seed (moss) 11 rows.

Row 89: Seed (moss) 5 sts, bind (cast) off 23 sts, seed (moss) to end.

Row 90: Seed (moss) 5 sts, cast on 23 sts, seed (moss) 5 sts.

Keeping patt correct, seed (moss) 14 rows.

Bind (cast) off.

Petal (make 5)

Using the cable cast on method and B, cast on 3 sts.

Row 1 and every alternate row (WS): Purl.

Row 2: K1, M1R, k1, M1L, k1.

Row 4: K2, M1R, k1, M1L, k2.

Row 6: K3, M1R, k1, M1L, k3.

Row 8: Knit.

Row 10: K2, skpsso, k1, k2tog, k2.

Row 12: K1, skpsso, k1, k2tog, k1.

Row 14: Skpsso, k1, k2tog.

Row 15: P3tog.

Bind (cast) off last st.

Finishing

Weave in loose ends of the WS. Press the bag pieces, pressing the pleats flat along the lines of slipped stitches. Do not press the petals.

Fold the pleats in along the lines of slipped stitches and, using the sewing needle and thread, baste them into position. Using mattress stitch, join the bottom edges of the front and back sections of the bag, sewing carefully through the pleats for a neat finish. Remove the basting threads. Join the side seams.

Turn the top of the bag in so that the bound (cast) off edge aligns with the top edge of the handle opening and slip stitch it in place all around.

Sew the bound (cast) off ends of the petals together to make a flower. Cut 4 lengths of A, each 6in (15cm) long. Knot them together ¾in (2cm) from one end. Thread 2 ends of yarn through each of the holes in the round button. Use the ends of yarn to attach the flower to the bag at the top of the right-hand pleat. Secure the ends of yarn on the inside of the bag. Trim the ends on top of the button and unravel them to make stamens.

Beaded beret

Once the beads are threaded this project is easy to knit. For added decoration, consider making a beaded tassel to hang from the center of the crown, or making the underside of the beret a contrasting color.

Size
To fit an adult head 20in (50cm)

Materials
Rowan wool cotton 1¾oz (50g) balls

Violet	2

1 pair of US 3 (3.25mm) needles
1 set of US 4 (3.5mm) dp needles
Button
Size 8 beads 4oz (100g) pack

Dark green	1 (1029 beads)
Light green	1 (413 beads)
Blue	1 (301 beads)
Grape	1 (581 beads)

Gauge (Tension)
24 stitches and 30 rows to 4in (10cm) over beaded st st using US 4 (3.5mm) needles.

Note It is important to keep the gauge (tension) tight. If when you start beading the weight of the beads means the gauge (tension) gets a bit looser, drop down a needle size from your swatch and try and take the weight of the project on a cushion or table top.

Abbreviations
Sl2tog, k1, psso = slip two stitches together knitwise, knit 1, pass the slipped stitches over.
See also page 157.

Brim
Using US 3 (3.25mm) needles and the thumb method, cast on 116 sts.
Row 1 (RS): K1tbl, (p1, k1) rep to last st, yf, sl1 purlwise.
Rep row 1 once more.
Row 3: K1tbl, (p1, k1) rep to last 7 sts, bind (cast) off 3 sts, p1, yf, sl1 purlwise.
Row 4: K1tbl, p1, k1, p1, cast on 3 sts to complete buttonhole, cont to last st keeping the rib patt correct yf, sl1 purlwise.
Rep row 1 three more times, ending with a RS row.
Row 8: Bind (cast) off 7 sts, cont to the last st keeping the rib patt correct yf, sl1 purlwise. *(109 sts)*
Row 9 (RS): (K3, M1) rep thirty-four more times, k4. *(144 sts)*
Change to US 4 (3.5mm) dp needles and join, taking care not to twist the sts.
Rounds 1–11: Knit.
Round 12: (K6, M1) rep twenty-three more times. *(168 sts)*
Rounds 13–23: Knit.
Cut yarn.

Threading instructions
Thread the second ball of yarn with beads following the chart. Work from left to right on every charted row, starting with 66 and working down the chart. Repeat the bead sequence on each row seven times in total.

TECHNIQUES: Shaping ◗ page 14 • Close beading ◗ page 69

Crown

Work chart beading seven times and foll the shaping below.

Round 24: (K10, k2tog) rep thirteen more times. *(154 sts)*

Work 7 rounds.

Round 32: (K19, sl2tog, k1, psso) rep six more times. *(140 sts)*

Work 5 rounds.

Round 38: (K17, sl2tog, k1, psso) rep six more times. *(126 sts)*

Work 5 rounds.

Round 44: (K15, sl2tog, k1, psso) rep six more times. *(112 sts)*

Work 3 rounds.

Round 48: (K13, sl2tog, k1, psso) rep six more times. *(98 sts)*

Work 3 rounds.

Round 52: (K11, sl2tog, k1, psso) rep six more times. *(84 sts)*

Work 3 rounds.

Round 56: (K9, sl2tog, k1, psso) rep six more times. *(70 sts)*

Work 3 rounds.

Round 60: (K7, sl2tog, k1, psso) rep six more times. *(56 sts)*

Work 1 round.

Round 62: (K5, sl2tog, k1, psso) rep six more times. *(42 sts)*

Work 1 round.

Round 64: (K3, sl2tog, k1, psso) rep six more times. *(28 sts)*

Work 1 round.

Round 66: (K1, sl2tog, k1, psso) rep six more times. *(14 sts)*

Break yarn, thread through rem 14 sts and draw the stitches together. Secure temporarily while the seam is stitched.

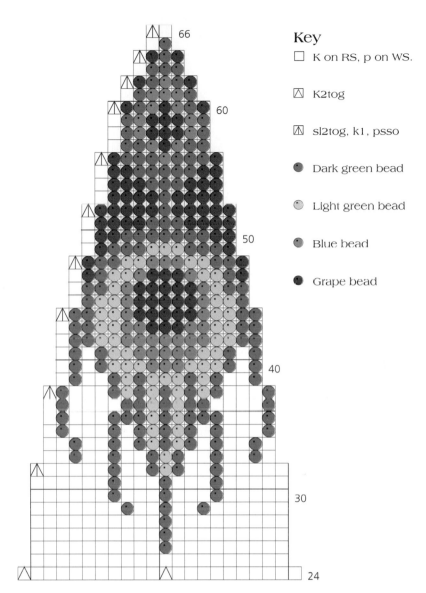

Key

- ☐ K on RS, p on WS.
- ◹ K2tog
- ◺ sl2tog, k1, psso
- ● Dark green bead
- ● Light green bead
- ● Blue bead
- ● Grape bead

Finishing

Insert a 12in (30cm) plate inside the beret and dampen it with a damp cloth. Lay a thin cloth over the knitting and steam it gently with a warm iron, pressing the damp cloth with a dry cloth between steam sessions. Do not press directly onto the beads with the iron as they, and possibly the plate, may shatter. Leave until completely dry.

Weave in the ends on the WS.

Sew on button to correspond to buttonhole.

After the first few washes, repeat the steaming process.

Table runner

This pattern is very simple to follow, but is very effective. For variations on the theme, consider threading beads, or even metal nuts, onto the ball chain before starting the next repeat.

Size
10 x 36in (25 x 90cm)

Materials
Jaeger siena 4 ply cotton
  1¾oz (50g) balls
    Pale blue   1

1 pair of US 0 (2mm) metal needles (metal needles are stronger than wooden ones)

Pliers with a cutting edge

19yds (20m) ½in (2mm) ball chain cut into 52 x 15in (37cm) lengths.

Note A quick method is to measure one length, tape it to a workbench and measure the remaining lengths of chain against it.

Gauge (Tension)
42 stitches and 48 rows to 4in (10cm) over st st using US 0 (2mm) needles.

Note It is important to keep the gauge (tension) tight. If the weight of the ball chain means the gauge (tension) gets a bit looser, drop down a needle size from your swatch and try and take the weight of the project on a cushion or table top.

Abbreviations
PB = place ball chain. Yarn forward, position the link between two balls on the ball chain between the working yarn and the knitted fabric and firmly purl the next st.

PBR = place ball chain. Yarn forward, position the fifth link from the last knitted in on the ball chain length to the left between the working yarn and the knitted fabric and firmly purl the next st.

PBL = place ball chain. Yarn forward, position the fifth link from the last knitted in on the ball chain length to the right between the working yarn and the knitted fabric and firmly purl the next st.
See also page 157.

First end section
Using the thumb method, cast on 103 sts.
＊**Row 1 (RS):** K1tbl, (PB 5in (12cm) from one end, with the longer length of ball chain to the front, k1, p1, k1) rep twenty-four more times, to last 2 sts, PB, sl1 purlwise.
Row 2 and every alt row (WS): K1tbl, (k1, p1, k1, p1) rep twenty-four more times, to last 2 sts, k1, yf, sl1 purlwise.
Rep the last 2 rows twice more but PB the next link up from the last, looping the longer length over the working yarn from back to front.

Pattern repeat
Row 7: Knit.
Row 8: Knit.
Row 9: K1tbl, (p1, k1, p1, k1) rep twenty-four more times, to last 2 sts, p1, sl1 purlwise.

Row 10: K1tbl, (k1, p1, k1, p1) rep twenty-four more times, to last 2 sts, k1, yf, sl1 purlwise.
Row 11: K1tbl, (PB the third link from the last knitted in, k1, p1, k1) rep twenty-four more times, to last 2 sts, PB, sl1 purlwise.
Row 12: K1tbl, (k1, p1, k1, p1) rep twenty-four more times, to last 2 sts, k1, yf, sl1 purlwise.
Row 13: K1tbl, (PB the next link from the last knitted in, k1, p1, k1) rep twenty-four more times, to last 2 sts, PB, sl1 purlwise.
Row 14: K1tbl, (k1, p1, k1, p1) rep twenty-four more times, to last 2 sts, k1, yf, sl1 purlwise.
Rep the patt repeat three more times.

Crossover pattern
Row 39: Knit.
Row 40: Knit.
Row 41: K1tbl, (p1, k1, p1, k1) rep twenty-four more times, to last 2 sts, p1, sl1 purlwise.
Row 42: K1tbl, (k1, p1, k1, p1) rep twenty-four more times, to last 2 sts, k1, yf, sl1 purlwise.
Rep the last 2 rows twice more.
Row 47: Knit.
Row 48: Knit.
Row 49: K1tbl, (p1, k1, p1, k1) rep twenty-four more times, to last 2 sts, p1, sl1 purlwise.
Row 50: K1tbl, (k1, p1, k1, p1) rep twenty-four more times, to last 2 sts, k1, yf, sl1 purlwise.
Row 51: K1tbl, (PBR, k1, p1, k1, PBL, k1, p1, k1) rep eleven more times, PBR, k1, p1, k1, PBL, sl1 purlwise.
Row 52: K1tbl, (k1, p1, k1, p1) rep twenty-four more times, to last 2 sts, k1, yf, sl1 purlwise.

Row 53: K1tbl, (PB the next link from the last knitted in, k1, p1, k1) rep twenty-four more times, to last 2 sts, PB, sl1 purlwise.

Row 54: K1tbl, (k1, p1, k1, p1) rep twenty-four more times, to last 2 sts, k1, yf, sl1 purlwise.

Rep the patt repeat four more times.
Rep the crossover patt repeat once more.
Rep the pattern repeat four more times. *
Cont without PB as folls.

Row 1: Knit.

Row 2: Knit.

Row 3: K1tbl, (p1, k1, p1, k1) rep twenty-four more times, to last 2 sts, p1, sl1 purlwise.

Row 4: K1tbl, (k1, p1, k1, p1) rep twenty-four more times, to last 2 sts, k1, yf, sl1 purlwise.
Rep the last 2 rows twice more.
Rep the last 8 rows seventeen more times.
Purl one row ending with a RS row.
Transfer stitches onto a stitch holder.

Second end section

Using the thumb method, cast on 103 sts.
Rep the first end section from * to *.
Knit one row, ending with a RS row.

Finishing

Weave in the loose ends on the WS. Transfer the stitches from the stitch holder onto the second needle and, using Kitchener stitch, graft the second end section to the middle section.
Steam the runner without letting the iron touch the fabric, and pin and block it to size.

embroidery

EMBROIDERY OFFERS BOTH A WONDERFUL WAY to add detail and decoration to a knitted fabric, and a chance to express yourself creatively without any fear of making an irreversible mistake.

Although duplicate stitch is the most commonly used embroidery stitch on knitted fabric, many of the others also lend themselves well to the grid that the knitted stitches and rows provide. Knit a few swatches and try out some of your own personal favorites.

You can embroider with almost anything that will go through the eye of a needle, though some materials will work better than others. Conventional embroidery threads and tapestry yarns work well, are easy to use, and come in a wide range of colors.

Both smocking and appliqué techniques and swatches are also included in this chapter, giving you an even wider range of decorative techniques to choose from.

Embroidery
TECHNIQUES

Surface decoration

Knitting and embroidery are natural companions. Almost any embroidery stitch can be used on knitted fabric, but a bold approach tends to work best. Embroidery can be added to a finished project that is missing a certain something, or it can be used to update an old favorite from the closet.

Generally the flat, even surface of st st offers the most opportunities, but any stitch pattern that offers large areas of repeated texture will provide an excellent backdrop for a motif. However, motifs are not the only way embroidery can be used. Consider using an embroidery stitch in stripes between bands of rib or cable, around a cuff or to highlight a shaping detail.

It is important to remember that all-over embroidery patterns with stranded lengths of thread on the reverse will reduce the elasticity of your knitted fabric. There is also the risk of long stranded threads catching.

TYPES OF THREAD AND YARN

The sensible approach is to match the weight of the embroidery thread to the yarn of a knitted fabric, checking fiber content and colorfastness. However, the sensible approach is not always the most creative one, and there are ways around most problems.

The silky sheen of embroidery thread will add a different texture and feel to a project worked in a soft chunky yarn. If a fine wool thread has caught your eye, then make sure the color and design you chose is bold enough to create a contrast between the two matte textures.

If you have decided to add a motif to a chunky knit sweater, but the knit stitches dictate a scale that is too large, then baste a piece of fabric to the wrong side and use that to anchor your embroidery

LEFT TO RIGHT
Large knitter's sewing needle;
small knitter's sewing needle;
tapestry needle.

stitches. The fabric can be as light as muslin and any excess is easily trimmed away. For a result that will look like clever shading, use a variegated thread with a color change that is frequent enough to suit the area being embroidered.

What does not work well is chunky or textured yarns used on a fine cotton or wool knitted fabric. The yarn tends to create ugly distortions and textured yarns can lose their charm when drawn repeatedly through knitted fabric. If the combination is irresistible, consider positioning the yarn over the fabric and securing it with small stitches.

When starting and finishing embroidery, sew the ends into the back of the knitted fabric, or the stitches, to secure it. One of the best parts of embroidery is that if the knitted fabric is not damaged, it is possible to gently pull out the embroidery stitches and start again if need be.

TYPES OF NEEDLE

The most important factor is that the point of the needle is blunt. This will help to avoid splitting stitches in a knitted fabric, which can spoil the fabric and distort the embroidery.

Knitter's sewing needles work well if you are embroidering with yarn. They come in different sizes, so select one to suit the thickness of the yarn.

You can also use tapestry needles to embroider with, and their smaller eyes make them ideal if you are embroidering with thread or fine yarn.

RUNNING STITCH AND BACK STITCH

Most knitters are familiar with these two stitches as they are often used for seaming at one time or another. However, they can be decorative as well as practical.

Used densely along an edge, these stitches will help to flatten the curl of st st. They can also strengthen areas vulnerable to wear, such as elbows and the heels of socks. Subtle but useful, these are not stitches to be forgotten.

DUPLICATE STITCH

Duplicate stitch, or Swiss darning, is worked on the knit side of st st, following the path of the stitches and covering them with the embroidery. For almost invisible results use the same or a similar weight of thread or yarn as that of the knitted fabric. For knitters who like the look of complex intarsia designs, but are put off by long vertical lines or isolated stitches, this is a wonder stitch. Large areas of duplicate stitch will stiffen the fabric.

1 **Working horizontally along a row**, bring the needle through the knitted fabric from back to front at the base of a stitch, leaving a 4 in (10 cm) tail of thread on the wrong side. Slide the needle behind the loops of the stitch above. Take the needle back through the base of the stitch from front to back and bring it up again at the base of the next stitch. Pull the stitch up tight, carefully matching the tension of the knitted fabric.

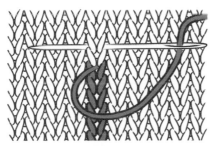

2 **Working vertically up a column of stitches**, bring the needle through the knitted fabric from back to front at the base of a stitch. Slide the needle behind the loops of the stitch above, then take it back through the base of the stitch from front to back. Bring it up at the base of the next stitch, carefully matching the tension of the knitted fabric. Complete the embroidery with the needle on the wrong side. Secure the end by oversewing over the back of the duplicate stitches. Cut the thread and re-thread the needle with the tail left at the beginning, then sew this in in the same way to avoid damaging the knitted fabric, in case you ever want to remove the duplicate stitches.

CROSS STITCH

A cross stitch is composed of two slanting stitches that cross each other. It does not have to be square, as in the charted cross stitch designs for fabric embroidery, but to create a square stitch, work it over approximately two stitches and three rows of st st.

1 Imagining the fabric as a grid of squares or rectangles, bring the needle though the knitted fabric from back to front at the top left of the proposed stitch. *Go through the fabric from front to back at the bottom right of the stitch and back to the front at the bottom left. Take the needle though to the back again at the top right of the completed stitch and come back to the front at the top left of the next stitch along to the left. Repeat from *.

FRENCH KNOTS

French knots are twists of thread secured by a small stitch running through them. The number of times the thread wraps around the needle can be varied, as can the length of the central stitch itself.

If the needle returns to the back of the fabric some distance from where it came up and has sufficient wraps to make a dense strand, it is called a bullion knot.

French or bullion knots can be used tightly packed together in the center of embroidered flowers, or as a "punctuation mark" in a design.

1 Bring the needle through the knitted fabric from back to front and wrap the thread round it two or three times. Then take the needle from front to back through the hole it came out of, or as close as possible to it, taking care not to split the yarn. Hold the thread taut at the tip of the needle to keep the wraps in place and draw the needle though the fabric, pulling the knot tight.

BLANKET STITCH

Usually known as an excellent stitch for neatening and strengthening edges, blanket stitch is a loop stitch that can also be worked on the surface of a knitted fabric.

For perfect blanket stitch, the stitches should be evenly spaced and of equal length, and a knitted fabric supplies a useful grid. However, varying the length and space between stitches can produce interesting results.

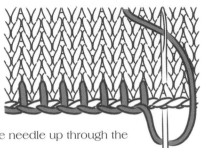

1 Bring the needle up through the knitted fabric from back to front, the required distance up from the edge. For the first stitch, take the needle to the back, slightly to the right of where it first came to the front. Pass the needle from back to front through the loop of thread and draw the stitch tight. Repeat along the row, keeping the distance, length, and tension of the stitches the same.

CHAIN STITCH

Chain stitch is a series of interconnecting loops. This stitch can be made to change direction very easily and is perfect for twisting and winding lines, and for filling shapes with blocks of color. As with all stitches, if used densely it will affect the drape of the fabric.

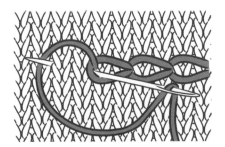

1 Bring the needle through the knitted fabric from back to front where the chain is to begin. Return through the hole the needle has just come out of, make a small forward running stitch and wrap the thread round the emerging point of the needle. Repeat, changing the direction of the running stitches as necessary, but trying to keep them all the same length.

FEATHER STITCH

Feather stitch is a variation on chain stitch, with two columns of open chain stitches worked alternately from top to bottom. This is a good stitch for giving emphasis to vertical lines and for creating an organic look.

1 Bring the needle through the knitted fabric from back to front. *Take it back down slightly to the right, make a running stitch to midway between the two points and catch the thread under the needle. Pull the stitch tight.

For the next stitch, go back down through the fabric slightly to the left. Make a small running stitch to the mid-point, catching the thread as before. Repeat from *.

LAZY DAISY STITCH

Lazy daisy stitch is a series of chain stitches, each anchored separately with a small straight stitch. The loops are usually all the same size, but varying their length and the colors used within one design can produce some creative results. This stitch is perfect for delicate borders and small flowers – embroider a French knot in the center to finish them off.

1 Bring the needle though the knitted fabric from back to front where the stitch is to start: if you are making a flower, this will be the center of it. Take the needle to the back again through the same hole, and draw the thread slowly through until a loop of the desired size is formed. Bring the needle through from back to front at the furthest point of this loop and secure it with a small straight stitch. Repeat as many times as required.

SATIN STITCH

Satin stitch is a series of straight stitches that sit next to each other, covering the fabric below. If long, the stitches are difficult to keep to a constant tension and may distort the fabric, as well as catching fingers or jewellery. Long stitches can be made into two smaller ones, the second stitch splitting the first by coming up halfway along it.

1 Bring the needle through the knitted fabric from back to front on one edge of the shape to be stitched. Take the needle to the back again at the opposite edge of the shape. Come back to the front a thread's width from where the needle last came to the front. Take the thread to the back a thread's width away from the stitch on the other side. Continue in this manner across the shape. For a slightly raised effect, work satin stitch in one direction and then again at right angles over the first stitches.

LADDER STITCH

Ladder stitch is a series of evenly spaced horizontal stitches that can be used to join two edges together, or to create a raised surface texture. It is worked from top to bottom, and the distance between the stitches and their width can be varied to good effect.

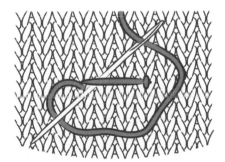

1 Bring the needle through from back to front at the top left of the ladder. Take a horizontal stitch to the right and come up again slightly above it. Take the needle to the back slightly below the long horizontal stitch, creating a small straight stitch. Bring the needle to the front again just below where it first appeared. From top to bottom, slide the needle under the left-hand edge of the horizontal stitch.

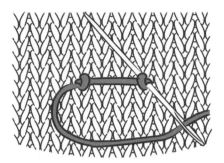

2 * On the right-hand side, pass the needle under the end of the horizontal stitch and the straight stitch.

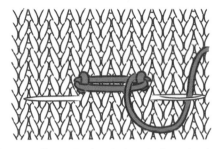

3 Take the needle to the back, just below the horizontal stitch on the right-hand side. Come back to the front just below the last horizontal thread on the left-hand side. Pass the needle under the straight stitch and the end of the lower horizontal stitch on the left-hand side. Repeat from *, taking care to keep the spacing even.

Transferring a motif onto knitted fabric

To visualize and check the scale of a design on a project, have likely areas for embroidery color photocopied. Draw possible designs and colors onto the copies, or onto a layer of tracing paper. If you have access to a computer and scanner, you can create endless variations until you are happy with the scale, size and color of the design.

You can also trace the design onto water-soluble embroidery facing using a water-soluble marker, then baste it onto the front of the knitted fabric. Stitch the design and then gently soak away the facing. Even if the design is densely stitched the facing will dissolve. However, as always, if possible test the facing on a swatch.

A cheaper option is to trace the design onto tissue paper using a permanent marker and then baste the outline onto the knitted fabric with small running stitches. Tear away the paper gently and embroider as before. Finally, remove the basting.

Smocking

Smocking is usually associated with 17th-century peasant clothing, which was made of large rectangles and shaped by gathering sections of the garment, such as the yoke, and embroidering the pleats thus formed.

This technique works well with knit fabrics, too, but they do have more bulk and a lot of smocking can become cumbersome. The great advantage is that a knitted fabric offers a natural grid of the type on which most traditional smocking patterns are based. It is not necessary to create regular gathers in the fabric before embroidering, just decide on a row and stitch distance and gather the fabric as you go. Of course, this is made easier if the base fabric is a rib or has some regular repeat you can work to.

Remember that true smocking requires a lot of fabric and the density of the gathers will be determined by the repeat you choose. A heavy yarn and wide repeat will create a very thick, stiff fabric.

One option is to cheat and give the impression of smocking by working a small repeat rib and not allowing the embroidery to draw the fabric too much.

HONEYCOMB STITCH

This popular smocking stitch nips the fabric together at regular intervals to create a lattice pattern. The distances between the stitches and the width of them can be varied, but it can create long strands on the reverse if the stitches are too far apart, making snagging a problem. If too wide an area of fabric is drawn together, then it can stretch, creating a hole at either end of the stitch.

Working from left to right, bring the needle through the knitted fabric from back to front. Make a back stitch over the required number of stitches and draw the fabric up. Insert the needle as if to repeat the stitch, but bring the point to the front again a few rows down. Repeat the sequence over the next area of stitches to the right, but to make the second stitch, bring the needle through level with the first stitch and work across the fabric in an up-and-down zig-zag pattern. One zig-zagging row is one row, not two, of honeycomb stitch. In theory it can be worked in reverse, from right to left, starting at the stated number of rows below the lower stitches. However, this rarely looks the same and it usually better to always start from the left.

SURFACE HONEYCOMB STITCH

This is a variation on honeycomb stitch, but the stranding appears on the front of the work rather than the back. It is usually worked with only one horizontal stitch, not two on top of each other, so it is not as strong as honeycomb stitch, but the stranding at the front can be attractive.

1 Working from left to right, make a horizontal stitch over the required number of stitches, inserting the needle from right to left and coming to the front at the left-hand end of the stitch. Draw the fabric up. Insert the needle from right to left a few rows down and make a stitch to secure the next section of fabric as before. Then insert the needle from right to left a few rows up. When inserting the needle a few rows up or down, it goes through a stitch below or above the last one.

OUTLINE STITCH

Outline stitch is a series of long back stitches that are used to gather the fabric together. There is no point in using this stitch to create faux smocking, as its principle purpose is to act as a firm locking stitch for a series of gathers and so it is often found top and bottom of smocking panels.

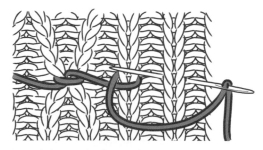

1 Working from left to right, bring the needle through the knitted fabric from back to front. Keeping the needle above the thread, make a horizontal stitch over the required number of stitches and draw the fabric together, returning to the front one stitch to the left. Continue working across to the right, repeating the sequence over each section of fabric. Keeping the needle below the thread will create a reverse barley twist effect.

TRELLIS STITCH

Trellis stitch is very similar in principle to outline stitch, but instead of just working horizontally across the knitted fabric to the right, each new stitch also moves a small distance up or down the fabric.

The trellis effect is created by stitching opposing zig-zags; where the first row has a zig-zag that starts by working up the fabric, the second row has a zig-zag that goes down the fabric.

This stitch looks equally good worked in parallel zig-zags in different colors, or in opposing zig-zags that slightly cross over each other.

VANDYKE STITCH

Vandyke stitch gathers the fabric together to create a square or rectangular line of stitching that moves across and then up or down, like castle battlements. The most impressive part of this stitch is how easy it is to do – especially if you have mastered surface honeycomb stitch – and how complex the end result can look.

The main difference in appearance between surface honeycomb stitch and vandyke stitch is the position of the stranding, which in vandyke stitch goes along the side of the column of stitches and in honeycomb stitch goes across the column of stitches.

As with all smocking stitches, there are strands of thread that can get caught, and drawing the fabric together at a constant tension is important for an even look.

1 Working from right to left, bring the needle through the knitted fabric from back to front. *Make a small back stitch, drawing up the first section of fabric to the left. Count down the rows to the required one and insert the needle into the stitch directly below the left-hand end of the first stitch. Repeat the back stitch to draw up the second section of fabric. Count up the rows and insert the needle into the stitch directly above the left-hand end of the second stitch. Repeat from *.

Appliqué

Appliqué is the application of shapes to a surface using glue, small stitches or bold embroidery techniques. The shapes can be made of many materials – the most commonly used being cotton fabric, leather or felt – and can be accompanied by braids, ribbon and beads. Try anything that is compatible with the knitted fabric in terms of laundering and colorfastness.

Shapes can be hemmed or overlocked, but this increases the stiffness of the finished result. However, this can be an advantage for some projects, such as a bag, which can benefit from some extra support to help hold their shape.

Using glue on a knitted fabric is just not a good idea. The amount of glue required will ruin the drape and will seep through to the reverse, creating a messy problem.

If the project is flat, with little or no movement, such as a cushion or small areas of an afghan, iron-on interfacing can be a useful way of securing the shapes. With cotton fabrics it has the added advantage of reducing the amount of fraying.

Smaller shapes can be secured with a line of running stitches down the middle, or a button in the center. If the fabric is one that does not fray, such as felt, then the edges will not need overlocking.

If the applied shapes are large, then they will need some additional sewing around the edges to ensure that they do not come away during the rigours of washing and general wear-and-tear. But it need not stop there.

Appliqué does provide an opportunity to use embroidery stitches to further enhance a design. Often the edges benefit from the use of feather or ladder stitch, or even a simple zig-zag stitch. Choose contrasting colors and make a feature of the stitches, it will all help to hold the viewer's attention for longer.

Even if a combination of sewing and embroidery is used, smaller shapes tend to have less of an impact on the drape of a knitted fabric. In addition, large shapes can detract from what is primarily a knitted project. What is the point of all that careful knitting if it is to be covered up and just used as a backdrop for something else?

Embroidery
SWATCH LIBRARY

Duplicate stitch, sometimes known as Swiss darning, is specifically for knitted fabric, and as such is the embroidery stitch most commonly used by knitters. However, many other embroidery stitches work well on knitted fabric, producing a very decorative finish for a small amount of work. Stitches can also be embellished with beads or ribbon, so experimentation is the order of the day.

As well as working in knitting yarn, these stitches also offer the perfect opportunity to use the enormous range of colors available in embroidery threads and yarns. The restrictions of mixing yarns↓ do apply, so if in doubt do a swatch and launder it to check the results.

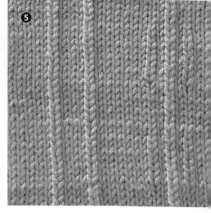

Running stitch and back stitch

It is easy to overlook the familiar and this is a mistake with running stitch and back stitch↓.

❶ SAMPLER

These flowing patterns make excellent edging designs, or focal points on knitted fabric.

Left panel, top to bottom

This is an example of whip stitch on back stitch. A line of back stitch is worked and then a contrasting thread is passed under the stitch loops from top to bottom.

Wave stitch is worked on a line of back stitch, but the contrasting thread is first passed under the stitch loop from top to bottom and then again from bottom to top. This example has two runs of contrasting thread worked in opposite directions.

This is an example of single wave stitch with one run of thread.

Even plain back stitch and running stitch can be decorative.

Right panel, top to bottom

This Pekinese stitch is worked on a line of back stitch with the contrasting thread brought from back to front under the second stitch from the right. *Pass the thread under the back stitch loop to the right of it from bottom to top and from top to bottom under the loop of the stitch three to the left. Repeat from * to the end of the row.

This linked back stitch is worked over two rows of back stitch with the contrasting thread worked in wave stitch over the two rows.

This linked running stitch is worked over four rows of running stitch with the contrasting thread worked over two rows, each in opposite directions.

Duplicate stitch

Worked with due care, duplicate stitch↓ can imitate a knitted stitch brilliantly. Worked poorly, it will look a mess. The secret is to take your time, work the stitches individually and tension each one correctly.

❷ DUPLICATE STITCH LETTER

Letters are an excellent example of how fantastic duplicate stitch is when it comes to working motifs made up of single stitches in a row of knitted fabric.

There are many alphabets to choose from, though if you are using letters graphed for cross stitch you will have to lengthen them, as the height of a knitted stitch is only 70 percent of its width.

❸ EMBROIDERED CABLE

With a little care, duplicate stitch can be worked over a textured or three-dimensional stitch pattern. Plan the design beforehand and practice on a swatch to ensure that your plan works before you start embroidering the project.

Left Duplicate stitch is worked down the centre of a cable, emphasizing the twist beautifully.

Right The edge stitch of a band of st st dividing cables is embroidered with duplicate stitch to draw more attention to the cable itself.

❹ BEADED DUPLICATE STITCH

This is a slightly different interpretation of duplicate stitch, with the stitches themselves being invisible and the beads they carry being the decoration.

Choose a beading thread to match the color of the yarn as closely as possible and thread a beading needle. Work vertical columns of

duplicate stitch, threading on a bead before going under the loops of the stitch above and then again before going back down through the base of the stitch being worked. As the beading needle has a sharp point, particular care must be taken to follow the knitted stitches without splitting them.

The beads can be nudged into neat horizontal rows, or left, as here, in more fluid columns.

On this swatch every fourth column of stitches is beaded, with the columns on either side being embroidered in duplicate stitch using a sparkly yarn.

❺ TARTAN
Duplicate stitch can be combined with simple stripes to create a much more complicated looking design.

The pattern is given here as a chart; all the horizontal lines are knitted, while all the vertical ones are added in duplicate stitch once the knitting is complete.

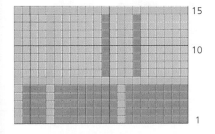

Cross stitch
A versatile embroidery stitch for knitters, cross stitch ↓ is quick to work and translates easily onto the grid provided by a knitted fabric. Do remember that if you are working a design that was originally graphed for conventional fabric cross-stitch, you may need to amend the height of it if you want to work over single stitches in the knitted fabric, as they are not square.

❻ ALL-OVER CROSS STITCH
This swatch is covered with a pattern of cross stitches worked over two stitches and two rows of the knitted fabric, with an equal amount of spacing between each row and column of cross stitches. Alternate rows are staggered to create a trellis.

The cross stitches are anchored in the middle with a tiny straight stitch in a darker yarn. This has the practical effect of holding the stitches close to the fabric, as well as adding interest to the design.

❼ CROSS STITCH WITH RIBBON
The nature of cross stitch makes it suitable for trapping lengths of ribbon or fiber and holding them against the knitted fabric in a decorative way.

Here, lengths of organza ribbon the width of two rows are laid across the knitted fabric and stitched over with cross stitches in two shades of pink embroidery thread.

❽ CROSS STITCH MOTIF
Along with duplicate stitch, cross stitch is ideal for working motifs. This heart is worked in variegated embroidery thread for added interest. When cutting a new length of thread, cut it so that the stitching continues from the same point in the color variegation as it ended.

French knots
French knots ↓ will add texture to plain knitted fabrics. Use them to create a decorative border or as way of enhancing an intarsia design.

❾ FRENCH KNOTS SAMPLER
These three rows of French knots are worked using the same method, but with design variations.

Top This French knot is made with two lengths of fluffy novelty yarn.
Middle Here, a bead is added before the thread is twisted around the needle and passed back through the knitted fabric.
Bottom The thread is wrapped around the needle four times before it passes back through the knitted fabric. This is called a bullion knot.

❿ BOBBLE FRENCH KNOTS
Instead of knitted-in bobbles, this cable pattern has French knots added, worked using four strands of the main yarn. The two great advantages of this are that the size

of the knots can be judged as part of the overall pattern at the end of a project, and that the knots can be used to add an extra element at the last minute.

⓫ FRENCH KNOTS ON RIB
This k1, p1 rib is embroidered with French knots worked into the side of the knit stitches on every second row.

⓬ FRENCH KNOT MOTIF
The bee is made from from alternate yellow and brown bullion knots worked side-by-side, with two white lazy daisy ↓ stitches for the wings.

The flower petals are created by wrapping the thread around the needle, but going back through the fabric ½in (12 mm) away from where the needle came out. These elongated French knots radiate around a flower center of yellow French knots. The stalk is embroidered in chain stitch ↓.

TECHNIQUES: Cross stitch ◗ page 97 • French knots ◗ page 97 • Lazy daisy stitch ◗ page 98 • Chain stitch ◗ page 98

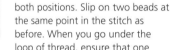

Blanket stitch

This edging stitch is particularly suited to knitted fabric, as the grid of stitches and rows makes it very easy to space the blanket stitches↓ evenly for a neat finish.

Remember that blanket stitch will affect the elasticity of an edge, so it is not suitable for items that need to be stretched; for example, a tight-fitting neckline.

❶ BEADED BLANKET STITCH

Beads can be placed on blanket stitches in two different positions to give different effects. Slip the bead onto the working thread at the appropriate point in the stitch.
Left The left-hand stitches hold the bead on the edge of the fabric. Slip on the bead before taking the needle through the fabric. When you go through the loop of thread, ensure that the bead is to the left of the needle so that it sits correctly.
Right The stitches on the right have the bead on the front of the knitted fabric. Slip on the bead at the same point in the stitch as before. When you go through the loop of thread, ensure that the bead is to the right of the needle so that it sits in the correct position.

Center These stitches have beads in both positions. Slip on two beads at the same point in the stitch as before. When you go under the loop of thread, ensure that one bead is on either side of the needle.

❷ EDGED LADDER

Add detail to a ladder by edging it with blanket stitch. Work the blanket stitches carefully around the top and bottom of the ladder with either a stitch to either side (top), or a vertical central stitch (bottom).

Faux darning

The second ladder on this swatch is faux darned. This makes the ladder opaque and adds a vintage effect. Work the darning in a lighter weight yarn than that of the knitted fabric or it can become very bulky.

Thread a knitter's needle with the darning thread and weave it under and over alternate "rungs" of the ladder, weaving into the very first and last stitches. On the next row, take the needle over the "rungs" it went under on the first row, and vice versa.

Use the tip of the needle to nudge the weaving over to one side of the ladder and repeat the process until the weaving fills the ladder.

❸ BLANKET-STITCHED FRINGE

Another practical and decorative use for blanket stitch is as an edging above an unpicked fringe↓.

If worked in st st, the last stitch before the fringe has a distinct tendency to work loose and blanket stitch will prevent this.

Here, the stitch is worked alternately over one and two stitches. As well as being decorative, this makes the edge of a knitted fabric even more secure.

Chain stitch

In Indian embroidery chain stitch↓ is often worked with a hook and is called tambour embroidery.

Push a crochet hook down through the fabric and draw up a loop of thread. * Put the hook through again a little further along and draw through a second loop. Slip the second loop through the first one and repeat from *.

This method is quick and is essential for working some of the following chain stitch techniques.

❹ CHAIN STITCH ON RIB

This is a very good way of keeping the elasticity of rib, but adding the decorative look of a complex Fair Isle or intarsia pattern.

A k1, p1 rib is worked in the light blue yarn and then chain stitch is worked vertically, one stitch for each row, in contrasting colors.

❺ BEADED CHAIN STITCH ON GARTER STITCH

This chain stitch pattern has to be

done using a needle and thread rather than a hook.

Work two lines of dark purple chain stitch between the garter stitch ridges. Then, using a lighter yarn, * work two chain stitches, thread on a bead, make a stitch and repeat from * taking particular care with the tension of the first stitch after the beaded stitch.

❻ ADDING OBJECTS

Using a hook to draw a loop of thread through from the back of the work offers an opportunity to attach objects with a hole in to a knitted fabric.

Work a chain stitch, put the object on the hook and draw a loop through from the back of the work. Slide the object down onto the stitch and then work another stitch, but this time on the other side of the object to secure it.

❼ CHAIN STITCH MOTIF

Chain stitch is easily worked in any direction and can be used to create solid blocks of color. However, if small, close stitches are used the fabric can become very dense.

This swatch is worked using a crochet hook and embroidery thread.

❽ CHAIN STITCH ON MOTIFS

Chain stitch can be used to add twiggy, wavy lines to an intarsia pattern or to "paint" with thread over a knitted design.

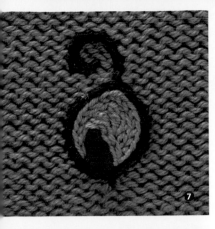

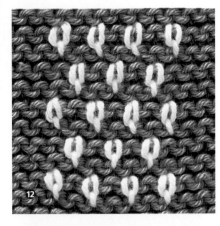

For this swatch a knitted intarsia square is freehand embroidered with a spiral design using a hook and knitting yarn.

Feather stitch

This stitch can be worked vertically or horizontally, following the grid provided by a knitted fabric. Alternatively, you can abandon the grid and work the stitch freehand. Either way, feather stitch ↓ is simple to embroider and gives instant interest to the plainest project.

⑨ BEADED FEATHER STITCH

Beads not only add glamour to a straight line of feather stitch, but if this stitch is worked along a hem, the weight of them helps the garment hang well. It is best to use a bead with a hole large enough for the embroidery needle to pass through, as adding the beads ↓ the traditional way is, while possible, very time consuming.

Bring the needle up through the knitted fabric as usual. Thread on an even number of beads (here, six are used), * make the running stitch and bring the needle up in the middle of the string of beads. Pull the stitch taut, thread on the same number of beads again and repeat from *.

⑩ FREEHAND FEATHER STITCH

Simply work the stitch, altering the direction of the running stitch that goes to the midpoint of the loop of thread to change the direction of the feather stitches.

⑪ TWO-COLOR FEATHER STITCH

This might look, and sound, a little complicated, but it is easy to work.

Thread two needles, one with each color of thread: A and B. Bring A up through the knitted fabric. * Take it down again to the right. Bring B up at the midpoint of the loop of thread and pull A taut around it. Take B down through the fabric to the left of where it came up and bring A up at the midpoint and repeat from *.

Lazy daisy stitch

An attractive stitch that is easy to work, lazy daisy stitch adds charm to any feminine project, particularly those designed for little girls.

⑫ LAZY DAISY LOOPS

This stitch is usually used to make flowers, but it can be worked as separate loops to create a border or an all-over design. Here, rows of stitches are worked over three rows of garter stitch, and are staggered on alternate rows.

⑬ LAZY DAISY FLOWERS

These flowers are worked in pink embroidery thread on knitted fabric and the center of each flower is filled with a yellow bullion knot.

⑭ RIBBON FLOWERS

Silk ribbon embroidery is a craft in itself, but can work well on knitted fabric. This flower in worked on cotton fabric to provide a contrast with the silk ribbon, and the center of the flower is filled with a stitched-on bead.

TECHNIQUES: Feather stitch ◆ page 98 • Threading beads onto the yarn ◆ page 66 • Lazy daisy stitch ◆ page 98

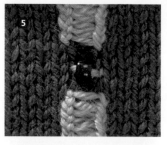

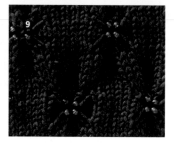

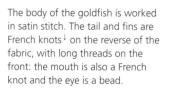

Satin stitch

This is a difficult stitch to get right. It is important to watch the tension of each stitch to make sure it does not draw up the fabric. A very flat finish can be difficult as you may be forced to split the yarn of a knitted fabric if the holes in it are not in the right places for the satin stitches↓.

It is best to work bold designs, and, if the drape is not important, back as small an area as necessary of the fabric with iron-on facing.

❶ PADDED SATIN STITCH
A raised effect can be achieved by working two layers of satin stitches in opposite directions.

Here, two stitches are worked over three rows of knitted fabric, and then more satin stitches are worked at right angles to them.

❷ SATIN STITCH MOTIF
Any design can be transferred onto the fabric and stitched, but avoid long strands and position the motif carefully on a knitted fabric.

The body of the goldfish is worked in satin stitch. The tail and fins are French knots↓ on the reverse of the fabric, with long threads on the front: the mouth is also a French knot and the eye is a bead.

❸ SPLIT SATIN STITCH
Stitch splitting solves some of the problems of satin stitch: long strands are lessened and subtle shading can be achieved.

Make the first stitches about a third longer than is required to fill the area. Then work the next row of stitches, bringing them through the first row two-thirds of the way up.

Look in books on English Jacobean embroidery for designs.

Ladder stitch

Ladder stitch↓ has a place in this book because it is such a useful way of sewing blocks of knitting together for an afghan or cushion. It is decorative, disguises baggy selvedges neatly and is suitably elastic.

❹ LADDER STITCH SAMPLER
This stitch is decorative in itself, but it can be further adorned.
Left This beaded ladder stitch has one square bead, one round glass bead and another square bead added to the first horizontal strand of the stitch sequence that appears at the front of the fabric.
Right Here, the front horizontal loops are bound together with back stitch↓. Bring a needle threaded with contrast yarn to the front three horizontal loops down the ladder. ✱ Pass the needle under the three loops above and then under the three loops below the start point. Repeat from ✱.

❺ BLOCKS OF LADDER STITCH
The distance between strands or blocks of ladder stitch can be varied. Here, beads are added to the first horizontal loop of the sequence between blocks.

❻ LOOSE LADDER STITCH
A gap is left between two pieces of knitted fabric that are ladder-stitched

together. This produces a very flexible seam that looks good on tight-fitting projects.

Smocking

Smocking is worked on a grid that can be made up of either beads, rib or carefully counted st st. The embroidery links points on this grid and can add texture and color, especially when stitches are mixed together in broad bands.

However, sometimes the best bit of a smocked design is where the fabric falls free of the stitching and flows in soft gathers. To create these soft gathers and prevent the smocked area from becoming too stiff, use a looser gauge (tension) and finer yarns than you might usually do – unless of course you want an upholstery-weight fabric.

TECHNIQUES: Satin stitch ◆ page 99 • French knots ◆ page 97 • Ladder stitch ◆ page 99 • Running stitch and back stitch ◆ page 96 • Smocking ◆ page 100

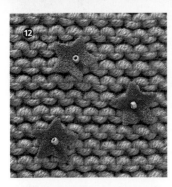

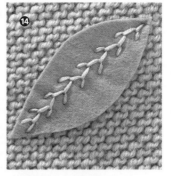

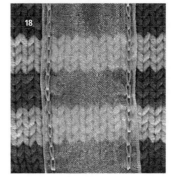

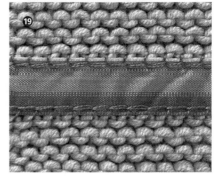

❼ HONEYCOMB STITCH

This swatch is worked on rib with a short repeat to create soft gathers. A denser fabric with pronounced pleats is formed if the pattern is worked over a larger repeat. The honeycomb stitch is worked on a k1, p2 rib in a yarn color used on subsequent rows as part of the knitted rib fabric.

❽ SURFACE HONEYCOMB

The width of the knitted fabric is reduced by the embroidery and soft pockets of excess fabric are created in the diamond shapes. On this swatch long strands of surface honeycomb are worked on k1, p3 rib.

❾ GATHERED BEADS

Using the slip stitch technique↓, place a bead every sixth stitch and every sixth row on the knitted fabric. Then, using strong sewing cotton and a needle, thread the needle through a group of four beads in a clockwise direction. Pass the needle through the beads again and secure the ends on the wrong side.

Close beaded fabric will hold the beads more securely, but you loose the long strands of yarn radiating out from the beads.

❿ BEADED OUTLINE STITCH

If the distances between beads are not too great, then beads can be used instead of folds in the fabric or knit stitches in rib to grid a pattern

On st st use the close beading technique↓, to place a bead every

third stitch and alternate row on the knitted fabric. Then use strong sewing cotton and a needle to sew a row of running stitches between the rows of beads. Secure one end and gather the knitted fabric up to the required width. This makes it easier to embroider the beads, as they are held firmly in position by the lines of running stitch.

Use embroidery threads and outline stitch to gather the beads, and the knitted fabric decoratively. Finally, remove the running stitches.

⓫ BEADED VANDYKE STITCH

The strands of smocking stitches offer an opportunity for embroidery, and this technique can also be used with surface honeycomb stitch.

Before each small horizontal stitch add one large bead, and before each long stitch strand add sufficient beads to cover the thread.

Adding more beads onto each strand than is required to cover the distance will make it stand proud of the fabric and add more texture.

Appliqué

Applying shapes in other materials to a knitted fabric is a quick and simple way to add color and interest to a project. Try as many different materials as you can find, though bear in mind the restrictions to laundering and elasticity that appliqué↓ can bring.

⓬ STARS

Punched out of suedette fabric with a hobby punch, these stars are attached to a knitted fabric with a single bead stitched on in the center. If each star is attached separately, the fabric's elasticity is not compromised.

⓭ FLOWERS

In the same way as the stars, these flowers are punched out of felt. A stitched-on button not only attaches a flower, it also gives it a center. Here, the flowers are positioned on the edge of knitted fabric to create a cheerful border.

⓮ LEAF

Embroidery stitches can enhance the design of an appliquéd shape. This leaf is cut out of felt and the central line of feather stitch↓ indicates the veins, as well as attaching it to the knitted fabric.

⓯ HEART

This leather heart is quite stiff, so a single central line of linked back stitch↓ will hold it in place without the sides drooping.

⓰ FRAYED FABRIC

The fraying qualities of some fabrics can be exploited to good effect in appliqué, if the project will not be subject to much wear-and-tear. Here, a rectangle of cotton is frayed on each side and running-stitched to a knitted fabric to create a vintage, patched effect.

⓱ KNIT ON KNIT

Knitted shapes are ideal for appliqué as they do not fray and

can, if necessary, be worked in a yarn that has exactly the same washing requirements as the background fabric.

For this swatch a geometric shape in mohair yarn is sewn on to a background of thicker cotton yarn using the mohair yarn and tiny oversewing stitches.

Knitted shapes can also be appliquéd onto ordinary fabric with great results. The shapes can be purely decorative or have a practical aspect, such as a knitted square to make a pocket. Decorative embroidery stitches or more discreet machine stitching can be used to attach the shapes.

⓲ ORGANZA RIBBON

Translucent ribbon allows a knitted fabric below to show through. In this swatch a length of pale blue ribbon is sewn on at right angles to the stripes of a knitted fabric with tiny chain stitches↓. Stitching ribbon over part of an intarsia design can also be very effective.

⓳ VARIEGATED RIBBON

Ribbons are available in a vast rage of colors, patterns, widths and fabrics. This pretty variegated pink ribbon is blanket stitched↓ to cotton knitted fabric, and the result would make a charming project for a baby.

TECHNIQUES: Slip stitch beading ⬧ page 68 • Close beading ⬧ page 69 • Appliqué ⬧ page 101 • Feather stitch ⬧ page 98
Running stitch and back stitch ⬧ page 96 • Chain stitch ⬧ page 98 • Blanket stitch ⬧ page 98

Crazy patchwork cushion

Although this is quite a complex intarsia design, it is a good project to choose if you have problems making neat color joins, as the embroidery will hide any baggy stitches beautifully.

Size

17¾ x 13¾in (45 x 35cm)

Materials

Rowan wool cotton 1¾oz (50g) balls

Pale green A	1	
Pale blue B	1	
Lilac C	1	
Purple D	1	
Red E	1	
Dark pink F	2	

1 pair each of US 5 (3.75mm) and
    US 4 (3.5mm) needles
Cable needle

Size 6 beads ⅓oz (9g) pack
    iridescent purple   1 (124 beads)

Tapestry needle
Selection of embroidery threads
Knitter's sewing needle
Two buttons
17¾ x 13¾in (45 x 35cm)
    cushion pad

Gauge (Tension)

25 stitches and 33 rows to 4in (10cm) measured over st st using US 5 (3.75mm) needles.

Abbreviations

C4F = cable 4 forward.
C4B = cable 4 backward.
MB = make bobble. Knit twice into front and back of st, turn work, purl 1 row, turn work, slip 2 sts, k2tog, pass slipped sts over.
PB = place bead. Use the slip stitch technique.
See also page 157.

Note Use the intarsia technique to change yarn colors.

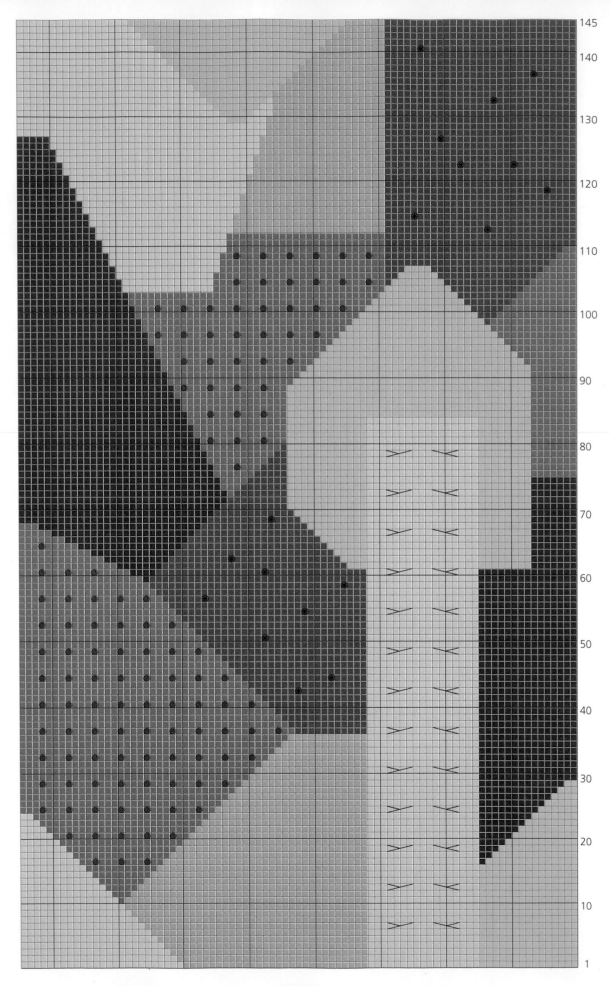

Front

Front

Using US 5 (3.75mm) needles and A, cast on 85 sts.

Work chart to row 145.

Bind (cast) off.

Buttonband panel

Using US 5 (3.75mm) needles and D, pick up 85 sts from last row of chart.

Work foll stripe patt in st st.

5 rows D.

15 rows C.

10 rows F.

9 rows C.

8 rows F.

Change to US 4 (3.5mm) needles and cont in F.

Row 48: P2, k1, (p1, k1) rep to last 2 sts, p2.

Row 49: K2, p1, (k1, p1) rep to last 2 sts, k2.

Rep rows 48–49 four more times.

Bind (cast) off.

Buttonhole panel

Using US 5 (3.75mm) needles and F, pick up 85 sts from first row of chart (not cast on row.)

Work foll stripe patt in st st.

17 rows F.

6 rows C.

6 rows D.

6 rows C.

15 rows D.

2 rows F.

5 rows D.

16 rows C.

10 rows F.

5 rows D.

Change to US 4 (3.5mm) needles and cont in D.

Row 89: K2, p1, (k1, p1) rep to last 2 sts, k2.

Row 90: P2, k1, (p1, k1) rep to last 2 sts, p2.

Rep rows 89–90 once more.

Row 93: K2, p1, (k1, p1) rep ten more times, bind (cast) off 5 sts, (k1, p1) rep eleven more times, bind (cast) off 5 sts, (k1, p1) to last 2 sts, k2.

Row 94: P2, k1, (p1, k1) rep ten more times, cast on 5 sts, (k1, p1) rep eleven more times, k1, cast on 5 sts, (k1, p1) rep to last st, p1.

Rep rows 89–90 twice more.

Bind (cast) off.

Embroidery

Weave in ends on the WS of the work. Using the embroidery silks doubled and a variety of colors, embroider over all of the intarsia joins in the cushion front. On this cushion, chain stitch, blanket stitch, feather stitch and whipped running stitch have been used, but take this opportunity to be creative and use your own favorite embroidery stitches.

Finishing

Steam the cushion with a warm iron. Do not place the iron onto the beads or they may shatter.

Using mattress stitch, sew the side seams of the buttonhole panel to the front. Sew the side seams of the buttonband panel to the front, tucking the rib buttonband under the buttonhole band and sewing it in place. Press the seams. Sew two buttons onto the buttonband to align with the buttonholes.

Key

☐ K on RS, p on WS.

 C4F

 C6B

✳ MB

● Place mauve bead

▨ Pale green A

▨ Pale blue B

▨ Lilac C

▨ Purple D

■ Red E

■ Dark pink F

TECHNIQUES: Bobbles ◆ page 10 • Cables ◆ page 12 • Slip stitch beading ◆ page 68 • Embroidery ◆ page 94

Smocked dress

Smocking is a traditional skill that can be updated and enlivened by working it in contemporary colors. This dress has a plain rib bodice that can be smocked using either the stitches given in the pattern, or any other combination of smocking and embroidery stitches.

To make this dress easier to wear, there are two buttons at the back attaching the sleeves to the bodice.

Sizes

Ages	2yrs	4yrs	6yrs
Chest	22in	24in	26in
	(56cm)	(61cm)	(66cm)
Length	20in	22in	25in
	(50cm)	(56cm)	(64cm)

Materials

Jaeger siena 4 ply cotton
1¾oz (50g) balls

Light green	5	6	7

US 2 (3mm) 32in (80cm)
    circular needle
US 2 (2.75mm) 32in (80cm)
    circular needle
US 2 (2.75mm) 15in (40cm)
    circular needle
Optional 1 pair US 2
    (2.75mm) needles
(The circular needles can be used to
    work back and forth)

3ft (1m) ¼in (6mm) ribbon
5⁄16in (8mm) buttons
    Green   2

Anchor embroidery cotton skeins

Leaf green	1
Warm pink	1
Gold	1

Embroidery needle

Gauge (Tension)

31 stitches and 42 rows to 4in (10cm) over k1, p2 st repeat using US 2 (2.75mm) needles.

Abbreviations

Sl2tog, k1, psso = slip the next 2 sts together knitwise, k1, pass the two slipped sts over.

Wrap st and turn = Wrap the working yarn in a counterclockwise direction around the next stitch, slipping it to and from the right-hand needle as required and finishing at the front or back ready to turn the work as if to continue back along the row and work the next stitch.
See also page 157.

Note Remember to pick up the wrapping loop around the stitch and work it together with the stitch either knitwise or purlwise as the stitch dictates and as they appear.

Edging

Using US 2 (3mm) circular needle and the cable method, cast on 576(608: 640) sts.
Work backwards and forwards on the circular needles.
Row 1: [K3, sl2tog, k1, psso, k3, p3, k1, p3] rep thirty-five (thirty-seven: thirty-nine) more times.
(504(532:560) sts)
Row 2: [K3, p1, k3, p7] rep thirty-five (thirty-seven:thirty-nine) more times.
Row 3: [K2, sl2tog, k1, psso, k2, p3, k1, p3] rep thirty-five (thirty-seven: thirty-nine) more times.
(432(456:480) sts)
Rows 4 and every alt row: Purl and knit stitches as pattern set.
Row 5: [K1, sl2tog, k1, psso, k1, p3, k1, p3] rep thirty-five (thirty-seven: thirty-nine) more times.
(360(380:400) sts)
Row 7: [Sl2tog, k1, psso, p3, k1, p3] rep thirty-five (thirty-seven: thirty-nine) more times. *(288(304:320) sts)*

Skirt

Change to US 2 (2.75mm) circular needle. Place marker, ensure that the sts are not twisted, and join to work in the round. The round join will become the center back.
Next round: [K1, p3] rep to the end of the round.
Cont until work measures 8¼in(9in:10½in), (21cm(23cm:26.5cm)) from cast on edge.
Dec round: [K1, p2, sl2tog, k1, psso, p2] rep to the end of the row.
(216(228:240) sts)
Next round: [K1, p2] rep to the end of the round.
Cont until work measures 9¼in(10¼in:12in), (23.5cm(26cm:30cm)) from cast on edge.
Dec round: [K1, p1, sl2tog, k1, psso, p1] rep to the end of the row.
(144(152:160) sts)
Next round: [K1, p1] rep to the end of the round.
Cont until work measures 11in(12in:14in), (28cm(30cm:35.5cm)) from cast on edge.

Bodice

Purl the next 2 rounds.

First size eyelet round: K2, (yo, k2tog, k3) rep ten more times, yo, k2tog, k23, (yo, k2tog, k3) rep eleven more times, k2. *(144 sts)*

Second size eyelet round: K2, (yo, k2tog, k3) rep ten more times, yo, (k2tog) rep once more k25, k2tog, (yo, k2tog, k3) rep eleven more times, k2. *(150 sts)*

Third size eyelet round: K2, (yo, k2tog, k3) rep eleven more times, yo, k2tog, M1, k29, M1 (yo, k2tog, k3) rep twelve more times, k2. *(162 sts)*

Next round: Knit.

Purl the next 2 rounds.

Next round: (P2, k1) rep to the end of the round.

Cont until work measures 16in(17½in:20½in), (40.5cm(44.5cm: 52cm)) from cast on edge.

Next round (buttonhole): K24(25:27), bind (cast) off 3 sts, k90(94:102) bind (cast) off 3 sts, k24(25:27).

Next round: K24(25:27), cast on 3 sts to complete buttonhole, k90(94:102), cast on 3 sts to complete buttonhole, k24(25:27).

Cont until work measures 18in(18½in:21½in), (45.5cm (47cm:55cm)) from cast on edge.

Picot bind (cast) off round: Bind (cast) off 2 sts purlwise, (cast on 2 sts, bind (cast) off 4 sts foll set patt) rep to the end of the round.

Sleeve (make two)

Using either US 2 (2.75mm) and the cable method, cast on 107(135:135) sts.

Edging

Row 1: (K3, sl2tog, k1, psso, k3, p2, k1, p2) rep six (eight: eight) more times, k3, sl2tog, k1, psso, k3.

((91(115:115) sts)

Row 2: [P7, k2, p1, k2] rep six (eight: eight) more times, p7.

Row 3: [K2, sl2tog, k1, psso, k2, p2, k1, p2] rep six (eight:eight) more times, k2, sl2tog, k1, psso, k2. *(75(95:95) sts)*

Row 4 and every alt row: Purl and knit sts as patt set.

Row 5: [K1, sl2tog, k1, psso, k1, p2, k1, p2] rep six (eight:eight) more times, k1, sl2tog, k1, psso, k1. *(59(75:75) sts)*

Row 7: [Sl2tog, k1, psso, p2, k1, p2] rep six (eight:eight) more times, sl2tog, k1, psso. *(43(55:55) sts)*

Row 9: [K1, p2, k1, p2] rep six (eight: eight) more times, k1.

Row 10–12: Work as patt set.

Shoulder shaping

Row 13: Work 34(46: 46) sts as patt set, wrap st and turn.

Row 14: Sl1, work 24(36:36) sts as patt set, wrap st and turn.

Row 15: Work 22(34:34) sts as patt set, wrap st and turn.

Row 16: Sl1, work 17(30:30) sts as patt set, wrap st and turn.

Row 17: Work 16(28:28) sts as patt set, wrap st and turn.

Row 18: Sl1, work 12(24:24) sts as patt set, wrap st and turn.

Row 19: Work 10(22:22) sts as patt set, wrap st and turn.

Row 20: Sl1, work 6(18;18) sts as patt set, wrap st and turn.

Row 21: Work 4(16:16) sts as patt set, wrap st and turn.

Larger two sizes only

Row 22: Sl1, work 12 sts as patt set, wrap st and turn.

Row 23: Work 10 sts as patt set, wrap st and turn.

Row 24: Sl1, work 6 sts as patt set,

Smocked panel

Use the smocking stitches shown here or devise your own pattern.

❶ FRENCH KNOTS

French knots worked in leaf green with gold linking stitches.

❷ SURFACE HONEYCOMB AND FRENCH KNOTS

Honeycomb worked in gold with pink French knots in the center of the diamonds.

❸ OUTLINE STITCH

Worked in warm pink towards the top and leaf green at the bottom of the panel.

❹ VANDYKE STITCH, FRENCH KNOTS AND LONG STITCHES

Vandyke stitch worked in pink with leaf green French knots. The center diamonds have diagonal stitches in leaf green and gold French knots in the center.

❺ OUTLINE STITCH

Worked in leaf green.

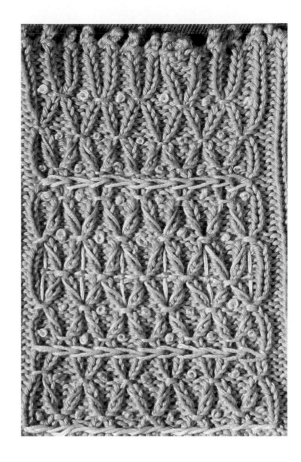

wrap st and turn.

Row 25: Work 4 sts as patt set, wrap st and turn.

All sizes

Next row: Sl1, work sts as patt set, now after each p st, k stitch-wrap and st together, rep four(six: six) times, work 8 sts in patt set.

Next row: Work 19(25: 25) sts as patt set, now after each k st, p stitch-wrap and st together, rep five(seven: seven) times, work 8 sts in patt set.

Next row: Purl. *(43(55:55) sts)*

Next row: Knit.

Cont in st st for 9 rows.

Next row: [K1, p1] rep to last st, k1.

Next row: [P1, k1] rep to last st, p1.

Rep the last 2 rows once more.

Bind (cast) off in rib.

Finishing

Press the edgings carefully, but avoid pressing the rib.

Using basting thread and starting and ending with a knit stitch, mark out vertically the center 31(33:37) sts to be smocked.

Then mark the 3rd row from the bodice and every subsequent 5th row. Using the chart as reference, smock the panel as indicated.

Attach the button to just inside the selvedge of each sleeve.

Slip stitch the sleeves in place 1 row down behind the picot bind (cast) off at the front of the bodice, so the decorative frill is to the outside.

Thread the ribbon through the eyelets, bringing the ends out to tie at the center front.

TECHNIQUES: Smocking ♦ page 100 • French knots ♦ page 97 • Short row shaping ♦ page 18 • Picot bind (cast) off ♦ page 128

Embroidered baby blanket

Combining three-dimensional pintucks and quick-to-work st st, this baby blanket will grow quite quickly on your needles. Once knitted, it is the ideal project for perfecting duplicate stitch, though if you prefer, the design can be worked in cross stitch, working one cross stitch over one stitch of the knitted fabric.

Size
27½ x 26in (70 x 66cm)

Materials
Rowan wool cotton 1¾oz (50g) balls

Green A	7
Dark pink B	1
Lilac C	1

1 pair of US 5 (3.75mm) needles

2 safety pins
Stitch holder
Knitter's sewing needle

Gauge (Tension)
25 stitches and 33 rows to 4in (10cm) measured over st st using US 5 (3.75mm) needles.

Abbreviations
See page 157.

To make
Using the thumb method and A, cast on 161 sts.

Work 14 rows in k1, p1 seed (moss) stitch.

Row 15 (RS): (K1, p1) rep four more times, M1L, inc, k139, inc, M1R, (p1, k1) rep four more times. *(165 sts)*

Row 16: (K1, p1) rep four more times, k1, p143, put last 11 sts on a safety pin.

Row 17: K143, put last 11 sts on a safety pin.

Working on these 143 sts, work 38 rows in st st.

Row 56 (WS): Knit.

Starting with a k row, work 3 rows st st.

Row 60 (WS): Knit.

Row 61 (RS): Knit.

Row 62: Purl.

Row 63: Work pintuck, picking up upper loops of sts of row 56.

Starting with a p row, work 6 rows st st.

Rep rows 56–69 once more.

Rep rows 56–63 once more.

Starting with a p row, work 40 rows st st, ending with row 131.

Rep rows 56–131 twice more, ending with row 283. Put sts on stitch holder.

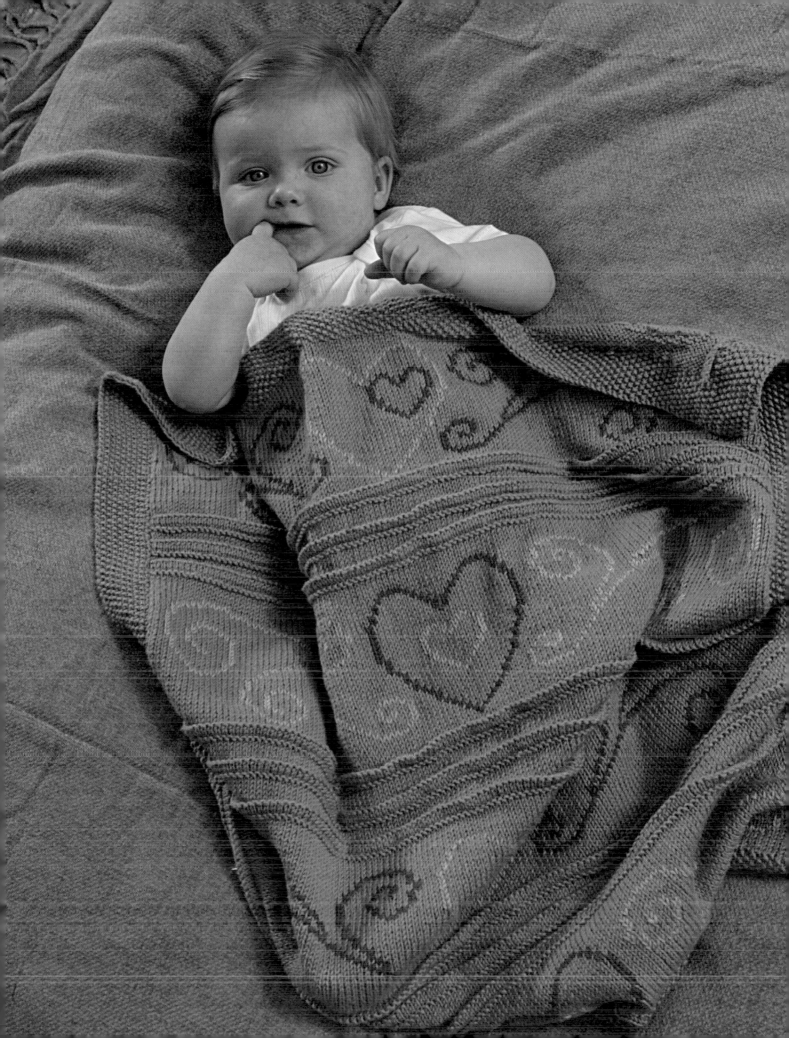

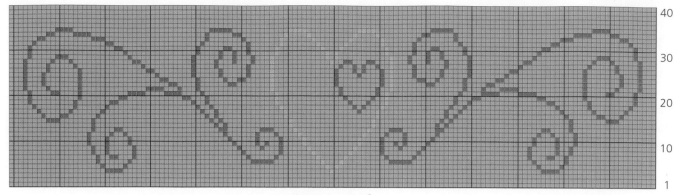

Top panel

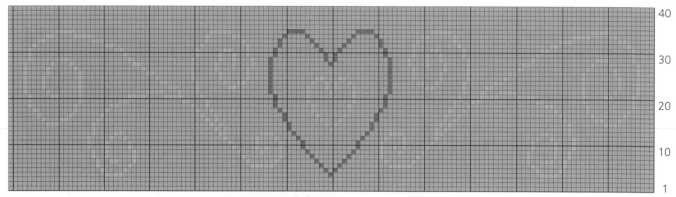

Second from top panel

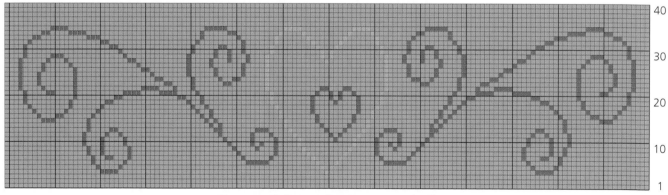

Second from bottom panel

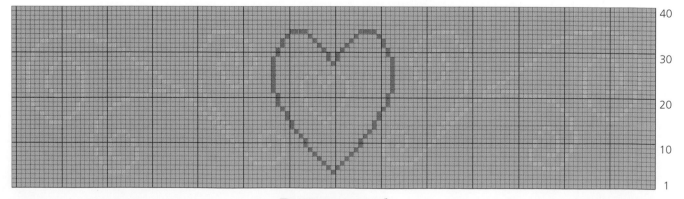

Bottom panel

Edgings

Slip the 11 sts on the left-hand side of the blanket onto a needle, starting at the outside edge. Rejoin yarn. Work in seed (moss) stitch until the band, when slightly stretched, fits along the edge of the blanket, ending with a right-side row. Put the sts onto a safety pin.

Rep on the 11 sts on the right-hand side of the blanket, ending on a wrong-side row, but do not put the sts onto a safety pin.

Next row: Seed (moss) 9 sts from band, p2tog, slip 143 sts from holder onto a needle, k2tog, seed (moss) across blanket to last 2 sts, k2tog, slip 11 sts from safety pin onto a needle, p2tog, seed (moss) to end. Keeping patt correct, work 13 rows seed (moss) stitch.

Bind (cast) off in seed (moss) stitch. Using mattress stitch and taking a 1 st seam on both the central area and the edgings, sew them together. Work carefully over the pintucks to sew them into the seam as smoothly as possible.

Key

- Green A
- Dark pink B
- Lilac C

Embroidery

Press the blanket, avoiding the pintucks. Following the charts, embroider each panel between the pintucks. Place the central bottom stitch of the large heart on the central 71st stitch of each panel (not including the stitch taken into the seam on each side), on the 4th row above the seed (moss) border and the pintuck rows; rows 19, 95, 171 and 247.

When working vertical columns of duplicate stitch, a neater, flatter finish is always obtained by starting at the bottom and working up. Therefore, embroider the hearts starting with the central bottom stitch and working up one side. When you get to the apex on one side of the heart, secure the yarn on the back of the work. Count the stitches carefully to ensure that you start in the right position and, using a new length of yarn, place the central stitch of the dip, leaving a long tail of yarn at the back. Work up one side of the dip to complete that side of the heart. Use the tail of yarn to work the other side of the dip. Then go back to the bottom and work the other side of the heart.

Work the scrolls on either side of the hearts in a similar way. Firstly, work the long diagonal line that connects all the scrolls, starting at the lower end. Then embroider the lines that branch off the long diagonal, finishing at the top of each scroll. Go to the bottom of each scroll and, leaving a long tail of yarn at the back, work up the shorter side. When you get to the top, secure the yarn on the back and use a new length to work the innermost part of the scroll, starting at the bottom. Go back to the

long tail of yarn and work the other side of the scroll. This method does involve careful counting of stitches to ensure that you start the embroidery in the right place each time, but it will produce a neater result.

Finishing

Press the embroidered blanket, avoiding the pintucks.

TECHNIQUES: Duplicate stitch ♦ page 97

Vintage laundry bag

Shaker colors, traditional motifs and a little faux darning are topped off with a delicate picot edge to create a vintage-style laundry bag. Made from washable cotton, it's roomy enough to hold laundry for a weekend away, making it practical as well as pretty.

Size
15 x 12in (38 x 30cm)

Materials
Rowan cotton glacé 1¾oz (50g) balls
   Pale blue   4

Rowan kidsilk haze 1oz (25g) balls
   Pale blue   small amount

24in (60cm) US 3 (3.25mm)
   circular needle

Tapestry needle
1 skein each of dark and light brown
   and 2 skeins of mid-brown
   embroidery thread
Knitter's sewing needle

Gauge (Tension)
25 stitches and 36 rows to 4in (10cm) measured over st st using US 3 (3.25mm) needles.

Abbreviations
See page 157.

To make
Using the thumb method, cast on 144 sts.
Place a marker.
Work 23 rounds in k1, p1 seed (moss) stitch.
Round 24: K72, make a cluster of 5 loops wrapped around two fingers, k71.
Round 25: Knit.
Round 26: K10, M1, k33, M1, k20, M1, k40, M1, k25, M1, k16. (*149 sts*)
Knit 23 rounds.
Round 50: K44, drop next st, k104.
Knit 10 rounds.
Round 61: K105, drop next st, k42.
Knit 12 rounds.
Round 74: K10, drop next st, k136.
Knit 16 rounds.
Round 91: K129, drop next st, k16.
Knit 14 rounds.
Round 106: K63, drop next st, k81. (*144 sts*)
Knit 11 rounds.
Work 23 rounds in seed (moss) stitch.
Round 141: [Seed (moss) 10 sts, yo, k2tog] rep eleven more times.
Keeping seed (moss) patt correct, work 9 rounds.
Picot bind (cast) off round: [Bind (cast) off 2 sts in seed (moss) stitch, cast on 3 sts, bind (cast) off 3 sts] rep forty-seven more times.

TECHNIQUES: Loop clusters ♦ page 13 • Ladders ♦ page 24 • Picot bind (cast) off ♦ page 128

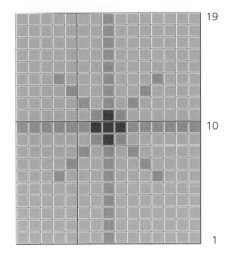

19

10

1

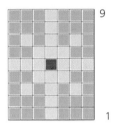

9

1

Key

■ Pale blue yarn

■ Mid-brown

■ Dark brown

□ Light brown

Embroidery

Weave in the loose ends on the WS of the work.

Press the knitting, folding it so that the cluster of loops is on one edge of the bag.

Using kidsilk haze and the tapestry needle, faux darn the ladders. As you work, use the point of the tapestry needle to push the rows of darning right up against the edge of the ladder or the previous rows of darning, so that the ladder is completely filled with darning. Ensure that you darn into the stitches at the very ends of the ladders for a neat, firm finish.

Embroider the charted stars using cross stitch, working one cross stitch over one stitch of the knitted fabric. Position the stars randomly on the bag, using the main photograph as a guide if you wish. Avoid embroidering the edge stitch of the ladders or the top and bottom bands of seed (moss) stitch.

Finishing

Press the bag. Using mattress stitch, join the bottom edge.

Cut 4 lengths of yarn, each 1 yard (1m) long and make a twisted cord. Thread the cord through the eyelets in the top of the bag, then knot the two ends together. Cut the cord 1¼in (3cm) below the knot and unravel the ends to make a tiny tassel.

TECHNIQUES: Faux darning ◗ page 104 • Cross stitch ◗ page 97 • Trimmings ◗ page 132

edgings and trimmings

ALL TOO OFTEN THE DESIGN FEATURES OF A knitted item are concentrated on the main areas of knitted fabric, and the edges are ignored. This really is wasting a great design opportunity, and the chance to give your knitwear real designer flair.

There are quite a number of different cast ons and bind (cast) offs, some of which will make just a subtle difference. Others will make such a strong statement that you may not need any further embellishment. So don't just use what you are familiar with – experiment.

Similarly, trimmings are too often overlooked, and yet can provide all the design appeal you need. A trimming can also be a perfect finishing touch to a simple or an intricate knitted project. From the most simple, such as a fringe on a plain scarf, to a wild and wooly band of knitted in tails, trimmings are great tools in any knitter's repertoire.

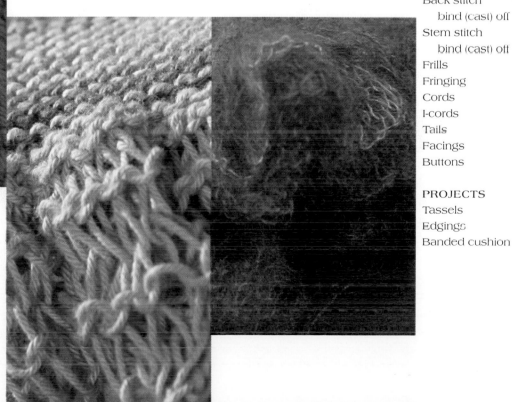

Edgings and trimmings
TECHNIQUES

Beginnings

Good beginnings make for happy edgings. Choosing the right cast on can greatly influence the look of a final project. The two basic cast ons that most of us use are the thumb cast on, with its subtle edge and elasticity, and the cable cast on, with its decorative qualities and strength.

However, there are a wealth of other possibilities which will add interest to your project, or just give a different twist to a pattern that you love and knit again and again. How many times does the same baby jacket pattern come out for friends and family?

Edgings can either grow from the cast on, be sewn on later or knitted on later. Experiment with a few edgings on swatches, considering carefully the project's final use and the practicalities of day-to-day wear and tear. The edging can be as subtle as a picot that grows from a practical rib, or it can be an elaborate lace design that will be finalized when there is a chance to view the project as a whole.

Rib is unbeatable as a way to give an edge grip and to create a smooth line from a wrist to a sleeve, but the depth, stitch repeat and style of the rib can be varied. The rolled edge of st st can be emphasized by a tight cast on worked with a smaller pair of needles, or it can be reduced by using the tubular cast on. If a motif is being worked, using occasional purl stitches above knit stitches of the same color will balance the twist of these stitches.

While you are thinking about the stitch technique, be sure not to forget the use of color. A contrasting edge will draw the eye, and colorful buttonhole facings can make you look leaner. However, a bright hip-level hem can add pounds to your appearance.

A good place for fancy edgings is where they will be seen. With garments the focus is usually on the person and their face, but with small children their faces are comparatively close to the hems of their garments, so those, too, can benefit from decoration. Do remember that very lacy patterns can be hazardous for little children's fingers.

PICOT CAST ON

Picot cast on is a series of tails created by casting on a number of stitches and then immediately binding (casting) some or all of them off again. The number of stitches, the number of cast on stitches between the tails and the tension of the picot edge can be varied to create different effects. A tight cast on and loose bind (cast) off on longer tails will give them a twist. Experiment using different needle sizes and gauges (tensions).

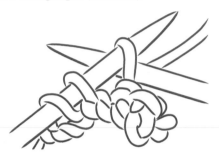

1 If there is to be a seam, then cast on a selvedge stitch. *Cast on three stitches, bind (cast) off three stitches, cast on three stitches then repeat from * until the number of stitches on the left-hand needle is the number required, remembering to add a selvedge stitch for the seam at the end. The number of stitches between each tail can be varied so that the row ends with only one selvedge stitch to make up the desired total of stitches.

INVISIBLE CAST ON

For those of us who don't like to commit too early and may have several ideas in mind for a final edging, this cast on leaves all your options open. It creates a temporary edge that can be unpicked to produce loops that can then be worked in the other direction from the knitted fabric.

This technique can be used to create a perfect rib bound (cast) off edge that matches the one at the neck, or to attach a decorative lace edge that is worked from a straight edge down, or to graft on an edging that has been worked horizontally. It can also be used to add a heavy beaded edging, and so reduce the distortion and strain on the yarn the weight of beads can cause while knitting.

However, it is important to allow sufficient depth for the edging and to calculate this into the depth worked before any shaping. Underestimate rather than overestimate what the depth might be; a few rows of a contrast stitch pattern such as seed (moss) stitch can be added before the edging design. Do not try to continue any pattern above the cast on as there will not be an invisible transition.

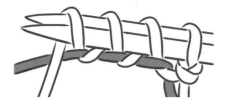

1 This method uses a length of waste yarn in a contrasting color to the working yarn. Holding two needles together, place a slip knot of the working yarn onto the needles. *Wrap the working yarn anti-clockwise around the needles, securing the waste yarn between the needles and the working yarn. Bring the working yarn down, in front of the waste yarn and right around it. Repeat from * until the desired number of stitches have been created. One larger needle can be used, rather than two, but it should be double the width of a needle size you intend using; it helps to create larger loops that are easier to pick up later on.

Using a third needle, work the stitches on the needles as usual for the first row, then work using two needles. When you are ready to work in the opposite direction, unpick the waste yarn carefully from the last stitch back to the first one, picking up the loops on a needle. When working the first row, ensure that no loops are twisted.

THUMB INVISIBLE CAST ON

For all those that have mastered the thumb method, this is an easy invisible cast on technique. A length of waste yarn in a contrasting color is used instead of the tail of the working yarn. On a needle twice as thick as the one you intend using for the subsequent rows, place slip knot of a length of waste yarn and then a slip knot of the working yarn. Cast on using the thumb method, but using the waste yarn instead of the tail of the working yarn; the loops on the needle will be in the working yarn. Cast on the required number of stitches, not counting the waste yarn slip knot. Work the next row using the correct needle size and when the waste yarn slip knot is reached, just drop it off the left-hand needle.

When you are ready to work in the other direction, unpick the waste yarn, starting at the end without the slip knot, and put the loops onto a needle. You may need to carefully cut the waste yarn every now and again. Check that no stitches are twisted and work the loops as normal.

CROCHET INVISIBLE CAST ON

This uses a foundation chain of crochet in a waste yarn as a base for a cast on. Chain a few stitches more than those required in the cast on. Using the working yarn, pick up one stitch through the back loop of each chain stitch. The front has the appearance of embroidered chain stitch. To unpick, pull on the loose thread of the foundation chain with the few extra stitches and the stitches will unravel.

TUBULAR CAST ON

Tubular cast on is a pintuck on the cast on edge. It uses waste yarn to support the first few rows of knitting, which will then appear on the wrong side of the work. The nature of this cast on creates a perfect knit one, purl one foundation row that will show if another stitch pattern is used and the edge is examined closely. However, it is strong and creates an edge similar to that found on many bought garments.

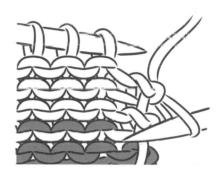

1 Cast on half the number of stitches you require using waste yarn in a contrasting color, plus one stitch to create an even number if necessary. Starting with a purl row, work two rows in st st in the waste yarn, then four rows of st st in the working yarn. On the next row, *purl one stitch and, using the right-hand needle, pick up one loop from the first row of the working yarn. Slip the loop onto the left-hand needle and knit it.

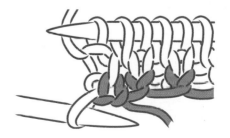

2 Repeat from * to the end of the row. Work a few rows of knit one, purl one rib, or another stitch pattern, and then unpick the waste yarn from the working yarn.

Endings

The bind (cast) off is always very exciting and we often, unwisely, work late into the night to reach that point and be able to release the work from the needles. In case, it has not been made clear, do not do this: take your time, enjoy your knitting and whatever you do, check over the work the night before binding (casting) it off.

The most common bind (cast) off is the knit two, pass the first stitch over technique. This works well and produces a strong decorative edge. To perform the same process in a slightly quicker way, use a crochet hook instead of the right-hand needle and use it to loop the last stitch through the first one, instead of passing the first over the last one.

However, if the bind (cast) off is not to be part of a seam, then consider working it, and maybe a few rows before it, in a different color. Alternatively, there are several other methods that can be employed, each with their own decorative qualities.

PICOT BIND (CAST) OFF

Picot bind (cast) off is the casting on and then binding (casting) off of tails along a bound (cast) off edge. The number of stitches cast on will vary the length of the tails. Long, droopy tails do not always look good in a single row, but can look better if the frequency of tails is increased. In order to bind (cast) off the row, more stitches need to be bound (cast) off than cast on in each repeat.

Pretty and durable, this edging is perfect for any edge you want to make a fuss of: try it on bags, necklines and on trims around afghans and cushions.

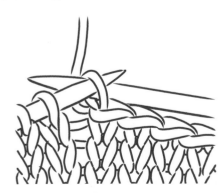

1 If there is to be a seam, bind (cast) off a selvedge stitch. Bind (cast) off to the first tail by knitting two stitches and passing the first one over the last. *Slip the stitch on the right-hand needle purlwise onto left-hand needle.

2 Cast on stitches using the cable method, bind (cast) off the new stitches and then the stitches to the next tail. Repeat from * to the end of the row.

To ensure that the number of repeats ends with one selvedge stitch, deduct two stitches from the total, if there is a seam on both sides. Each tail grows from one stitch, which is cast off in addition to the stitches making up the tail, so one more stitch appears to be cast off than was cast on. Add this cast off number to the number of stitches cast off between tails to work out how many stitches to cast off from the end of one tail to the start of the next.

TUBULAR BIND (CAST) OFF

Tubular bind (cast) off is where a pintuck is made with the last few rows to create a rolled edge. It stiffens and strengthens the edge, but it can be a bit inflexible for snug necklines and does affect the drape of the fabric. If the last few rows are worked in a different color, then not only is it easier to pick up the loops, but stylish detail is added to the top of bags or pockets.

The depth of the tuck can be varied, but do allow for it in your measurements before binding (casting) off. For added definition, thread a cord through the pintuck, cutting the ends slightly short so they remain hidden.

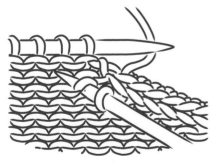

1 Work two extra rows for a two-row pintuck, ending with a purl row. *Purl one stitch and, using the right-hand needle, pick up the aligning upper stitch loop from the row two rows down. Slip the loop onto the left-hand needle and work it together with the next stitch. Repeat from * to the end of the row.

I-CORD BIND (CAST) OFF

An I-cord bind (cast) off is a series of extra stitches knitted as an I-cord along an edge, binding (casting) off the edge stitches as it goes. The effect is of a French knitting cord attached to an edge. It can be worked in a contrasting color and can be used to maintain the width of stitch patterns that are likely to shrink across a row when bound (cast) off. Like all I-cords, this bind (cast) off can be beaded and striped to create different textures, and the number of extra stitches can be varied.

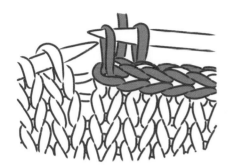

1 Using the thumb loop cast on, add extra stitches to the left-hand needle holding the stitches to be bound (cast) off. *Knit the first stitch through the back of the loop and then knit the extra stitches, minus one. This stitch is knitted together through the backs of the loops with the first of the original stitches to be bound (cast) off. Slip all the stitches on the right-hand needle back onto the left-hand needle. Repeat from * to the end of the row, pulling the the yarn tight after the first stitch of each repeat to close the I-cord. When no more of the original stitches remain, either knit all the remaining stitches together through the backs of the loops, or, if there are too many stitches, knit two together through the backs of the loops twice and pass the first stitch on the right-hand needle over the last stitch on the right-hand needle. Continue to bind (cast) off in this way until no more stitches remain.

BACK STITCH BIND (CAST) OFF

Back stitch bind (cast) off is an edge based on the back stitch used in sewing and embroidery. This method is quick and can be used as a temporary bind (cast) off, or to create a very subtle and flat edge that is not obviously bound (cast) off, or as a base for a beaded edge.

Back stitch bind (cast) off is also useful because it forces stitch patterns with a tendency to shrink across the width to hold their shape, and it can act as a useful blocking guide, for instance on some laces and rib. On rib,

the effect can be to create a funnel shape. On lace shawls, if it is worked loosely, it creates a softer edge that will drape in a similar way to the lace fabric.

1 Thread a knitter's sewing needle with a length of yarn five times the width of the edge to be bound (cast) off; the working yarn from the last knitted stitch can be used. *Insert the needle into the first two stitches on the left-hand knitting needle purlwise and pull through: if not using the working yarn, leave a tail to be sewn in later. Insert the needle into the first stitch again knitwise, drop the stitch off the left-hand knitting needle, and pull the yarn tight. Repeat from * to the end of the row, then sew in the ends.

STEM STITCH BIND (CAST) OFF

Stem stitch bind (cast) off is sewn edging with more decorative qualities than back stitch bind (cast) off, but with all the other advantages. It is also an edge along which stitches can easily be picked up, and it is less bulky and stiff than the usual knit two, pass the first stitch over bind (cast) off. Experiment with contrasting thread weights and colors, or perhaps use two threads together.

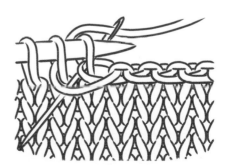

1 Thread a blunt knitter's needle with a length of yarn five times the width of the edge to be bound (cast) off. *Insert the needle into the the second stitch on the left-hand needle knitwise and then into the first stitch purlwise and under the sewn strand at the front. Pull the the yarn tight and drop the first stitch off the needle. Repeat from * to the end of the row, then sew in the ends.

KITCHENER STITCH

Kitchener stitch, or grafting, is the sewing together of two rows of stitches to create a seamless join. It can be done on any stitch pattern, but as it follows the path of knitted yarn over two rows, it can be quite difficult to work over a combination of knit and purl stitches facing one another.

This technique is often used on the shoulder seams of baby garments to reduce the bulk, but on adult garments mattress stitch adds some desirable stiffness to the seam. The other common use of Kitchener stitch is to attach an edging with stitch loops to an invisible cast on so that the reduced bulk gives a smoother seam.

1 Thread a knitter's sewing needle with a length of yarn four times the width of one of the edges to be joined. Lay the two pieces of knitted fabric to be joined in position, still on the needles. From right to left, insert the knitter's needle through the first stitch on the lower piece from back to front and repeat on the first stitch on the upper piece. *Insert the needle into the the first stitch on the lower piece again, but this time from front to back and from back to front through the second stitch on the lower piece. Drop the first stitch on the lower piece off the knitting needle.

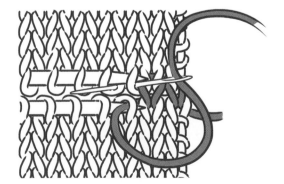

2 Insert the needle into the the first stitch on the upper piece again, but this time from front to back and from back to front through the second stitch on the upper piece. Drop the first stitch on the upper piece off the needle. Repeat from * to the end of the row. Sew in the ends.

INVISIBLE BIND (CAST) OFF

Invisible bind (cast) off is where the last two rows are worked separately and then are grafted together to create a tube on the edge of the work. If worked loosely it is a good edging for neckline rib and, as for tubular cast on, is at its most invisible when worked on knit one, purl one rib.

It is easier if, on the two rows before the bind (cast) off, the knit stitches of knit one, purl one rib are knitted, and the purl stitches slipped purlwise with the yarn in front. Therefore, each stitch is only worked once over two rows.

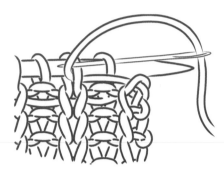

1 Thread a knitter's sewing needle with a length of yarn four times the width of the edge to be bound (cast) off. *Insert the needle into the first stitch knitwise and drop the stitch. Insert the needle into the third and then the second stitch purlwise. Drop the next stitch on the left-hand needle.

2 Bring the needle to the front between the next two stitches and insert the needle knitwise into the next stitch not sewn. Repeat from * to the end of the row.

This technique basically grafts knit stitches from the right side to the knit stitches on the wrong side using Kitchener stitch. It can be adapted for other stitch patterns, but it is easier if like stitches can be grafted together.

Invisible bind (cast) off can be made easier by slipping both sets of stitches onto double-pointed needles. Remember to go through each stitch twice and follow the route the yarn takes, using the pattern set on previous rows as a guide.

Finishing touches

Some of these techniques will be well known to any knitter, and indeed to other crafters, but try to be creative with the familiar as well as the unfamiliar and look at them in a new light.

Fringing is most commonly found in a single layer on the edge of a project, but it can be used within the main knitted fabric; for example, as a trim on a yoke. With traditional fringing the yarn and colors can be decided once a knitted fabric is complete, but with unpicked fringing they have to be chosen at the outset. Both provide an opportunity for beading and complex knotting.

TRADITIONAL FRINGING

Traditional fringing is the looping of strands of yarn through the edge stitches of knitted fabric. Waiting until the project is finished before working the fringe allows you to choose the perfect colors and strand length.

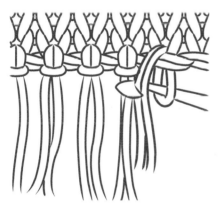

1 To make strands of an equal length, wrap yarn round a piece of card of the correct strand depth, starting and ending on the same edge. Cut the yarn along this edge of the card. Fold one or more strands in half and draw the loop through the fabric using a crochet hook. Then draw the loose ends through the loop and pull them firmly. Repeat along the edge, then trim the ends to level them.

UNPICKING STITCHES TO CREATE A FRINGE

In this technique, stitches are worked and then unravelled to create a fringe on what would usually be a side edge of a knitted fabric. It works on any stitch pattern, though with st st the last stitch in a knitted fabric can be baggy. Each stitch will produce a fringe three times its width, so work a swatch, calculate how deep the fringe needs to be and add the required number of stitches to the cast on.

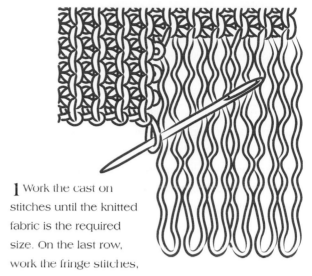

1 Work the cast on stitches until the knitted fabric is the required size. On the last row, work the fringe stitches, then bind (cast) off the remaining stitches. Remove the knitting needle from the fringe stitches and use the tip of a knitter's sewing needle to pull them loose and unravel them.

TASSELS

Tassels can add a finishing touch to home furnishings such as cushions and afghans, and are also useful on bags, hems, or hats. They look best when they hang freely.

Cut a piece of card the depth of the tassel and wide enough for the skirt bulk. Wind yarn around the card; the number of times depends on the yarn. Tassels are yarn hungry, but less of a fluffy yarn than a smooth one is needed. When the the skirt is full enough, stop winding on the same edge of the card (the bottom) as you started.

Cut a length of yarn about 8 in (20 cm) long and thread a knitter's needle. On the top edge, slide the needle between the card and skirt and tie the length of yarn tightly around the top of the skirt. Cut the loops along the bottom.

Thread the needle with 16 in (40 cm) of yarn, double it and knot the ends. Decide how deep you want the head of the tassel to be and wrap the yarn around it at this point, taking the needle through the loop formed by the knotted ends and pulling it up tight. Wrap the yarn round the skirt several times, then secure the end with a few back stitches. Cut off the needle and hide the ends of yarn in the skirt. Fluff out the skirt and trim any loose ends.

Experiment with different yarn combinations for the skirt, perhaps using two yarns from the project. For a more prominent head, insert a large bead into the head and secure the second yarn around its base. A skirt can be attached to a pom-pom head by tying the yarn securing the skirt loops around the middle of the pom-pom.

POM-POMS

Pom-poms are fluffy balls of yarn that many of us made as children. They can be attached to edges or used to create false buttons, be multicolored or one color. Fluffy yarn will make them look denser and more even textural.

Draw two circles the size you wish the pom-pom to be onto card. Then, using the same center point, draw a second smaller circle. The size of this circle will determine the density of the pom-pom and how much yarn it will need. An inner circle about a third of the size of the outer one will make an average pom-pom.

Cut out the inner and outer circles. Place them together and wrap yarn through the center hole and around the disc, working around the circle. Continue until the yarn will not pass through the center hole any more.

Using sharp scissors, cut the yarn around the edge of the pom-pom and part the two discs slightly. Tie a length of yarn 8 in (20 cm) long tightly around the center of the pom-pom, between the discs. Cut the discs off the yarn strands. Fluff up the pom-pom and trim any long ends.

TRIMMINGS

Ribbons and braids can be bought or made using some of the techniques described in previous chapters. For example, use embroidery thread and a Fair Isle pattern with a small stitch repeat to create your own brocade, or the weaving technique and silk to make a ribbon. I-cords can be used to create frog closures, to weave in and out of eyelets, or even to edge or outline a design.

To make twisted cord, take a length of yarn 60 percent longer than the required finished length, fold it in half and hook it round a secure nail or door handle. Twist the two ends in the same direction until the yarn is tightly coiled. Hold the ends together, unhook the loop and allow the yarn to coil up into a cord. Any number of yarns can be twisted together and it is worth experimenting with different yarn weights and colors.

Knitted I-cords and tails

I-cords are knitted tubes that can be applied later to a project, or knitted in as you go. Tails are two rows of knitting that hang free of the project and are worked as you go. Both can be used to create a chunkier fur texture, or a texture like a bobble but with more movement.

I-CORDS

I-cords are very similar to French knitting, but the number of stitches is variable and it is worked on double-pointed needles. It is important to have a firm gauge (tension) and to take particular care with the first stitch in each row, as they have a tendency to be baggy and reveal the join.

1 Cast on the required number of stitches using the thumb method and work one row. *Slide the stitches along the right-hand needle until they are at the right-hand end and the working yarn is on the left of the work. Stretch the yarn across the back of the work and knit the first stitch. Pull the working yarn tight and continue knitting the remaining stitches. Repeat from * until the cord is the required length.

INTEGRATED KNITTED TAIL

This tail is a series of stitches that are cast on and bound (cast) off within a row of knitting, using either the working yarn, or a yarn stranded across the back. They can be densely packed, or used as a focal point on a single row. A contrasting yarn or color is also effective.

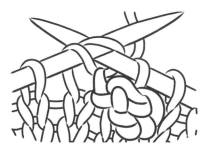

1 Knit to the position of the tail, cast on the required number of stitches onto the left-hand needle using the cable method and bind (cast) them off again. Continue along the row to the next tail.

SEPARATE KNITTED TAIL

This tail is worked separately by casting on a few stitches and then binding (casting) them off again, but not fastening off the final loop. A series of these tails can be created using ends of yarn as short as 12 in (30 cm), and stored on a spare needle by their loops. These tails can then be knitted into a fabric by working to the position of the tail, slipping the loop of the tail onto the left-hand needle and knitting it together with the next stitch.

Edgings and trimmings
SWATCH LIBRARY

The design of anything, whether it be a sweater, a car or a house, can be made or broken by the detailing. A neat finish that complements the item as a whole, and creative use of trimming can turn the simplest project into a stylish statement.

All cast ons or bind (cast) offs can be embellished in one way or another. From simply working them in a contrast color or yarn texture, to adding beads, cords or patterns, there is a huge range of possibilities, which should be given as much consideration as any other design feature you are using in the project.

Equally, trimmings – whether they be fringe, buttons added to a finished item, or knitted in elements – need careful planning to be successful.

❶ THUMB CAST ON METHOD
This cast on produces an elastic edge that resembles a row of garter stitch. Here, it is used to secure a length of decorative cord to the edge of a knitted fabric.

Work thumb cast on, but before each stitch ensure that the cord is positioned over the cast on tail.

❷ ST ST EDGE
A st st edge without support will roll towards the knit stitches and the right side. This can be an attractive feature, but it makes it difficult to knit a motif close to the cast on edge. The reason for the curl is the bias of the knit and purl stitches, which are pulling the fabric in the same direction.

If occasional purl stitches are worked on the right side, they will help to counteract the bias. The purl stitches need to be positioned carefully so they do not interrupt the motif, and ideally should be worked in the background color only and into a stitch of the same color.

Picot cast on
There are several variations of picot cast on↓ here, and these are only a few of the possibilities. Remember to consider beading and contrast colors as well as altering stitch repeats and the length of picots.

❸ LIGHT PICOT EDGE
"Light", in this case, means that the picots are spaced further apart than they are on some of the other variations shown.

∗Cast on 4 sts for the space between the picots and 4 sts for the picot using the cable cast on method.
Bind (cast) off 4 sts.
Rep from ∗ until the required number of sts are on the left-hand needle.

❹ DOUBLE PICOT EDGE
Two picots are worked at every picot position. This also creates a row of eyelets along the edge of the work, just above the picots.

Use cable cast on throughout.
Cast on 2 sts for the selvedge.
∗Cast on 4 sts for the picot.
Bind (cast) off 4 sts.
Cast on 4 sts for the picot.
Bind (cast) off 4 sts.
Cast on 1 st for the space between the picots.
Rep from ∗ until the required number of sts are on the left-hand needle.

❺ PICOT EDGE ON RIB
This picot edge is worked using the same pattern as the previous swatch. The k2, p2 rib grows very smoothly out of the picots.

❻ LONG DOUBLE PICOT EDGE
This picot is forked at the end, which gives it bulk, but this is away from the edge of the knitted fabric.

Use a cable cast on throughout.
Cast on 2 sts for the selvedge.
∗Cast on 10 sts for the picot.
Bind (cast) off 4 sts.
Cast on 4 sts for the second point.
Bind (cast) off 10 sts.
Cast on 2 sts for the space between the picots.
Rep from ∗ until the required number of sts are on the left-hand needle.

❼ TIERED PICOT EDGE
Two picot cast ons are knitted together to create a double edge.

Picot in a contrast color
Use a cable cast on throughout.
∗Cast on 6 sts.
Bind (cast) off 3 sts.
Rep from ∗ until the required number of stitches are on the left-hand needle.
Work 4 rows of st st. Leave the sts on spare needle.

Picot in the main color
Work in the main color.
Rep from ∗ until the required number of sts are on the left-hand needle.
Purl 1 row.
With the contrast color at the back and the main color at the front, ∗ k1 st from the main color together with 1 st from the contrast color.
Rep from ∗ to the end of the row.

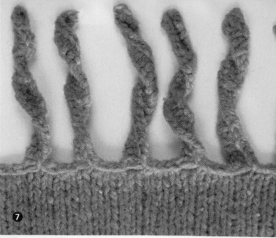

and then bound (cast) off tightly to make twisted tails.

❽ FLUFFY PICOT BIND (CAST) OFF

This picot bind (cast) off is quite dense. Increasing the number of stitches bound (cast) off from the original knitted fabric before casting on will produce a less dense finish. Try also using less thick yarn or another novelty yarn.

Using a thicker fluffy yarn, bind (cast) off sufficient stitches for the selvedge, if required.

✴ Cast on 4sts using the cable cast on method,
Bind (cast) off the 4 extra sts plus 1 st from the original knitted fabric.
Rep from ✴ leaving selvedge sts if necessary on the other edge of the knitted fabric.

I-cord bind (cast) off

This creates a lovely rolled edge with stitches at right angles to that of the knitted fabric. An I-cord bind (cast) off is very durable. Look at the I-cord ideas on page 139 for some more variations.

❾ I-CORD BIND (CAST) OFF ON RIB

This three-stitch I-cord bind (cast) off↓ is worked in a contrasting color on a k2, p2 rib. The horizontal bias of the I-cord bind (cast) off splays out the rib slightly and will create a funnel neck shape on a polo neck collar.

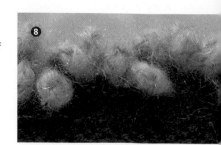

Invisible cast on

Invisible cast on↓ can also be used to create a decorative edge.

❶ FLUFFY INVISIBLE CAST ON

In this swatch a chunky-weight yarn is used as the waste yarn. The ends can be secured by weaving them into a seam or back along the reverse of the knitted fabric. Alternatively, the waste yarn can be a ribbon or threaded with beads.

Tubular cast on

This durable edge is very popular for cuffs. It is usually used with k1, p1 rib, but a k2, p2 rib can also be worked – the edge just will not be a smooth continuation of the pattern.

❷ BEADED RIB

As tubular cast on↓ works so well with k1, p1 rib, and beading between stitches↓ is a quick way to add glamour to a cuff; this pattern combines the two.

Cast on the required number of sts using the tubular cast on.
Row 1 (RS): [K1, p1] rep to the end of the row.
Row 2: [K1, p1] rep to the end of the row.
Row 3: K1, [p1, with the yarn in front, slide a bead along the yarn to the base of the right-hand needle, p1] rep to the last st, p1.
Rep rows 2–3.

❸ CLOSE BEADED RIB

This beaded rib looks more like a conventional rib with the beads↓ proud of the knitted fabric.

Cast on the required number of sts using the tubular cast on.
Row 1 (RS): K1, [p1, slide a bead along the yarn to the back of the right-hand needle, k1tbl drawing the bead through the stitch loop] rep to the last st, p1.
Row 2: K1, p1 to the end of the row.
Rep rows 1–2.

❹ SEED (MOSS) STITCH

Seed (moss) can be worked on a tubular cast on, but the rolled edge is detectable.

❺ BOBBLE RIB WITH TUBULAR CAST ON

This decorative bobble↓ rib pattern is a useful way to add extra design detail to a project.

Abbreviations

mb = knit into the front, back, front and back of the next st. [Transfer the loops onto the left-hand needle and knit] rep three times more. Transfer the sts onto the left-hand needle, k2tbl, bind (cast) off to the last 2sts, k2tog, bind (cast) off the last st.

Cast on the required number of sts using the tubular cast on method.

Row 1 (RS): [K1, p1 mb, p1] rep to the end of the row.
Rows 2–4: Cont in rib patt set.
Row 5: K1, p1 [k1, p1 mb] rep to the end of the row.
Rows 6–8: Cont in rib patt set. Rep rows 1–8.

❻ TUBULAR CAST ON ON A ST ST EDGE

A st st pattern after the cast on will roll towards the right side. The added support of a tubular cast on reduces this, particularly if it is worked on needles one size smaller than the needles used for the st st pattern. This edge has very little elasticity and the tubular cast on will be visible to the keen observer.

Here, a Fair Isle pattern is worked, which can further reduce curling if some strands are woven into the back as work progresses.

Picot bind (cast) off

Nearly all the ideas discussed for the picot cast on can also be used for a picot bind (cast) off↓.

❼ EDGE TAILS

This is a picot with a large number of stitches cast on and bound (cast) off.

✴ Bind (cast) off 4sts.
Cast on 24 sts.
Bind (cast) off 24sts.
Rep from ✴.
The 24 stitches are cast on loosely

TECHNIQUES: Invisible cast on ◈ page 126 • Tubular cast on ◈ page 127 • Beading between stitches ◈ page 69 • Close beading ◈ page 69 • Bobble ◈ page 10
Picot bind (cast) off ◈ page 128 • I-cord bind (cast) off ◈ page 129

⑩ WIDE I-CORD BIND (CAST) OFF

This I-cord bind (cast) off is worked using five extra stitches and a slightly thicker contrasting yarn on a st st fabric. Relatively small knitting needles are used, so the edge is very stiff. This reduces the curl of the selvedges of the knitted fabric. Larger needles would create an even larger I-cord that would be more flexible.

⑪ I-CORD BIND (CAST) OFF SEAM

This may seem a bit complicated when you first read it through, but it is worth trying with some yarn and the book in front of you because it is an exciting way of joining blocks of knitted fabric together. Depending on the gauge (tension), it supplies some stiffening to the seam that can be used to hold shapes flat and straight. This example is also worked in a contrasting color.

Work two blocks of knitting to the required size and leave the stitches on the needles. Hold them in your left hand with the wrong sides together.

Cast on the extra stitches onto the front needle using the thumb loop cast on method. ＊ Insert a third needle, held in the right hand, into the back of the first stitch on the front needle and the back of the first stitch on the back needle, and knit them together.

Knit until one extra stitch remains on the front needle. Knit this together with the next stitch.＊

Transfer the extra stitches onto a cable needle.

Starting with the stitch on the right of the cable needle, rep from ＊ to ＊ remembering to pull the yarn tight after each repeat.

This technique can be worked on selvedges, too, if stitches are picked up along it first.

Back stitch bind (cast) off

This sewn bind (cast) off is slightly less flexible than stem stitch bind (cast) off, but it is stronger and more discrete.

⑫ BACK STITCH BIND (CAST) OFF ON ST ST

A contrasting thread is used to bind (cast) off this edge using the back stitch bind (cast) off.

⑬ BACK STITCH BIND (CAST) OFF ON RIB

This k1, p1 rib is bound (cast) off using back stitch bind (cast) off. Note how the back stitches reinforce the edge and curl it slightly to the back.

⑭ BEADED BACK STITCH BIND (CAST) OFF

The beads on this sewn cast off edge sit slightly forward on the fabric, but adding beads to a back stitch bind (cast) off is slightly stronger than adding them to a stem stitch bind (cast) off. These beads are slightly wider than a stitch, so the fabric is stretched slightly across its width.

Use the back stitch bind (cast) off but, before inserting the needle into the first stitch knitwise, thread on a bead. Beading thread is used here for extra strength.

Stem stitch bind (cast) off

This stitch can be used in the same way as back stitch to create a temporary or permanent, flexible bind (cast) off. However, its real beauty is that the stitches are worked in two directions, which makes beading a double band very easy.

⑮ STEM STITCH BIND (CAST) OFF ST ST

A contrasting thread is used to bind (cast) off this edge using the stem stitch bind (cast) off.

⑯ STEM STITCH BIND (CAST) OFF ON RIB

This k1, p1 rib is bound (cast) off using stem stitch bind (cast) off. Note how the edge has the appearance of a cable cast on, but is still elastic.

⑰ LOOP BEADED STEM STITCH BIND (CAST) OFF

This is quite a heavy cast off edge that should be worked on a tight gauge (tension) and reinforced on the wrong side with cotton bias tape for a flat finish – unless you find the natural wavy, undulating edge part of the appeal.

The beaded loops are created by using the standard stem stitch bind (cast) off, but threading seven beads onto the thread before inserting the needle into the second stitch knitwise, or the first stitch purlwise.

Beading thread is used here for extra strength.

TECHNIQUES: Back stitch bind (cast) off ⬧ page 129 • Stem stitch bind (cast) off ⬧ page 129

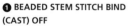

Frills

Another effective way to shape an item, frills also add a fullness that is particularly pretty. Frills can be worked in the same yarn as the main body of the item, but a toning or contrasting yarn emphasizes the feature and adds interest.

❺ FRILL CAST ON

This technique uses shaping↓ to create a pronounced but unstructured frill on the cast on edge that can work well instead of rib on loose-fitting garments.

It is shown here on garter stitch, and could be worked on st st, but not on rib or seed (moss) stitch as the stitch pattern will be disrupted.

Using the thumb method, cast on two and a half times as many stitches (this must be an even number) as are required for the main body of the knitted fabric, plus one more stitch.

Row 1 (WS): Knit.
Row 2: [k2tog] rep to last st, k1.
Row 3: Knit.

❶ BEADED STEM STITCH BIND (CAST) OFF

This swatch is worked in one color of bead, but a variety of color combinations can be used.

Use the standard stem stitch bind (cast) off, but thread a bead onto the needle before inserting it into a stitch loop.

❷ BEADED STEM STITCH BIND (CAST) OFF ON THE CAST ON EDGE

This beaded edge is created using an invisible cast on↓. Unpick the waste thread and work a few rows of seed (moss) stitch.

To make the beaded fringe, use the stem stitch bind (cast) off, but thread a pearl onto the needle before inserting it into the second stitch knitwise. Then thread seven clear beads, one larger blue bead and one pearl bead onto the thread and secure the fringe by skipping the pearl bead and threading the needle back through the other

beads, before inserting it into the first stitch purlwise.

Beading thread is used here for extra strength.

❸ INVISIBLE BIND (CAST) OFF ON RIB

The invisible bind (cast) off hides the raw edge at the back of the work. This example is worked on k2, p2 rib.

❹ INVISIBLE BIND (CAST) OFF ON MOCK CABLE RIB

This rib is an easy way to add interest to what would otherwise be a very functional edge.

Cast on using the thumb method.
* Work 4 rows of k2, p2 rib.
Next row (RS): Cross 1 st right, p2, work to the end of the row.
Rep from *.
This rib is finished with an invisible bind (cast) off, which hides the raw edge at the back of the work.

Row 4: [k1, k2tog] rep to last st, k1. Work main body of the knitted fabric as required.

❻ SINGLE FRILL

This is the most straightforward frill. Here, it is worked in double-knitting-weight cotton yarn on a background of Aran-weight wool yarn. This change in thickness and texture serves to further emphasize the frill.

Pick up 1 st between and 1 st from the center of every stitch in the background fabric, so that you have double the number of sts as in the background, minus 1.

Work the required depth of the frill in st st.

Work a border in seed (moss) stitch to prevent the edge of the frill from curling.

❼ TIERED FRILL

For an even fuller, frillier look, work one frill off the bottom of another to create tiers.

Pick up and knit the first frill in the same way as for Single Frill, but do not work the seed (moss)

TECHNIQUES: Invisible cast on ◗ page 126 • Invisible bind (cast) off ◗ page 130 • Shaping ◗ page 14

stitch edge, bind (cast) off the st st edge.

Pick up 1 st between and 1 st from the center of every stitch along the bottom edge of the frill.

Work the required depth of the second frill in st st.

Work a border in seed (moss) stitch to prevent the edge curling.

Fringing

A classic way of finishing the edge of a piece of knitting, fringing can also be applied to the main body of a piece of knitted fabric to create texture or a decorative detail.

Contrasting colored or textured yarns are a quick and easy way of adding still more interest.

❽ BEAD AND TASSEL FRINGE

The traditional fringing technique↓ is used here to make a basic fringe from chunky yarn. A bead is then threaded onto each strand of fringe and held in place by a knot below

it: the beads and knots are positioned at different heights on the strands of fringe. The yarn below each bead is unravelled for a tasseled finish.

❾ PLAITED FRINGE

This fringe is made with the traditional technique using a repeat pattern of three colored yarns. To add texture, adjacent strands, selected at random across the fringe, are plaited together and finished with a knot.

❿ STRIPED UNPICKED FRINGE

Stripes work rather well with the unpicked fringe technique↓, as they extend naturally into the fringe strands. The yarn is carried along the edge on the side of the work that will not be unravelled.

This sample is knitted in garter stitch and takes advantage of the way the yarns join to produce an intricate-looking fabric with a fringe that is five stitches deep.

A = blue
B = pink

Cast on in A.
K 3 rows in A.
K 2 rows in B.
K 4 rows in A.
Rep the last 6 rows as required.
Rep the first 3 rows.
K5 in A, bind (cast) off rem sts.
Unpick fringe.

⓫ UNPICKED FRINGE WITH EYELETS

Here, a row of yarnover↓ eyelets sits just above the fringe, which is five stitches deep. The two stitches before the yarnover are knitted together, which helps prevent the last row of stitches above the fringe from becoming baggy.

Row 1: K5, k2tog, yo, k to the end of the row.
Row 2: Purl.
Rep rows 1–2 as required.
Next row: K5, bind (cast) off rem sts.
Unpick fringe.

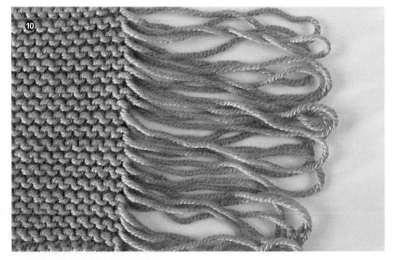

TECHNIQUES: Traditional fringing ♦ page 131 • Unpicking stitches to create a fringe ♦ page 131 • Yarnover ♦ page 15

❶ BEADED UNPICKED FRINGE
Beads not only add a decorative element to this swatch, but the weight of them helps the three-stitch fringe hang neatly, and gives it a lovely swing. The row of beads on the knitted fabric are placed using the slip stitch technique↓, while those on the fringe are just slid up to the back of a stitch.

Here, there are two beads on each loop, but you could slide one up to the back of the work on the purl rows only to give just one bead on each loop.

Abbreviations
PB = place bead using the slip stitch technique.

Row 1 (RS): K2, slide bead up to back of work, k2, PB, k to the end of the row.
Row 2: P to last 2 sts, slide bead up to back of work, p2.

Rep rows 1–2 as required.
Next row: K3, bind (cast) off rem sts.
Unpick fringe and slide beads down to sit at the bottom of the loops.

❷ EYELET FRINGE
Fringe can be attached within the body of a piece of knitted fabric, as well as at the edge. This yarnover↓ eyelet technique allows specific, individual fringes to be positioned wherever they are wanted.

On this swatch different yarns are used to show how different effects can be created.

On a knit row [knit to position of fringe, yf, k2tog] rep as required.
Next row (WS): Purl.
Next row: [Knit to position of eyelet on previous knit row, yf, k2tog] rep as required.
Complete work.
Using the traditional fringe technique, fold a bundle of yarn in

half, push the looped end from front to back through the top eyelet and then back through the bottom one. Tuck the cut ends through the loop and pull them to tighten the fringe. Do not pull them too tight or you will distort the knitted fabric.
Fringes left to right Chunky yarn; cotton yarn, mohair yarn, chunky yarn with the strands unravelled once the fringe has been made.

❸ LOOP CLUSTER FRINGE
This fringe method uses the loop clusters↓ technique to place fringe within the body of a piece of knitted fabric. The clusters are further decorated with ½in (12mm) brass plumbers' fittings that are pushed up to the top of the loops and hammered to clamp them in place.

[On a wrong-side row, work to the position of the first fringe, make a

cluster of four loops] rep as required.

The loops can be cut to make fringe, as in the three central fringes. The yarn of the loops on the left is unravelled to make a fluffy fringe, while on the right the loops are left uncut.

Cords
Cords can be created by casting on a number of stitches to match the length of the cord, and then binding (casting) them off. A small number of stitches can also be knitted in a variety of ways to create long strips and ribbon-like fabrics.

❹ SPIRAL CORD
To make this cord, cast on a number of stitches, which are then increased before they are bound (cast) off. This means the length has to be determined before casting on.

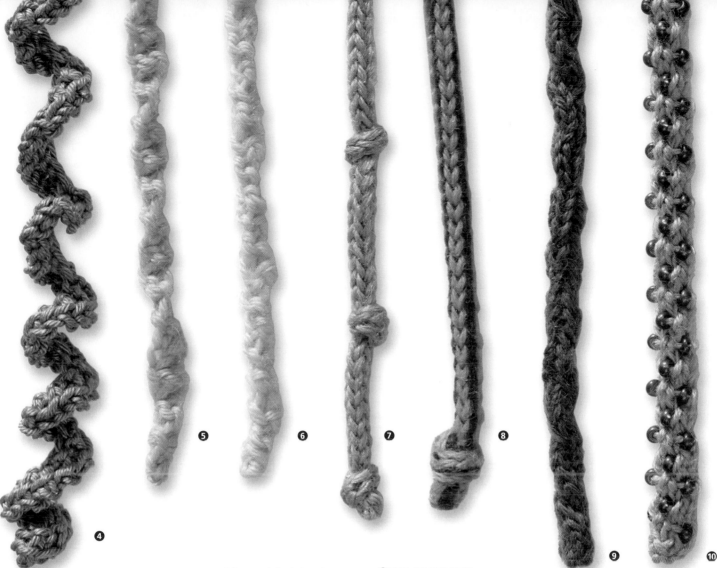

Use a gauge (tension) swatch to calculate the number of stitches to cast on for a given length and then multiply this by four. This is only a rough guide, as it will vary depending on your gauge (tension).

Use the thumb method to cast on the number of stitches required.
Row 1: Inc each st.
Bind (cast) off loosely.
For a more pronounced spiral, use a cable cast on.

I-cords

The basic I-cord technique can be adapted to create elements from bags and drawstrings to ties and edgings that will suit any project. I-cords work best with 3 to 6 cast on stitches, any more than this and the stretch between the first and last stitch tends to sag. To create a thicker, stranded cord, either twist or plait several single I-cords together. These could vary in color and technique to add extra interest.

All of the I-cords shown are knitted in double knitting yarn

❺ SINGLE STITCH TWIST KNIT I-CORD
This is very quick to knit and creates a fine, flexible cord that is perfect for drawstrings on small projects. It can also be worked in chunky yarn or a combination of yarns to make an edging.

Cast on 2sts.
Row 1: Yo, k2tog, do not turn work. Rep this row.

❻ SINGLE STITCH TWIST PURL I-CORD
Cast on 2 sts.
Row 1: Yo, p2tog, do not turn work. Rep this row.

❼ KNOTTED I-CORD
Knitting a simple I-cord and knotting the length as desired can create a very textural cord. Experiment with macramé or sailors' knots for variety.

❽ TWO-COLOR I-CORD
This is a good way to coordinate with a multicolored project and add color to a long I-cord.

Cast on 5 sts. Work the first and last stitches in the same color to link the stitches round, but the center 3 sts can be worked in any combination of colors. Here, colors A, B, A, B, A are repeated on every row to create a vertical stripe. The end of the cord is knotted.

❾ DOUBLE TWIST I-CORD
With its distinct twist, this I-cord works well in most projects, but does not lie flat unless secured as an edging or held in tension. It can be a bit fiddly to knit, but it is made a lot easier if worked using three cable needles rather than full-length double-pointed needles.

Cast on 5sts.
Row 1-3: Knit.
Row 4: K1, C4F.
Row 5: Knit.
Rep rows 4–5 as required.

❿ BEADED I-CORD
Beading stiffens an I-cord, but is perfect for bag handles and edgings that do not require flexibility. This feature can be used also to help maintain a shape or form that has a tendency to sag, such as cushion edgings or hats.

Abbreviations
PB = place bead. Use the slip stitch method.

Thread the beads onto the yarn.
Cast on 5 sts.
Rows 1-3: K3, do not turn work and rep, starting with first st on the right again.
Row 4: K2, PB, k2.
Row 5: K.
Row 6: K1, PB, k1, PB, k1.
Row: 7: K.
Rep rows 4–7.

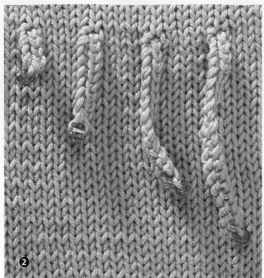

Tails

These can be knitted to any length and do not distort the gauge (tension) of the fabric, making them a useful ingredient in a knitter's collection of embellishments. If the tail is to be more than half-a-dozen stitches long, it is best to use a third needle to make it or you will stretch the background fabric.

❶ STRAIGHT AND CURLY TAILS

Depending on the tension used on the cast on and bound (cast) off rows, tails can be given a twist or made to lie flat. If the stitches are cast on loosely then bound (cast) off firmly, the tail will be curly. If the same tension is used on both rows, the tail will be straight (though you may need to press it to make it completely flat).

Left to right A straight 10-stitch tail; a curly 10-stitch tail; a curly 20-stitch tail; a straight 20-stitch tail.

❷ BEADED TAILS

A bead on the tail gives it a little weight – as well as decoration – to help it hang in place and swing gently when moved.

Thread beads onto the yarn. Cast the tail on in the usual way, then slide a bead up to the last st. Knitting the first st tightly, bind (cast) the tail off in the usual way.

Left to right A 5-stitch tail; a 10-stitch tail; a 15-stitch tail; a 20-stitch tail.

❸ ALL-OVER TAILS

This produces a highly textured fabric that keeps a good degree of flexibility. As well as the all-over pattern, this technique works well

as a band within plain knitted fabric. Here, all the tails are ten stitches long, but they can be any length you wish.

Abbreviations
MT = make tail.

Multiple of 5 sts + 6.
Starting with a k row, work 4 rows st st.
Row 5 (RS): K2, MT on 3rd st, [k4, MT on 5th st] rep to last 3 sts, k3. Work 5 rows st st.
Row 11: K5, MT on 6th st, [k4, MT on 5th st] rep to last 5 sts, k5. Work 5 rows st st.
Rep rows 5–16 as required.

❹ TWO-COLOR OR TWO-YARN TAILS

Care needs to be taken in mixing yarns↓ for this; two thick yarns will make the fabric stiff and two different colors can look untidy.

Here, a cotton yarn and toning mohair yarn produce a good result. The pattern is the same as that for All-over Tails, but the tails are made in the mohair yarn only.

Abbreviations
MT = make tail.

A = cotton yarn
B = mohair yarn

Multiple of 5 sts + 6.
Starting with a k row, work 4 rows st st in A and B.
Row 5 (RS): K2 in A and B, MT on 3rd st in A only, [k4 in A and B, MT on 5th st in A only] rep to last 3 sts, k3 in A and B. Work 5 rows st st.
Row 11: K5 in A and B, MT on 6th st in A only, [k4 in A and B, MT on 5th st in A only] rep to last 5 sts, k5 in A and B.

Work 5 rows st st in A and B.
Rep rows 5–16 as required.

❺ SEPARATE TAIL EDGING

Making small separate tails is an excellent way of using up odd lengths of yarn: each of these tails requires only 12 in (30 cm) of yarn.

Cast on 7 sts using the thumb method.
Bind (cast) off 7 sts, and draw the yarn through the last loop. Trim the ends to about the same length as the tail. Repeat and store the separate tails on a spare needle.

To make the edging. *Cast on 1 st using the cable method. Transfer one tail onto the left-hand needle. Rep from * until the combined total of cast on sts and tail loops equals the required number of sts on the needle.
Next row: Knit each stitch and loop as usual.
For a more dense tail edge, count only the cast on sts towards the required number of sts, and on the next row, knit one loop together with one cast on st through the back of the loop.

❻ CABLE TAILS

Add a little extra to a simple cable↓ pattern by incorporating tails. The tail is cast on and bound (cast) off

onto the cable needle, so you do not end up having to use four needles.

Abbreviations
CTF = cable tail forward. Slip next 3 sts onto cable needle and hold at front, k3 from the right-hand needle, cast 5 sts onto the cable needle, cast these 5 sts off knitwise, k2.
CTB = cable tail back. Slip next 3 sts onto cable needle and hold at back,

TECHNIQUES: Tails ◗ page 132 • Mixing yarns ◗ page 40 • Cables ◗ page 12

7)

8)

9)

10)

k3 from the right-hand needle, cast 5 sts onto the cable needle, cast these 5 sts off knitwise, k2.

Left Panel of 6 sts and repeat of 7 rows on a background of st st.
Row 1: Knit.
Row 2: Purl.
Rep rows 1–2 twice more.
Row 7: CTF.
Rep rows 1–7 as required.

Right Panel of 6 sts and repeat of 7 rows on a background of st st.
Row 1: Knit.
Row 2: Purl.
Rep rows 1–2 twice more.
Row 7: CTB.
Rep rows 1–7 as required.

Facings

Facings need not always be vertical edges; with a bit of shaping↓ patterns can be adapted to create a variety of shapes and textures.

All the buttonholes in this section are made by working to the position of the buttonhole, binding (casting) off the required number of stitches to fit around the button and then casting them on again on the next row using the thumb loop cast on. For a neater finish, pass the yarn between your thumb and the needle before putting the last cast on stitch on the needle.

❼ CABLE FACING

This facing is a stylish alternative to the traditional buttonhole. It can be worked on any cable↓ pattern, but less than 6 sts may make the design less distinct.

Measure the edge for the facing, calculate the distance between the buttons and divide by two. This is the distance between cables. Ensure that this distance is also big enough to accommodate a button.
Cast on 3 sts for the rev st st to the left of the cable, sts for the cable, (in this case 6 sts), and 1 st for the right selvedge.✳✳
✳ **Row 1 (RS):** K to the last 3 sts, p3.
Row 2. K3, p to the end of the row.
Rep the last two rows to the position of a cable, ending with a WS row.✳
Next row: K1, C6B, p3.
Rep from ✳ to ✳ to the position of the next cable and buttonhole.
Next row: K1, C6B, p3.
Next row: K3, p3, slip the remaining 4 sts onto a stitch holder.
Turn and continue working on these 6 sts as set by the pattern to the position of the next cable. End with a WS row and cut yarn. Slip these 6 sts to a stitch holder.
Wrong-side facing and working from the left of the stitch holder, transfer the 4 sts from the stitch holder onto a knitting needle Rejoin the yarn.
Work on these 4 sts as set by the pattern to the position of the next cable. End with a WS row.
Right-side facing and working from the left of the stitch holder, transfer the 6 sts from the stitch holder onto a knitting needle

Next row: K1, slip 3 sts onto a cable needle and hold at the back of the work, knit the next 3 sts on the left-hand needle and then the stitches from the cable needle, p3.
Rep from ✳✳ to end of facing.

❽ UNPICKED FRINGE VARIATIONS

An unpicked fringe↓ can be cut and secured in a variety of ways.

Top to bottom
The fringe can be knotted in groups of two or three strands using a slip knot close to the facing edge.

It can be beaded and then knotted, using a slip knot on groups of two or three strands.

Two cut strands can be knotted using a reef knot.

❾ GARTER STITCH RIGHT-ANGLE TRIANGLE FACING

This facing can be worked on st st, too, but the proportions of the triangle will be elongated.

Measure the edge for the facing, calculate the distance between the buttons and divide by three, in this case 14 rows. This is the distance from the buttonhole that the increasing starts at.
Cast on the number of sts required for the facing.
Work the facing to the start of the increasing.
✳**Next row (WS):** Work to the last stitch, knit into the back of the stitch, but instead of dropping the loop off the left-hand needle transfer it onto the right-hand needle.
Next row (RS): K1tbl, k to the end of the row.

Rep the last 2 rows, working a buttonhole as required, until there are an equal number of rows before and after the buttonhole. In this case there are 14 rows, ending with a WS row.
Next row: Bind (cast) off the extra stitches so that only the original facing sts remain on the left-hand needle. Knit to the end of the row. Cont in garter stitch for a third of the distance to the next buttonhole and rep from ✳.

❿ GARTER STITCH TRIANGLE

This is very similar to the Garter Stitch Right-angle Triangle Facing. However, the extra stitches are not bound (cast) off, but decreased by working two stitches together through the back of the loop at the the beginning of each row after the buttonhole has been created.

TECHNIQUES: Shaping ◗ page 14 • Cables ◗ page 12 • Unpicking stitches to create a fringe ◗ page 131

Buttons

Buttons should not be overlooked as a way of adding a note of individuality to a project. There are many decorative buttons available, but a little imagination is all that is needed to turn a plain button into a fancy one.

❶ FLOWER BUTTON

This button is quite large, although the scale and size could be reduced by using a different weight of yarn or an embroidery thread for the tassel. It may not be not the most practical of fastenings because of its limited durability, but it would add an element of fun to a project. This button is created by making a tassel↓ with yarn and attaching a button to the head of the tassel, through the center of the skirt.

❷ FLUFFY BUTTON

This button is very decorative, though not suitable for heavy wear-and-tear. Experiment with other color combinations or try using beads on the loops.
Using double thickness yarn, knit a square of looped fur↓. The square is then filled with washable filler and made into an attach-later bobble↓.

❸ BUTTON PANEL

These are just a few of the many possible ways of decorating and attaching buttons.

First row, left to right.
This wooden button is attached using individual French knots↓ of yarn worked through each of the four holes in the button.

Thread a needle and use the thread doubled. Bring the needle through the button from front to back, leaving a 1in (2.5 cm) tail at the front. Make a French knot on the back of the button, then return the needle to the front of the work. Cut the yarn.

Repeat for each hole in the button. Trim and fluff the ends.

Then, with sewing cotton, sew the knots together and bind them to the button with small stitches to the front. Secure to the fabric.

This wooden button is secured to the fabric with French knots on the front. It is important to make the knots large enough not to pass through the button's holes. If necessary use the thread doubled.

Bring the needle through the button and fabric from back to front and make a French knot. Repeat with each of the holes in the button.

Look out for decorative buttons at craft shows and in artist's workshops. This button is made from ceramic and should be removed if the project is being laundered in a washing machine.

This shell button is another craft show find. It is made from a limpet shell that has been filled with resin, into which a button shank has been pushed.

Second row, left to right.
Large buttons can be adorned with beads, as here, or other smaller buttons. Attach the button to the fabric through both fixtures.

This button is stitched to the fabric with thread in a cross pattern.

This wooden button is stitched to the fabric using two horizontal straight stitches.

This metal button is stitched to the fabric with four straight stitches, using the holes in the button to create a square.

Third row, left to right.
This heart button has a fabric rose attached to the thread that is securing it to the fabric.

This metal button is attached to the fabric and then the holes are used to string beads across its radius and around the back to the hole again. A second bead is strung between the two holes. Beading thread is used for added strength.

This vintage button is attached to the fabric and then two beads are strung between each of its four holes in a circular direction. A larger bead is placed in the center

A star bead is attached to the top of this button.

Fourth row, left to right
This clear bead has a ribbon bow tied between its two holes. Thread the ribbon through the holes and then attach the button to the fabric by passing the needle through the back of the ribbon and through the holes in the button. A bow is then tied and the ends of the ribbon are trimmed.

Two small pearl beads are threaded between each of the two holes in this pearl button.

This button is made from a large flat bead with a smaller circular bead on top to secure it.

An appliqué shape is cut from felt and the button attached to the fabric through the shape. The shape will not show when the button is closed, but it adds an element of fun the rest of the time.

Fifth row, left to right
This button is an attach-later bobble↓ knitted in variegated ribbon yarn.

Embroidery thread is used to knit this button cover in stripes of 1 row in each of light blue, glitter pink and purple, and with every third row worked in rev st st. The knitted square is wide enough to go across the diameter of the button, plus a quarter.
The square is then treated like an attach-later bobble, but a button inserted into the pocket before it is drawn tight.

A single color square is knitted using embroidery thread, as described above. A motif is duplicate-stitched onto the front.

Sixth row, left to right
A square is knitted using embroidery thread strung with beads and the beading between stitches technique↓. The technique described above is then used to turn it into a button.

A square is knitted using seed (moss) stitch and alternate rows of green and yellow embroidery thread. Use the attach-later bobble technique to turn it into a button.

A square is divided into four panels of alternate st st and rev st st using untwisted cotton yarn. The technique described above is then used to turn it into a button.

The cover for this button is made from embroidery cotton and is shaped by increasing the stitches from the center.

Cast on 4 sts using the thumb method.
Divide between four dpn and, working in the round, inc into each stitch for the first 3 rounds.
Work two rounds.
Inc into every second stitch.
Work three rounds.
Cont in this patt until the circle is wide enough to fit across the button and a quarter of the way across the back.
Cut the yarn, thread a needle with it and pass the needle through the stitches. Draw the knitting tightly around a button.
Embroider the top with a French knot and four lazy daisy stitches↓ to cover the increases.

TECHNIQUES: Tassels ◆ page 131 • Looped fur ◆ page 13 • Attach-later bobble ◆ page 11 • French knots ◆ page 97 • Beading between stitches ◆ page 69
Lazy daisy stitch ◆ page 98

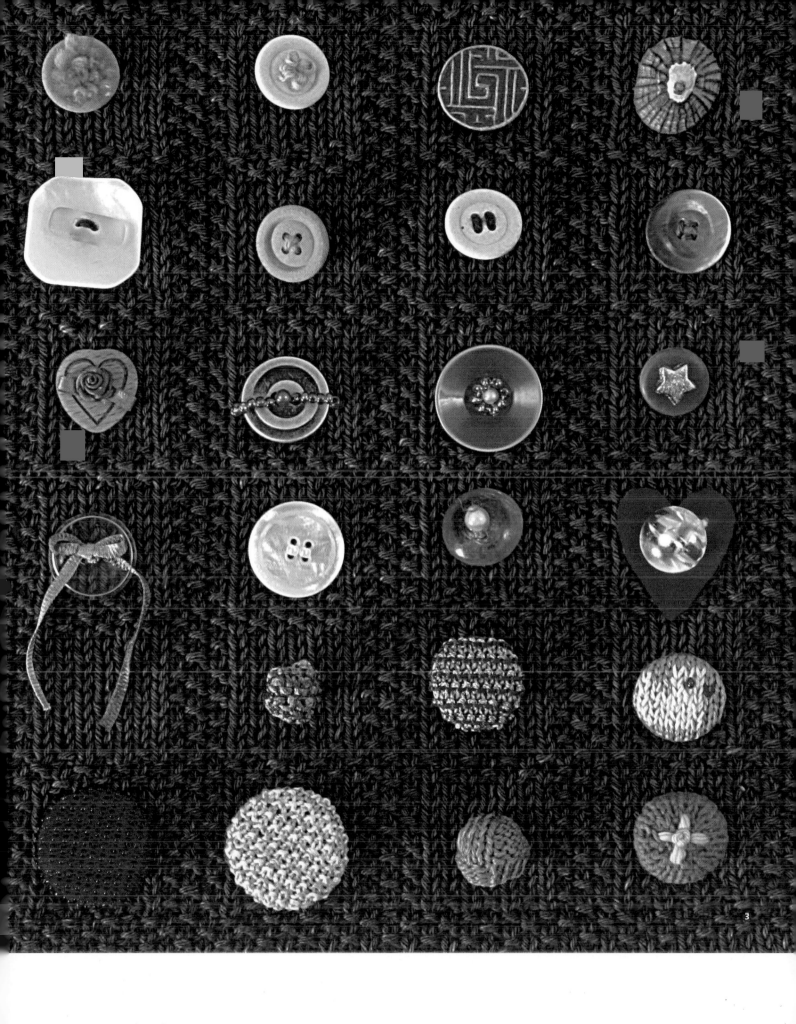

Tassels

There are four different versions of this elegant tassel, from a plain one worked in tweed yarn to a more complex beaded and cabled design. Choose the one you prefer, or adapt a pattern to include your own choice of embellishments.

All the tassels are quick to make, can be customized to coordinate with your interior color scheme, and will cost just a small fraction of their store-bought counterparts.

Each tassel has a different hanging cord, including one that works as a curtain tieback, but any cord can be used on any of the tassels. The tassels are best made from a fluffy yarn to create a full skirt, while the head covers work well in smooth yarns that show up stitch detail.

All the tassels are the same size; approximately 8½in (22cm) long. Gauge (tension) is not particularly important, though the tassel cover should be firmly knitted, so if you have a naturally loose tension, you may want to go down a needle size.

Tweed tassel

Materials

Rowan yorkshire tweed dk
1¾oz (50g) balls
Pink A 1

Rowan kid classic
1¾oz (50g) balls
Fawn B 1

1 pair of US 3 (3mm) needles
1 pair of US 3 (3mm) dp needles

Piece of cardboard 10in (26cm) deep

Abbreviations

MT = make tail. Cast on 6 sts, bind (cast) off 6 sts.
See also page 157.

Head cover

Using US 3 (3mm) needles and A, cast on 10 sts.
Row 1 (WS): Purl.
Row 2: [K1, M1] rep to last st, k1. *(19 sts)*
Row 3: Purl.
Row 4: [K1, M1] rep to last st, k1. *(37 sts)*
Starting with a p row, work 15 rows st st.
Row 20: [K2tog] rep to last st, k1. *(19 sts)*
Row 21: Purl.
Row 22: [K2tog] rep to last st, k1. *(10 sts)*
Row 23: [MT] rep to the end of the row.

Picot bind (cast) off row: [Using the cable method, cast on 25 sts, bind (cast) off 26 sts, slip st on right-hand needle back onto left-hand needle] rep to the end of the row.

Hanging cord

Using US 3 (3mm) dp needles and A, cast on 2 sts.
Row 1: Yo, k2tog, do not turn work.
Rep row 1 until cord measures 12in (30cm) long.
Bind (cast) off.
Fold the cord in half and tie a knot 2¼in (6cm) from the ends.

Tassel

Wind approximately half the ball of B around the card to make the tassel. Tie the ends of the cord around the top of the wound yarn so that the knot sits on top of the tassel. Bind off the head of the tassel with A.

Finishing

Using mattress stitch and taking a 1 st seam, join half the seam on the head cover, stitching down from the cast on edge. Slip the cover over the head of the tassel, then join the rest of the seam. Stitch through the tassel at the base of the head to anchor the cover to the tassel.

TECHNIQUES: Integrated knitted tail ➧ page 132 • Picot bind (cast) off ➧ page 128 • I-cords ➧ page 132 • Tassels ➧ page 131

Beaded tassel

Materials

Rowan wool cotton 1¾oz (50g) balls
    Cream A   1

Rowan kid classic 1¾oz (50g) balls
    Pale blue B   1

1 pair of US 3 (3mm) needles

Jaeger knitting beads
    500-bead pack
    Bronze   1 (199 beads)

Piece of cardboard 10in (26cm) deep

Abbreviations

PB = place bead. Use the close beading technique.

MB = make bobble. Knit twice into front and back of st, turn work, purl 1 row, turn work, slip 2 sts, k2tog, pass slipped sts over.

See also page 157.

Head cover

Thread beads onto A, then cast on 10 sts.

Row 1 (WS): Purl.

Row 2: [K1, M1] rep to last st, k1.
(19 sts)

Row 3: Purl.

Row 4: [K1, M1] to last st, k1.
(37 sts)

Row 5: Purl.

Row 6: K1, [PB] rep to last st, k1.

Row 7: P1, [PB, p4] rep six more times, p1.

Row 8: K5, [PB, k4] rep five more times, PB, k1.

Rep rows 7–8 twice more.

Row 13: As row 6.

Rep rows 7–8 three times.

Row 20: As row 6.

Row 21: Purl.

Row 22: (K2tog) rep to last st, k1.
(*19 sts*)

Row 23: Purl.

Row 24: (K2tog) rep to last st, k1.
(*10 sts*)

Row 25: (MB) rep to the end of
the row.

Picot bind (cast) off row: (Using the
cable method, cast on 15 sts, slide a
bead up to the last st, bind (cast) off
16 sts, slip st on right-hand needle
back onto left-hand needle) rep to the
end of the row.

Hanging cord

Using 6 strands of B, make a twisted
cord long enough to tie back your
curtain, plus 4in (10cm).

Tassel skirt

Wind approximately half of the ball of
B around the card to make the tassel.
Slip the cord between the card and
the yarn and pull half of it through.
Tie the cord around the top of the
tassel. Bind off the head of the tassel
with A.

Finishing

As for Tweed Tassel.

Striped tassel

Materials

Rowan classic yarns cashsoft 4 ply
1¾oz (50g) balls
Dark blue A   1

Rowan lurex shimmer 1oz (25g) balls
Dark blue B   1

Rowan kid classic 1¾oz (50g) balls
Purple C   1

1 pair of US 3 (3mm) needles

Piece of cardboard 10in (26cm) deep

Abbreviations

MT = make tail. Cast on 6 sts, bind
(cast) off 6 sts.
See also page 157.

Head cover

Using A, cast on 10 sts.

Row 1 (WS): Knit.

Row 2: (K1, M1) rep to last st, k1.
(*19 sts*)

Row 3: Knit.

Row 4: (K1, M1) rep to last st, k1.
(*37 sts*)

Rows 5–8: Change to B, knit.

Rows 9–12: Change to A, knit.

Rep rows 5–12 once more.

Rep rows 5–8 once more.

Row 25: Change to A, knit.

Row 26: (K2tog) rep to last st, k1.
(*19 sts*)

Row 27: Knit.

Row 28: (K2tog) rep to last st, k1.
(*10 sts*)

Row 29: (MT) rep to the end of the row.

Picot bind (cast) off row: Change to
B, (using the cable method, cast on
25 sts, bind (cast) off 26 sts, slip st on
right-hand needle back onto left-hand
needle) rep to the end of the row.

Hanging cord

Make a 12in (30cm) plaited cord from
1 strand of A and 2 strands of B. Fold
the cord in half and tie a knot 2¼in
(6cm) from the ends.

Tassel skirt

Wind approximately half of C and a
little of B around the card to make the
tassel. Tie the ends of the cord
around the top of the skirt so that the
knot sits on top of the tassel. Bind off
the head of the tassel with B.

Finishing

As for Tweed Tassel.

TECHNIQUES: Integrated knitted tail ◆ page 132 • Picot bind (cast) off ◆ page 128 • Tassels ◆ page 131

Beaded and cabled tassel

Materials

Jaeger aqua cotton 1¾oz (50g) balls

     Purple A   1

Rowan kid classic 1¾oz (50g) balls

     Pink B   1

Rowan kidsilk haze 1oz (25g) balls

     Dark pink C   1

1 pair of US 3 (3mm) needles

Cable needle

Piece of cardboard 10in (26cm) deep

Size 6 beads ⅛oz (5g) pack

     Purple   1 (78 beads)

Abbreviations

PB = place bead. Use the close beading technique.

C4B = cable 4 back.

MT = make tail. Cast on 3 sts, slide a bead up to the last st, bind (cast) off 3 sts.

See also page 157.

Head cover

Thread beads onto A, then cast on 11 sts.

Row 1 (WS): Purl.

Row 2: Inc in every st to last st, k1. *(21 sts)*

Row 3: Purl.

Row 4: Inc in every st. (42 sts)

Row 5: Purl.

Row 6: K5, PB, (k4, PB) rep to last st, k1.

Row 7: Purl.

Row 8: K1, (C4B, PB) rep seven more times, k1.

Row 9: Purl.

Rep rows 6–9 twice more.

Row 18: As row 6.

Row 19: Purl.

Row 20: (K2tog) rep to the end of the row. *(21 sts)*

Row 21: Purl.

Row 22: (K2tog) rep to last st, k1. *(11 sts)*

Row 23: (MT) rep to the end of the row.

Picot bind (cast) off row: (Using the cable method, cast on 20 sts, slide a bead up to the last st, bind (cast) off 21 sts, slip st on right-hand needle back onto left-hand needle) rep to the end of the row.

Hanging cord

Make a 12in (30cm) twisted cord from 2 strands of A. Fold the cord in half and tie a knot 2¼in (6cm) from the ends.

Tassel skirt

Wind approximately one-third of the ball of B and quarter of the ball of C around the card to make the tassel, ensuring that the top layer of yarn is B. Tie the ends of the cord around the top of the skirt so that the knot sits on top of the tassel. Bind off the head of the tassel with A.

Finishing

As for Tweed Tassel.

Edgings

The swatches in the libraries need not be used as they are seen. Many of them make excellent edgings, and with a little imagination and a selection of different yarns they can add style to a project. Here there are three versions of one edging, showing how different it can look worked with different yarns, slightly different techniques and with varied applications.

The gauge (tension) is not important for these edgings, because if they are attached later the edging can be eased to fit: the stitch count is the main factor that will determine length. However, if you are in any doubt, work a swatch.

Basic edging

This edging has consecutive rows worked on progressively smaller needles and is based on swatch seven from the Yarn Plus Library on page 45.

Length

The length is determined by the number of cast on stitches, which should be double the number required to complete the project if it is to be knitted on from the edging.

Materials

1 pair each of US 15 (10mm),
US 10½ (7 mm),
US 10 (6mm),
US 7 (4.5mm),
US 5 (3.75mm), and
US 2 (3mm) needles

The needle sizes will vary depending on the yarn used, but the principle is always the same.

Using the thumb method, US 15 (10mm) needles and A, cast on twice the required number of sts.
Using US 10½ (7mm) needle, knit 1 row.
Using US 10 (6mm) needle, knit 1 row.
Using US 7 (4.5mm) needle, knit 1 row.
Using US 5 (3.75mm) needle, knit 1 row.
Change to US 2 (3mm) needles.
Row 6: (K2tog), rep to the end of the row.

Lacy edging

This was used for the edge of an afghan to give it a border that is both light, and drapes beautifully.

Length

The length is determined by the number of cast on stitches, which should be double the number required to complete the project if it is to be knitted on from the edging.

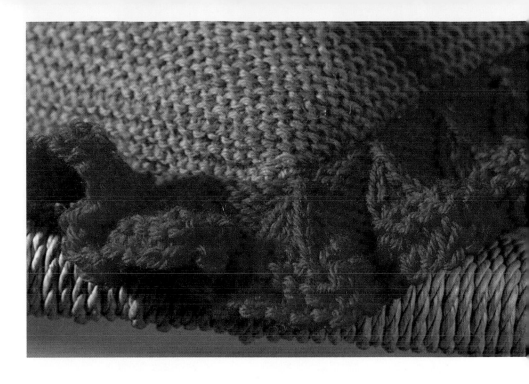

Materials

Rowan 4 ply cotton 1¾oz (50g) balls
Turquoise A
Blue B

1 pair each of US 19 (16mm),
US 17 (12mm),
US 15 (10mm),
US 11 (8mm),
US 10½ (6.5mm),
US 9 (5.5mm), US 7 (4.5mm), and
US 3 (3.25mm) needles

Abbreviations

See page 157.

Edging

Using the thumb method, US 19
(16mm) needles and A, cast on twice
the required number of sts.
Using US 17 (12mm) needles, knit
1 row.
Using US 15 (10mm) needles, knit
1 row.
Using US 11 (8mm) needles, knit
1 row.
Using US 10½ (6.5mm) needles, knit
1 row.
Using US 9 (5.5mm) needles, knit
1 row.
Using US 7 (4.5mm) needles, knit
1 row.
Using US 3 (3.25mm) needles, knit
1 row.
Row 8: (K2tog) rep to the end of
the row.

Stripe pattern

Row 9: Knit.
Change to B.
Knit 4 rows.
Change to A.
Knit 12 rows.
Cont in stripe patt as set as required.

Frilly edging

This edging is a combination of that
used on the Smocked Dress on page
114, but with some volume added by
working a few rows on decreasing
needle sizes.

Length

The number of cast on stitches
determines the length.
For this 12in (30cm) cushion cover,
the edging measures 48in (120cm).

Patt repeat
Cast on repeat: 13 sts + 4 sts.
Completed edging repeat:
1 st + 4 sts.

Materials

Jaeger baby merino dk
1¾oz (50g) balls
Red A   1

1 pair each of US 15 (10mm),
US 10½ (7 mm),
US 10 (6mm),
US 7 (4.5mm),
US 5 (3.75mm), and
US 2 (3mm) needles

Abbreviations

Sl2tog, k1, psso = slip two stitches
together knitwise, knit 1, pass the
slipped stitches over.
See also page 157.

Edging

Using the thumb method and US 15
(10mm) needles, cast on 628 sts.
Using US 10½ (7mm) needle, knit 1 row.
Using US 10 (6mm) needle, knit 1 row.
Using US 7 (4.5mm) needle, knit 1 row.
Using US 5 (3.75mm) needle, knit 1 row.
Change to US 2 (3mm) needles.
Row 6: (P4, k3, sl2tog, k1, psso, k3)
rep to last 4 sts, p4.
Row 7 and every alt row (WS): Purl.
Row 8: (P4, k2, sl2tog, k1, psso, k2)
rep to last 4 sts, p4.
Row 10: (P4, k1, sl2tog, k1, psso, k1)
rep to last 4 sts, p4.
Row 12: (P4, sl2tog, k1, psso) rep to
last 4 sts, p4.
Row 13: Bind (cast) off.

Finishing

Weave in the loose ends.
Sew the edging to the cushion with a
line of decreases from a pattern
repeat aligned on each corner.

Second frill

Using the thumb method, US 11 (8mm) needles and B, cast on the same number of sts.

Row 1: Knit.

Row 2: Change to US 10½ (6.5mm) needles, purl.

Joining frills

Holding the second frill in front of the first one and using the spare US 9 (5.5mm) needle, knit 1 st from each needle together until all the sts are knitted onto the US 9 (5.5mm) needle.

Cont in B.

Next row: Change to US 6 (4mm) needles, purl.

Next row: Change to US 2 (3mm) needles, knit.

Next row: Purl.

Next row: (K2tog) rep to the end of the row.

Rep these last two rows once more.

Work 3 rows st st.

Bind (cast) off.

Finishing

Weave in the loose ends.

Sew the edging in place along the bound (cast) off edge. Here, it is sewn to the back of a scarf, so the fringe on the end of the scarf falls over the frills and adds more detail.

Tiered edging

Materials

Rowan kidsilk haze 1oz (25g) balls

   Olive green A

   Lime green B

1 pair each of US 11 (8mm),

   US 10½ (6.5mm),

   US 9 (5.5mm),

   US 6 (4mm), and

   US 2 (3mm) needles

First frill

Decide on the number of sts required, this must be an even number.

Using the thumb method, US 11 (8mm) needles and A, cast on four times the required number of sts.

Row 1: Knit.

Row 2: Change to US 10½ (6.5mm) needles, purl.

Rows 3–6: Change to US 9 (5.5mm) needles and work in st st.

Break yarn and leave sts on needle.

Banded cushion

Yarns of a similar appearance, but of different weights and colors, are mixed to good effect in this sophisticated cushion. Finishing the picked-up bands with a contrast, softly scalloped edge adds a neat detail.

Size

15½ x 15½in (40 x 40cm)

Materials

Rowan yorkshire tweed chunky
    3½oz (100g) balls
    Gray A   2

Rowan felted tweed
    1¾oz (50g) balls
    Green B   1
    Brown C   1
    Blue D   1

1 pair each of US 10 (6mm),
    US 10½ (6.5mm),
    US 5 (3.75mm), and
    US 2 (2.75mm) needles

Knitter's sewing needle
2 1¼in (29mm) self-cover buttons
15½ x 15½in (40 x 40cm)
    cushion pad

Gauge (Tension)

11 stitches and 18 rows to 4in (10cm) over st st on yorkshire tweed chunky using US 10½ (6.5mm) needles.

Abbreviations

See page 157.

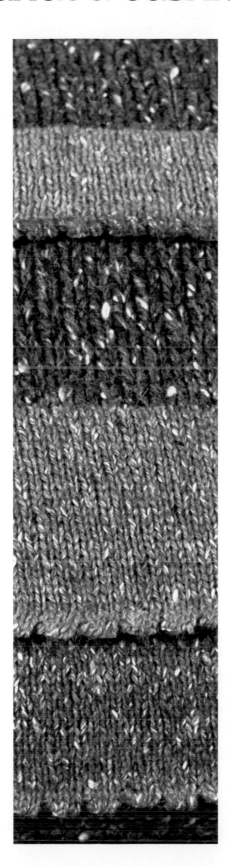

Back and front

Using the thumb method, US 10 (6mm) needles and A, cast on 43 sts. Work 9 rows in k1, p1 seed (moss) stitch for buttonband.

Change to US 10½ (6.5mm) needles. Starting with a k row, work 27 rows st st.

Row 37 (WS): Knit to form fold line. Starting with a k row, work 63 rows st st for front.

Row 101: Knit to form fold line. Starting with a k row, work 27 rows st st.

Change to US 10 (6mm) needles. Work 3 rows seed (moss) stitch.

Row 132: Seed (moss) 13 sts, bind (cast) off 4 sts, seed (moss) 8 sts, bind (cast) off 4 sts, seed (moss) to end.

Row 133: Seed (moss) 13 sts, cast on 4 sts, seed (moss) 9 sts, cast on 4 sts, seed (moss) 13 sts. Work 4 rows seed (moss) stitch. Bind (cast) off in seed (moss) stitch.

TECHNIQUES: Mixing yarns ◗ page 40 • Frills ◗ page 136 • Tubular bind (cast) off ◗ page 128

Bands

Right-side up, lay the knitted fabric
flat with row 1 towards you.

Using US 5 (3.75mm) needles and B,
and working from right to left, pick up
1 st from the center of and between
every st of row 57. (85 sts)

Starting with a p row, work 16 rows
of st st.

Break B, join in C.

Work 3 rows st st.

Next row: K3, (yo, k2tog, k1) rep to
last st, k1.

Work 3 rows st st.

Tubular bind (cast) off row: Pick up
first upper stitch loop of first row of C
and knit together with first st on right-
hand needle, (rep with next upper
stitch loop and stitch, pass first stitch
on left-hand needle over second st)
rep to the end of the row.

Rep band on row 77, using D instead
of B and B instead of C. Work
24 rows of D before changing to B.

Rep band on row 90, using C instead
of B and D instead of C. Work
16 rows of C before changing to D.

Back trim

With row 137 towards you, using
US 5 (3.75mm) needles and D, and
working from right to left, pick up 1 st
from the center of and between
every st of last row of st st. (85 sts)

Work 3 rows st st.

Next row: K3, (yo, k2tog, k1) rep to
last st, k1.

Work 3 rows st st.

Tubular bind (cast) off row: Pick up
first upper stitch loop of pick up row
of D and knit together with first st on
right-hand needle, (rep with next
upper stitch loop and stitch, pass first
stitch on left-hand needle over
second st) rep to the end of the row.

Buttons (make 2)

Using the cable method, US 2
(2.75mm) needles and C, cast on
18 sts.

Work 26 rows st st.

Bind (cast) off.

Following the manufacturer's
instructions, cover each button with a
square of knitted fabric.

Finishing

Weave in loose ends on the WS.
Press the cushion, pressing the
bands and back trim flat.

Using mattress stitch, sew the
side seams of the buttonhole panel
to the front. Sew the side seams of
the buttonband panel to the front,
tucking the buttonband under the
buttonhole band and sewing it
in place.

Turn the cushion cover inside
out and press the seams.

Sew two buttons onto the
buttonband to align with the
buttonholes.

Yarn information

Rowan Kidsilk Haze
Very lightweight yarn
70% super kid mohair,
30% silk
Approximately 230yds
(210m) per 1oz (25g) ball

Rowan Cotton Glacé
Sport-weight yarn
100% cotton
Approximately 125yds
(115m) per 1¾oz (50g) ball

Rowan Denim
Double knitting-weight
cotton yarn
100% cotton
Approximately 101yds
(93m) per 1¾oz (50g) ball

Jaeger Trinity Cotton
Double knitting-weight
40% silk, 35% cotton,
25% polymide fiber
Approximately 218yds
(200m) per 1¾oz (50g) ball

Rowan Wool Cotton
Double knitting-weight yarn
50% merino wool,
50% cotton
Approximately 123yds
(113m) per 1¾oz (50g) ball

Rowan Handknit Cotton
Worsted-weight yarn
100% cotton
Approximately 93yds (85m)
per 1¾oz (50g) ball

Jaeger Matchmaker Baby
Merino DK
Double knitting-weight yarn
100% merino wool
Approximately 130 yd
(120 m) per 1¾ oz (50 g) ball

Rowan Yorkshire
Tweed Chunky
Bulky yarn
100% pure new wool
Approximately 109yd
(100m) per 3¾oz (100g) ball

Rowan Polar
Chunky-weight yarn
60% pure new wool,
30% alpaca, 10% acrylic
Approximately 109yd
(100m) per 3¾oz (100g) ball

Rowan Kid Classic
Worsted-weight yarn
70% lambswool,
26% kid mohair, 4% nylon
Approximately 151yd
(140m) per 3½oz (100g) ball

Rowan Lurex Shimmer
Fingering-weight yarn
80% viscose, 20% polyester
Approximately 104yd (95m)
per 1oz (25g) ball

Rowan Cashsoft 4 Ply
Fingering-weight yarn
57% extra fine merino,
33% microfiber, 10%
cashmere
Approximately 197yd
(180m) per 1¾oz (50g) ball

Jaeger Aqua Cotton
Double knitting-weight yarn
100% mercerised cotton
Approximately 115yd
(106m) per 1¾oz (50g) ball

Rowan Yorkshire Tweed DK
Sport-weight yarn
100% pure new wool
Approximately 123yd
(113m) per 1¾oz (50g) ball

Jaeger Siena 4 Ply
Fingering-weight yarn
100% mercerised cotton
Approximately 153yd
(140m) per 1¾oz (50g) ball

Rowanspun DK
Sport-weight yarn
100% pure new wool
Approximately 219yd
(200m) per 1¾oz (50g) hank

Rowan Felted Tweed
Sport-weight yarn
50% merino wool,
25% alpaca,
25% viscose/rayon
Approximately 191yd
(175m) per 1¾oz (50g) ball

Rowan Cotton Tape
Chunky yarn
100% cotton
Approximately 71yds (65m)
per 1¾oz (50g) ball

Rowan Cotton Braid
Bulky yarn
68% cotton, 22% viscose,
10% linen
Approximately 55yds (50m)
per 1¾oz (50g) ball

R2 Braid
Bulky yarn
70% viscose, 30% nylon
Approximately 16yds (15m)
per 1¾oz (50g) ball

Jaeger Fur
Bulky yarn
47% wool, 47% kid mohair,
6% polymide
Approximately 22yds (20m)
per 1¾oz (50g) ball

**Suppliers of Rowan
Yarns and Jaeger
Handknits**

USA
Westminster Fibers Inc.
4 Townsend West
Suite 8
Nashua, NH 03063
Tel: 603 886 5041
Fax: 603 886 1056

Canada
Diamond Yarn
9697 St Laurent
Montreal
Quebec H3L 2N1
Tel: 514 388 6188

Diamond Yarn (Toronto)
155 Martin Ross
Unit 3
Toronto
Ontario M3J 2L9
Tel: 416 736 6111

Australia
Rowan at Sunspun
185 Canterbury Road
Canterbury
Victoria 3126
Tel: 03 9830 1609

UK
Rowan Yarns and Jaeger
Handknits
Green Lane Mill
Holmfirth
West Yorkshire
HD9 2DX
Tel: 01484 681881
www.knitrowan.com

Abbreviations

alt	alternate	skpsso	slip one, knit one, pass the slipped stitch over
beg	beginning/begin		
col	color/colorway		
cont	continue	sl	slip
cm	centimeter	sppsso	slip one, purl one, pass the slipped stitch over
Cr	cross		
C4B	cable four (or number stated) back		
		ssk	slip, slip, knit two stitches together
C4F	cable four (or number stated) forward	ss p2tog tbl	slip, slip, purl two stitches together
dec	decrease	st/sts	stitch/stitches
dp	double pointed	st st	stockinette (stocking) stitch
foll/folls	following/follows		
g	grams	s2tog k1 psso	slip two together, knit one and pass the slipped stitches over
In	inch		
inc	increase		
incr	increase right		
incl	increase left	s2tog p3tog	slip two, purl three stitches together
K	knit		
k1 pnso	knit one, pass the next stitch over	tbl	through the back of the loop/s
k2tog	knit two stitches together	T2B	twist two (or number stated) back
MB	make bobble	T2F	twist two (or number stated) forward
ML	make loop		
mm	millimeter	WS	wrong side of work.
MT	make tail	yb	yarn back
M1	make one (stitch)	yf	yarn forward
M1L	make one (stitch) left	yfon	yarn forward and over needle to make a stitch
M1R	make one (stitch) right		
oz	ounces	yo	yarnover
P	purl	*	repeat instructions between * as many times as instructed
patt	pattern		
PB	place bead		
pnso	pass next stitch over	( )	repeat instructions between ( ) as many times as instructed
PS	place sequin		
psso	pass slipped stitch over		
p2tog	purl two stitches together		
p2tog tbl	purl two stitches together through the backs of the loops		
rem	remaining		
rep/reps	repeat/repeats		
rev st st	reverse stockinette (stocking) stitch		
RS	right side of work		

CONVERSIONS
Needle sizes

US SIZE	METRIC SIZE	OLD UK & CANADIAN SIZE
15	10	000
13	9	00
11	8	0
11	7½	1
10½	7	2
10½	6½	3
10	6	4
9	5½	5
8	5	6
7	4½	7
6	4	8
5	3¾	9
4	3½	–
3	3¼	10
2/3	3	11
2	2¾	12
1	2¼	13
0	2	14

Weights and lengths

oz	=	g × 0.0352
g	=	oz × 28.35
in	=	cm × 0.3937
cm	=	in × 2.54
yd	=	m × 0.9144
m	=	yd × 1.0936

Index

Illustrations are indicated by italic numerals and technique drawings by bold numerals.

Author acknowledgments

Creating this book was no small task and the authors sincerely thank and appreciate the efforts of everyone involved.

Matthew Dickens for his patience, unerring eye for detail and composition and for bringing both humour and Olive Oil to our photography sessions. Abi Holroyd and her daughter India, the adorable baby who appears in some of the photographs and Claire Wilmot and her daughter Daniella, who modelled the Smocked Dress. The artworks were drawn by Kate Simunek, who took the reference supplied and created illustrations that magically combine beauty with instructive accuracy. At Rowan Yarns, Ann Hincliffe, who dealt day to day with our requests, and Kate Buller, who saw the potential of the project at such an early stage and encouraged us with yarn and support. Marie Clayton at Collins & Brown, who has been unerringly confident and supportive from the very first proposal meeting, and Katie Cowan at Collins & Brown, whose enthusiasm and skill were a tonic to the book. We especially appreciate the contributions of Ann Haxell, Margaret Roberts and Margaret Crawford who knitted, advised, and suggested improvements based on their combined one hundred and fifty years of knitting wisdom. Marilyn Wilson who questioned and pattern checked with an admirable love of detail. The legendry Elvis, for a special guest appearance on the Denim Afghan.